PRAISE FOR

THIS IS ALL

"Sandler wisely lets Camila's story stand on its own without lecturing us. Not to sound clichéd, but we walk in Camila's shoes. We come to understand what Sandler recognized early on: If Camila can't navigate the dearth of housing, how can others?"
—*The New York Times*

"A passionate cri de coeur . . . Camila's story is both uniquely her own and illustrative of the grindingly dictatorial public assistance programs that are determined not to assist."
—*The New York Review of Books*

"Lauren Sandler wrote *the* book about poverty in America. . . . an intimate illustration of the gutting inequalities that define the American social service system." —*InStyle*

"Left me breathless." —*Los Angeles Review of Books*

"Great . . . vivid . . . powerful." —*Salon*

"A stunning, depressing examination of the scramble for affordable housing in an era of gentrification and late-stage capitalism, and of a New York divided by race and class . . . Shook up my inherited assumptions about racial injustice." —*The Jewish Week*

"Harrowing, heartbreaking and riveting." —*The Trentonian*

"Forthright . . . a window into the American underclass . . . *This Is All I Got* is emphatic about the need for policy change, specifically the need to orient welfare systems to encourage education over work and to expand housing subsidies." —*National Review*

"[An] engaging and moving new book . . . Sandler deftly includes context, history and clearheaded explanations of the public welfare system and its dysfunctions in her detailed account of Camila's life. . . . The 'system,' ostensibly there to help Camila, who became a ward of the state at age fifteen, almost becomes a character in the book. . . . Ultimately, the story of her first year of motherhood is heartbreaking, inspiring and infuriating, all at once."   —Minneapolis *Star Tribune*

"A vivid, heartbreaking account . . . Sandler scrupulously documents Camila's efforts to navigate underresourced, byzantine, and dehumanizing public assistance programs, and examines her own conflicted feelings about bearing witness to a less-privileged woman's pain. . . . Readers will be moved by this harrowing and impassioned call for change."   —*Publishers Weekly*

"A closely observed chronicle . . . Sandler displays her journalistic talent by unerringly presenting this dire situation. . . . An impressive blend of dispassionate reporting, pungent condemnation of public welfare, and gritty humanity."   —*Kirkus Reviews*

"Sandler is frank from the start that it became difficult to maintain journalistic distance from a woman who became her friend. But even with this tangle, their collaboration leads to a rich, sociologically valuable work that's more gripping, and more devastating, than fiction. Readers will be struck by both the sheer impossibility of what Camila faces . . . and her ability to maintain hope as she does so. Sandler frequently juxtaposes Camila's struggles with tableaux of New York's encroaching wealth, with stunning statistics, giving readers an unusually personal view of an inarguably failing system."   —*Booklist*

"Meticulously crafted and brilliantly reported, Lauren Sandler's *This Is All I Got* exposes the Kafkaesque cruelties of America's disintegrating social safety net. It is a gut punch of a narrative, an electrifying summons to policy action, and an instant classic."

—DAN-EL PADILLA PERALTA, associate professor of classics, Princeton, and author of *Undocumented: A Dominican Boy's Odyssey from a Homeless Shelter to the Ivy League*

"A timely and empathetic act of journalism, brimming with moral conundra and posing an urgent and implicit question: How could we do better for this mother? How could we do better for this child?" —TED CONOVER, director of NYU's Arthur L. Carter Journalism Institute and author of *Newjack: Guarding Sing Sing*

"This is the very human story of a single family that at the same time is the broad and important story about the ravages of inequality in this country. This is also a book you cannot put down: Lauren Sandler's remarkable, intimate reporting and her lyrical, specific prose shine." —ALISSA QUART, author of *Squeezed: Why Our Families Can't Afford America*

"A stunning portrait of homelessness in America, and an unforgettable account of one mother's quest to find shelter in the contemporary city, *This is All I Got* is an urgent, myth-shattering book about what happens when we refuse to deal with urban poverty. Read it, share it, don't let the story disappear." —ERIC KLINENBERG, Helen Gould Shepard Professor in Social Science at NYU and author of *Palaces for the People*

BY LAUREN SANDLER

This Is All I Got: A New Mother's Search for Home

*One and Only: The Freedom of Having an Only Child,
and the Joy of Being One*

Righteous: Dispatches from the Evangelical Youth Movement

THIS IS ALL I GOT

THIS IS
ALL I GOT

A NEW MOTHER'S
SEARCH FOR HOME

LAUREN SANDLER

RANDOM HOUSE

NEW YORK

2021 Random House Trade Paperback Edition

Copyright © 2020 by Lauren Sandler
Book club guide copyright © 2021 by Penguin Random House LLC

Published in the United States by Random House, an imprint and
division of Penguin Random House LLC, New York.

RANDOM HOUSE and the HOUSE colophon are registered trademarks
of Penguin Random House LLC.

RANDOM HOUSE BOOK CLUB and colophon are trademarks
of Penguin Random House LLC.

Originally published in hardcover in the United States by Random House,
an imprint and division of Penguin Random House LLC, in 2020.

LIBRARY OF CONGRESS CATALOGING-IN-PUBLICATION DATA

Names: Sandler, Lauren, author.
Title: This is all I got: a new mother's search for home / by Lauren Sandler.
Description: | New York: Random House, [2020]
Identifiers: LCCN 2019045309 (print) | LCCN 2019045310 (ebook) |
ISBN 9780399589973 (trade paperback) | ISBN 9780399589966 (ebook)
Subjects: LCSH: Homeless women—New York (State)—New York. |
Homelessness—New York (State)—New York.
Classification: LCC HV4506.N6 S25 2020 (print) | LCC HV4506.N6 (ebook)
| DDC 305.48/442092 [B]—dc23
LC record available at lccn.loc.gov/2019045309
LC ebook record available at lccn.loc.gov/2019045310

Printed in the United States of America on acid-free paper

randomhousebooks.com
randomhousebookclub.com

2 4 6 8 9 7 5 3 1

First Edition

Book design by Jo Anne Metsch

To anyone who might see themselves reflected in these pages

CONTENTS

FALL

WINTER

SPRING

INTRODUCTION

met Camila in 2015 at a shelter in Brooklyn, as spring was melting into summer. I would know her for much longer than a year, but this story is of the first twelve months, in which she fought to build a life of basic stability for herself and the baby who was about to be born.

With finishing-school posture, she walked into the weekly evening meeting for shelter residents in a fresh white blouse and a pair of twill short-shorts, slim but for her pregnant belly. She didn't look like she needed to be there, or that's what one of the new mothers in the room muttered to no one in particular. Camila took a seat, surveying the room, and began to advise another pregnant resident on maternity patients' rights and natural birthing techniques. She was generous with a conspiratorial glance, maintaining just enough snap in her neck to remind the world she was Dominican, a constant portrait of double consciousness. But no matter how tall she carried herself, her feet remained anchored in a place she didn't want to be. She was born into struggle and deeply tethered there.

What set her apart? Was it her charisma? Her slightly preppy style? The world couldn't see her as someone who belonged in a shelter. Let's be straight: No one belongs in a shelter. Name any cliché about fated futility, they all apply to the individual experience of managing poverty in America. But Camila's caseworkers would tell you that they'd never seen anyone as knowledgeable about the system in which she was stranded. They marveled at how she kept policy and dates and addresses and caseworkers' names in her head like a savant, as she navigated waiting rooms and obtuse paperwork in her search for affordable housing, in her securing of public assistance, in her endeavors to establish legal paternity and procure child support, in her efforts to stay in school.

Camila held my eye contact as I explained to the group of women in the room that, if they were willing, I wanted to know their stories, to witness their lives. Some of them shrugged. Some of them shook their heads. Some nodded, open to the invitation, if skeptical. But Camila sat up even taller and folded her long fingers over the baby-blue purse resting on her lap. I could feel a light switch on and, with it, her mind revving, her thoughts lurching forward as she composed herself. Her cheeks, pale for Dominican skin, flushed slightly, like heat was building inside her. She waited politely for me to finish and for others in the room to speak. She set her jaw through the awkward silence that followed. And then, perched on the edge of her seat, her sandals firmly on the floor, Camila spoke. She said she had a story to tell.

As I came to learn, she had grown up mainly in apartments in Queens paid for by her mother's Section 8 housing voucher, back when a single mother could count on such support. No more. Her father had never lived in any of those apartments; he had his own life, and plenty of other kids, most of them with their own single mothers. Her mom had three other children of her own, too, and each had a different father, one more absent than the next. Camila's unfinished college years offered a succession of dorms at first, and once she got pregnant, a succession of shelters.

Here she was now, weeks before giving birth, making plans to stay off welfare and finish her degree in criminal justice. From that first meeting, I sensed that she was a woman who was hell-bent on propelling herself out of this shelter, away from the circumstances of her past, toward something solid, ambitious. And as I came to experience her, within and beyond her story, one thing was clear to me: If Camila couldn't use her wits and persistence to make the system work for her, no one could.

I was at the shelter where Camila was temporarily living because I wanted to witness and understand how deepening inequality is lived in America, and particularly in New York, a city that gets richer as the poor get poorer. This city is a fun-house mirror of national inequality, displaying class differences in their most exaggerated forms. At the shelter, I met women whose backgrounds varied but who all had nowhere to go when they showed up with their bags, and nowhere to go when they packed them once it was time to leave.

I first moved to the city in 1992, when homelessness was considered a national crisis. The night I unpacked my bags, 23,482 people slept in the city's public shelters. By the evening I met Camila in 2015, that number had ballooned to over sixty thousand people in the city's mainstream shelters, where in total, that year, over 127,000 people spent at least a night. That year, thousands more were housed in specialized shelters for domestic violence survivors, homeless youth, or people with HIV/AIDS. And thousands more, housed in hotel rooms or dilapidated apartments awaiting an eligibility determination for Temporary Housing Assistance, were denied ongoing aid. On the streets, in parks, on subway trains, over sidewalk vents, thousands more tried to find comfort on a strip of cardboard, a bag stuffed with whatever could be carried or scrounged.

A crisis of far greater magnitude is growing.

We see men, mostly, their stench pushing passengers to the other side of the train car or sitting on the edge of the sidewalk behind a cardboard sign. That man continues to be the emblem of homelessness and has been for decades. But there's a much larger homeless population in the city, an invisible one. One carefully made up, often headed to work or school, clustered down at the other end of the subway car with everyone else, avoiding that man in a greasy parka on a summer's day.

Homeless: What word more obliterates the nuances and trials of complicated relationships, of ambitions, of plans? It means failure rather than perseverance; homelessness as an end, even at a young age. But the homelessness crisis is a single lens in the kaleidoscope of American poverty—more specifically the catastrophe of urban American poverty, and even more specifically the poverty of women in urban America. The story of every person who has found themselves homeless, or in a place of serious housing instability, is individual, and yet each story is its own keyhole view of this country's deepest flaws: the vanishing safety net, the scourge of housing inequality, the yoke of which family you're born into, the stubbornness of entrenched racism, and the burdens that women are forced to carry utterly alone.

Theoretically, poverty doesn't discriminate. The data, however, tells a different story. It tells us that most people in poverty are women, specifically women of color. Furthermore, they're single mothers. And many of them are homeless, which means their kids are, too. One in thirty children in America is homeless, a population of 2.5 million kids in total. Three-quarters of New York's shelter population is made up of families, with few fathers to be seen. There's no doubt that it's hard being a man in poverty, but most don't do it as single parents.

Among developed countries, no nation fails its single mothers as gravely as does the United States. Here, they receive paltry social income support, the fewest early-childhood education and care options, minimal paid family leave and healthcare. More single mothers work in the United States than in other countries, but they are still impoverished by egregiously unequal low wages. Only one-third collect child support. No wonder single mothers make up the vast majority of our homeless population—whether we see them sleeping on the street or not.

This is information that any concerned citizen can find with a quick Internet search. But the data doesn't tell the whole story. We encounter so few stories about the homeless who apply lipstick, change a diaper, and go to work, or to class, or to the infinite linoleum-floored fluorescent-lit waiting rooms of our failing social-services system. Data can tell us who is on welfare, sure. But it doesn't tell us that a person becomes synonymous with welfare, is defined by it, a life's narrative distilled into a number, devoid of humanity, of individuality.

Poverty, on a day-to-day, hour-to-hour basis, is often numbingly boring. Hours spent in waiting rooms, just to learn an appointment has been canceled, and having to feel time slow in the same space again the next day. Evenings after shelter curfew, alone in a room with a sleeping baby. Miles of subway tracks followed from one remote neighborhood to another, searching for resources and information. This was a life that was familiar to Camila long before she arrived at the shelter where I met her. It was her mother's childhood. It was her own childhood. Now it was to be her child's childhood.

Homelessness is a crisis about housing, first and foremost. And housing in our age is about the inheritance of our families: how they care for or abuse us, how they uplift or resent us, how they can or can't—or will or won't—help us. It's the story of children and their parents. In poverty, where single-parent families are the norm, it's the story of children and mothers—and the nagging elusiveness of participatory and responsible fatherhood. Her mother delivered her a life of impossible circumstances. But Camila was determined to disrupt that cycle, to pass down a different fate.

What would it take?

Picture yourself at twenty-two with no margin for error. Picture yourself shouldering the stress of caring for an infant while attempting to navigate the system, utterly on your own. Picture facing such anxiety and fear with only your baby's cries as a partner.

Each of the women I met ended up at the shelter via a different path. One had a drug-addicted mother who couldn't take her in. One had witnessed the violent death of every close member of her family in the United States. One had parents who could no longer live with her mental illness, who perhaps saw her pregnancy as a last straw. One was evicted. In most of these cases, their babies' fathers said they'd stick around at the beginning, only to fade away by the birth. They all have harrowing, meaningful stories to tell, as do the millions of other women in their circumstances. But among them, Camila demonstrated a level of determination and resourcefulness that signaled that she might be able to find her way through the labyrinth to make a future on the other side. I wanted to see if she could.

It goes without saying, though it's important to say it anyway: Mine is a life lived in marked contrast to Camila's. I am not a woman of color. Nor am I a woman in poverty. It goes without saying as well that this is thorny territory, when power—of skin and access and economics—is so markedly unequal. And despite my relative privilege, I was not there to help her. It was a hard relationship to navigate. There were some ground rules I set: During my time with Camila, I paid for meals when we were together, I gave her holiday gifts, and I helped her move boxes and bags of belongings from one temporary residence to another. As with all the women I met over the course of my reporting, I gave her no money, no shelter, and no intentional advice. With Camila, those rules became increasingly difficult to maintain. But they served as a boundary and a reminder that, while I cared deeply for her, I was in her presence as a journalist. I was there to witness.

Other elements came into play when I began writing. I chose to protect Camila's identity, and that of every person I write about in the book. In doing so, I changed every name and some small identifying characteristics, as well as some addresses. I also adjusted some small elements of chronology for clarity. I changed no events that took place. Most of what I describe I witnessed, or it was described to me. When I reconstruct dialogue at times, I'm often relying on what Camila told me, sometimes corroborated by others, sometimes more than once, in uncanny repetition over time. Her mind is something to behold.

I didn't set out to write about someone who would be a stand-in for statistics. Individuals are not sociology, even if they are governed by social systems. If I were hewing to the demographics of homelessness, this book would likely be about an African American woman, not a Latina. It would not be about someone with such exceptional resilience or sparkle. The stories of other experiences in our broken system are also vital. (How does one manage this life with clinical depression, or a criminal record, or a physical disability, or an eighth-grade education?) But as much as I didn't choose someone with a different profile, that someone didn't choose me. Camila did. We made that relationship together, even if I write this book alone. I walked into a room one Wednesday evening. I didn't know then, or for some time to come, if the story would be how she could make the system work or how it could fail even her, despite her tenacious attempts to build security out of every resource available to her, scheming each new possible solution when every prior one fell through.

SUMMER

SUMMER

1

NATIVITY

At six o'clock in the morning, alone in her twin bed, Camila began active labor. Breathing the way she'd learned on You-Tube, she made a path to the bathroom. At least she had a private one here. Camila pushed aside the polyester shower curtain, a riot of ruffles and butterflies mismatched with the industrial green tiles. She turned on the tap. As the water rushed into the low tub, she found a playlist of spa music to soothe her through her contractions and pulled up the app she'd downloaded to time them.

She tapped out a text message to Kevin. *Good morning. I think today is the day.*

It was June 5.

Camila called the doula who had volunteered to coach her through labor. She didn't answer. Another contraction came, quicker than the last. She climbed into the tub, her long body lean but for the protrusion of her midsection. She closed her eyes and brushed her tight curls from her forehead. She lay there, listening to the new-age plucking of a harp, focusing on her breathing, tracking her contractions, calling the doula again and again.

Then the phone rang. She was jubilant to see Kevin's name on her screen. It was unusual for him to call; he usually texted. He said he needed to get some money and then he'd fly down from Buffalo tomorrow. The bus was much cheaper, but it was a ten-hour trip. Maybe he had some more money coming his way—he was getting signed to the Canadian Football League, or at least that's what he'd told her. He was graduating the following week. Camila was supposed to graduate the following week, too, but that's not how it had worked out.

She hung up and sank deeper into the bath, breathing as she'd practiced. The next contraction rocked her with its intensity. She splashed water on her neck and over her chest to try to calm herself down. Her breasts, usually so small, were engorged, ready. She tried to meditate the pain away. Camila had become interested in organic foods, homeopathy, natural childbirth—all hallmarks of Park Slope, the Brooklyn neighborhood she'd moved to a month before, when she was admitted to the shelter. She'd studied up on the data supporting breastfeeding, watched spiritual midwifery videos online, and toured a birthing center—alone—only to learn her pregnancy was too far advanced by then for her to deliver there.

It was eight o'clock already. She realized she'd been in the tub for two hours, the water long cooled. The other women would be up now—maybe not the pregnant ones, but the ones with babies. Rose, who ran the shelter, would soon be unlocking her office downstairs. On the sidewalk outside, the bums—as Camila called them—were lined up for breakfast at the soup kitchen. She thought about how no one in the building knew she was in labor.

Camila wasn't bothered that nobody would be accompanying her to the hospital, aside from her doula. Kevin would be there to meet the baby the next day; that was enough. Her mother, Geraldine, never had one of her four babies' fathers beside her. Camila's father certainly wasn't there when she was born. Motherhood was something that most women got into alone, at least most of the mothers she knew.

Suddenly she was ravenous. She pulled on her ratty terry-cloth bathrobe, wrapped her hair in a towel, and waddled to the kitchenette. Even at full term, her posture was rigidly erect, as though she was braced for oncoming conflict. While she waited for water to boil for oatmeal, she double-checked to make sure everything was ready. Her bag was packed for the hospital. The donated car seat stood beside it. Between her next two contractions, she sent Kevin airport information and the address of the hospital. Another contraction. The pain was escalating quickly.

She called her doctor, who told her to go straight to the hospital. It was in Forest Hills, a good forty-five minutes away, considering the usual morning gridlock. Her doula was supposed to drive her out there, to Queens, when the time came. She'd have to wait.

Camila reached for the box of rolled oats in the otherwise-empty cabinet, measured out a cup, and shook it into the boiling water. After stirring for a couple of minutes, she sat at the desk in the room and ate, sipping water from her Audrey Hepburn mug. The crib opposite her twin bed was lined with baby blankets and stuffed animals. One white teddy bear had his paws stitched together in prayer. When she pressed his belly, a scratchy recording of the Lord's Prayer buzzed from a speaker box inside his stuffing. Most everything for the baby had been donated by a mission of nuns in a brownstone uptown, where a shelf of anti-abortion pamphlets greeted you at the door. She had to remember to bring the blue-and-white shawl one of the sisters had knit.

The open shelving beside the crib was stacked with what she'd carried back to her room from the mission: a humidifier, diapers, a little plastic toy truck. Behind the shelves, the wall was painted a spring green, perhaps intended to calm, but there was a sharpness to the color. The opposite wall was painted a powder blue that she preferred. The twin bed was pushed against that wall. A wooden dorm dresser stood by the foot of the bed. On top of it lay a dozen nail polishes, a lint brush, and a Bible open to the page blessing the house of the servant of God. The dresser was filled with secondhand onesies and tiny pairs of pants. There would soon be a person to dress in all that neatly folded cotton. Her son. She wouldn't be alone in this room anymore.

The phone rang; her doula, finally. They were excited to hear each other's voices, to know that the moment had arrived. Over the weekend, they had walked for hours in Prospect Park, laughing about men, talking about new motherhood. They had the kind of intimate connection Camila made easily. Holding fast to those connections was another thing, partly because her life was so itinerant, untethered to family, moving along to the next temporary place to stay, but also because she could coax a grudge from something minor, even imagined, into something that pushed her from fight straight to flight. Her dark eyes would lose their luminescence, suddenly murky and shadowed, like a heavy curtain had tumbled over a bright window.

From earliest childhood, Camila had been an emotional pugilist. She'd been hurt too many times not to be. Few things agonized her more than feeling like the fool, thinking she should have known better. She had little control over her housing, her finances, her days spent in the infinite waiting rooms of aid bureaucracy, and even less control over the family she was born into. But she could control relationships, if she stayed on high alert for signs of disrespect, for the smallest implication of mistreatment. Getting played was the most unbearable of her life's myriad humiliations, the one that she avoided at all costs.

And yet, despite her own guardedness, she was a romantic. She couldn't help herself. That spirit led to how she imagined having a son: She'd have the most everlasting relationship there was. Not that her mother had approached parenthood that way. But it was yet another way Camila could demonstrate that she was nothing like her mother.

As Camila dressed, she heard Irina's baby crying across the hall. She dressed in shorts and a maternity blouse and banged on her door.

Irina opened it. She'd given birth to her son just a few weeks earlier.

"This is it!" Camila announced, grinning cheerfully through the pain.

"I knew it! I saw it on your face last night! Don't be scared," Irina said, her Ukrainian accent still thick despite her decade in New York. "I'm going to pray for you."

Through the doorway, Camila could see Irina's room. It looked like a warehouse from a baby-goods catalog: a crib filled with stuffed animals and blankets, a floor crowded with play mats and infant swings, her son's name in individual plush letters hanging on a wall. Irina's churchgoing may not have yielded her a home or a job, but it did offer a bounty of baby presents. In the framed photos covering the dresser, Irina's family was as present as Camila's was absent. The iPad Irina used to FaceTime her husband and her mother sat propped on the table, yet she was here alone. Purple smudges under Irina's eyes made them appear bruised by exhaustion; the long mousy-brown roots of her dyed-blond hair suggested it had been many months since she cared much about her appearance. The picture on the dresser of a woman in a wedding dress, flaxen hair in curling-iron twists, barely resembled her. Yet under Irina's haggard mask, her cheekbones remained broad, her pale-green eyes remained wide, her chin remained proud.

As they hugged, Camila's doula called to say she was searching for parking. Camila went back into her room to look out the window for the car. Across Fourth Avenue, the fancy kids' play space was opening for the day. The grates were already up next door at the pharmacy selling organic beauty products.

Then she felt a release. Her water had broken. She called her doula to tell her not to worry about parking. Camila suddenly realized that without Wi-Fi she wouldn't be able to communicate with anyone; her calling plan had been cut off weeks ago. Hopefully the hospital would have Internet.

Camila texted her sisters, hoping they would come. She knew better than to expect her mother to show up.

In the delivery room, a mantra looped through her mind: He's coming, Kevin is coming. She felt exhilaration, despite the pain. The hours passed. The doctor examined her and said it was too dangerous to wait any longer. He knew Camila had counted on a natural birth, but the umbilical cord was wrapped around the baby's shoulder like a purse.

Camila needed a C-section immediately. She wouldn't let herself be scared; it was information, just like all other information. As the nurse scooped Camila's curls into a surgical cap, prepared her for surgery, and wheeled her through the maternity ward, Camila chatted continuously, asking questions about the nurse's family, her background and training, the procedure about to begin. She followed the nurse's instructions to stretch her arms out onto the metal trays attached to the surgical table, making a cross with her body. A thick curtain hung halfway down her torso, hiding the doctor and the incision he was making below. She felt a tugging deep within, followed by a wail.

There, in the operating room, Camila became a single mother.

After the surgery and the post-op, and the initial thrill of having survived the procedure and having a boy who survived it, a boy that was hers, Camila occupied herself for a little while by taking selfies with her son on her chest. She shared his name on Facebook: Alonso Alvarez. She posted the selfies. The doula and doctor had left, and the nurses changed shifts. She was bored. She was lonely. Then it struck her hard: No one was there for her. Her sisters hadn't come. Her mother hadn't come. That wasn't a surprise, but still. Kevin was on his way, at least. She tried to take solace in the fact that he'd be there soon to meet Alonso in the hospital, just like a real father. Camila took some more selfies, trying to distract herself from how slowly the minutes were passing. It's hard for many of us to imagine that things could get worse than going into labor in a homeless shelter and giving birth utterly alone. But Camila would look back upon this time in the hospital with nostalgia. And she'd be alone then, too.

2

FOURTH AVENUE

n the mid-nineteenth century, soon after their completion of Central Park, Frederick Law Olmsted and Calvert Vaux laid out a 585-acre park on Prospect Hill in Brooklyn. Fill allowed streets to form a grid across the boggy land that sloped down to Gowanus Creek. Elevated train tracks quickly shadowed Third and Fifth Avenues, but in between them, Fourth Avenue—where Camila's shelter would stand one day—was cultivated into a grand European boulevard. A wide median of grass and trees rolled down its center, a place for a stroll or a bicycle ride. The wonder of electric lights illuminated the walkways in the evenings.

By 1910, the parkway was gone in the name of progress. Fourth Avenue had been entirely excavated to extend Manhattan's subway into Brooklyn. Trees had been uprooted, never to be replanted, and grass dug up and discarded. Once construction was finished underground, the subway tunnel was paved over, replacing greenery with ventilation grids. Fourth Avenue became a newly industrial avenue for a newly industrial time, with auto-body shops and garages studding the street alongside tenements that would stand for another hundred years.

Nobody chose to live on Fourth. Those who could afford it lived up the hill, closer to the park, in ornate houses on tree-lined blocks. If you found any success along the avenue in the fifties, chances were you moved up and out to one of the new suburban developments on Long Island. If you grew up closer to the park in the sixties or seventies, you knew to stay away from Fourth Avenue's barren seediness.

Fourth was where McDonald's planted its golden arches in Park Slope, both for the cheapness of the lot and the budget of the Brooklynites it wished to draw. And it was where that same McDonald's was razed a few decades later, after the neighborhood was rezoned for luxury towers. On that lot, red and yellow plastic was replaced by glass and steel: a residential building that offered stroller valet service in addition to wine refrigerators in every unit. The cheapest condos in the building started at $1.3 million—if you wanted a view with what the developers called "unlimited horizons," it cost $2 million more. These offering plans, and many more like them, were birthed the year Camila's baby was brought home to Fourth Avenue, homeless.

Several blocks up Fourth that same year, a two-story institutional rectangle of a building sold for $25 million to a private developer. Until the sale, it had been the area's Medicaid office. A block south, a new rental building offered a pet spa and a roof deck with cabanas and outdoor showers, where one-bedrooms cost $4,000 a month. That was the median rent for an apartment in Manhattan that year; in Brooklyn it had climbed almost 11 percent since the prior year, to over $3,000. And rents weren't rising highest and fastest in the upper end of the market but at the lower echelon, in the crumbling tenements with mice and roaches instead of pet spas. Brooklyn was building more apartments than anywhere else in the country, adding 24,575 units to its housing stock. But for anyone who was struggling, it made little difference. It was a developer's game. What wasn't being torn down to be rebuilt as bulk luxury was available to private buyers at sums that had been unthinkable just a decade before, when market-watchers declared that housing had hit a peak.

The borough that immigrants had once fled as soon as they'd climbed up into the American middle class was becoming a gated community. And yet people were still from here. People bought their groceries at the Key Food supermarket on Fifth—people who'd never stepped into the massive new Whole Foods on Third. But they wouldn't be able to shop at Key Food much longer; that low-slung brick building had just been sold to developers, too. It was pretty much the only place in the neighborhood the women at the shelter walked to, beating a triangular path between their temporary residence, the supermarket, and the subway up on Atlantic. They knew what was for them and what wasn't. They wouldn't so much as glance in the windows at the craft butchery or the Swedish espresso café as they passed by—the café I would walk to with Rose, who ran the shelter, so we could discuss the lives of those same homeless women over four-dollar coffees.

In the mid-seventies, a group of nuns running a soup kitchen in a nearby storefront let it be known they were looking for a new space, one that could offer overnight accommodation to Brooklyn's increasing homeless population—a fairly typical arrangement before zoning laws intervened. An Italian American family in the neighborhood offered them one of the dilapidated factory-and-warehouse buildings they owned. The sisters set up a kitchen in the back, with just a regular stove like you'd find in someone's home. They put pots of water on the burners and added anything they could scrounge up to turn the water into soup. During the day, tables lined the floor. At night, the nuns would stack up the tables and set cots in their place. Then in the morning, they'd stack up the cots and replace them with the tables again.

A generation passed. In the nineties, the family's children inherited the buildings and saw they could make money off a sale. They approached Sister Mary, who had taken over operations. The nuns had no money; the bank account dedicated to the soup kitchen held only three hundred dollars. Sister Mary asked for three months to find cash for a down payment. A local nonprofit got wind of the effort and applied for a grant from the state. They received money to properly equip the soup kitchen, and beyond that, they secured funding to establish nine small residences on the floors above, to house new mothers. Those mothers would be permitted to stay for a year with their babies. But only so long as they worked and looked for permanent housing.

Several years before I started visiting the shelter, sparks ignited a five-alarm fire inside the auto-body shop next door. For two days, firefighters attacked the flames from the residents' windows, as their rooms filled with fumes from car batteries and burning paint. The insurance settlement for the shelter's damage was almost enough to pay off the mortgage and make the shelter habitable again; donations covered the rest. Meanwhile, Sister Mary had fallen out of favor with the Franciscan Sisters of the Poor: She was an eccentric who resisted direction from the higher authorities of the order. In 2013, another woman was hired to replace her. Her name was Rose.

Rose was the daughter of Italian Americans who had been lured away from Brooklyn decades before by the new suburbia. In her early twenties, in the late days of disco, she had been fascinated by the city and found a cheap apartment in the borough. She spent the next few decades working in the city, eventually as an executive vice president for a large homeless-advocacy group. She'd become an expert in discerning differences—between the desperate and the merely struggling, between heartbreaking true stories and lies, between those who were raised in the system and those who ended up there through poor choices. She liked to say that she'd seen it all. Running the soup kitchen and the shelter, she suffered no fools. Long ago she'd perfected the art of listening with a suspicious ear, her mouth curved into a dubious smile. Her love was tough, and to most of the women who lived above her office, it didn't feel like love at all; it felt like arbitrary rules arbitrarily enforced. "They think I don't know them, but I know them," she'd often say to me.

I liked Rose—the stories she'd tell me were accented with both warmth and skepticism, a New Yorkese of Ebbets Field and the IRT rather than this moneyed Brooklyn. But I was aware, too, that her office was often dark by late afternoon. Rose had been drawn to her work from a sense of social justice, but she'd been at it most of her adult life. Her attention was focused now on a restaurant she was planning to open in Cobble Hill, a nearby neighborhood where diners and Italian bakeries had been replaced by high-end boutiques. There was even the very definition of a luxury department store, a Barneys New York, in a newly constructed building marketed as a "mews." To the zip code's current denizens, the poverty Rose encountered at the shelter had become as anachronistic as it was invisible.

Sometimes when I'd stop into her office, she'd show me pictures of stools she was considering for the restaurant's bar rather than discuss the various ordeals of the mothers living upstairs. She was tired of it all, the excuses, the desperation, the dramas. Over her career, she'd seen the chances for women like them go from bad to worse. And she saw the "girls"—always the "girls"—develop an entitlement that stretched in the opposite direction, she said. Her job was to keep the shelter afloat and make sure there was no trouble. She wasn't going to hang around Fourth Avenue any more than she had to.

The "girls" under her oversight might not have realized it, but she was the reason they had housing there. They weren't aware she had nearly single-handedly resurrected the place from near-ruin at the hands of the nun who preceded her. Or, in other words, that she had worked to give them a place to live for their child's first year in a safe building in what had become a safe neighborhood. The residents only saw her as a fickle landlord, someone who could find reason to kick them out before their year was up. It was an image she cultivated. "I'm the enforcer," she'd say—a five-foot-tall enforcer who loomed large in her crisp white oversized button-downs.

Certain rules were clear: You had to be in your room for the night by nine o'clock. You had to clean daily and submit to weekly room inspections. You had to attend the house meeting every Wednesday evening. You had to be working by the time your baby was three months old. You had to be actively looking for permanent housing. After your baby was three months old, you needed to be employed full-time or in school full-time. Otherwise it was simply Rose's call whether you were in or out.

Her windowed office was crammed with ephemera that home-less men would bring as offerings when they frequented the soup kitchen. A Barbie doll dressed as a nun. A chipped coffee cup. A picture of the pope. A discarded Valentine's Day garland. Presiding over it all was an oval-framed portrait of a woman in a black habit, Mary Frances Schervier, a sweet-faced young German nun, born in 1819, whose order was the genesis of this place and others like it around the world. Schervier's biography was a lesson in profound empathy verging on martyrdom. Rose's philosophy of how to best aid the poor diverged from the nineteenth-century nun's, at least when it came to those who lived upstairs. Namely, if the residents were comfortable, they'd never find their way on their own. At least that's how she explained it to me: They needed to be on edge; oth-erwise they wouldn't work to find permanent housing. And so her rules changed constantly.

Prospective residents could apply by referral, usually by one of the city's Catholic service organizations. They'd come to fill out an application detailing the reasons for their homelessness, their family backgrounds, their mental health, their criminal histories. If any-thing suggested a woman would cause drama, Rose would just shake her head. If you were accepted, you got a room with a bath-room and a kitchenette for $258 a month. You had to pay to use the stacked washer-dryer that was tucked into a closet by the front desk. It cost about the same as a laundromat, and you had to wait your turn—it was constantly in use, all those burp cloths, all those onesies—but it beat dragging a newborn to the laundromat. No social services were provided; meals were your own responsibility. The soup kitchen downstairs was open to all, but none of the resi-dents used it. That place was for the bums, the men off the street. Upstairs, homelessness had a very different status.

Many of the women upstairs had already done time at other shelters. They described the filth and infestations they'd encoun-tered at city shelters, where overcrowding, mental illness, and de-spair meant the very air vibrated with the constant threat of violence. I'd seen it myself, as an occasional volunteer, relegated only to activity rooms and common areas, never the residential areas. Some said the private shelters where they'd been before this one, ones still run by various Catholic orders, were even worse. They described punitive nuns, draconian rules, and single beds crammed together in Dickensian quarters. Privacy was a privilege, and the shelter on Fourth Avenue offered plenty of it.

I hadn't had much luck finding a shelter that would open its doors to a journalist. It was easy to presume why. There was an interest in protecting residents' safety and privacy, of course, but furthermore an unwillingness to expose to the light whatever darkness might lie within, whether conflicts and outbursts between residents or questions of staff abuse and cleanliness. I've seen plenty of slights amplified, accusations thrown, fury trained on minutiae, situations mishandled. It's hard to imagine that any organization would choose to manage such fire under observation, much less to reveal the physical and psychological circumstances of shelter life in institutions that have no oversight or governance beyond what a board or church chooses to scrutinize. And that's just the private shelters. City shelters don't permit journalists, period.

I'd gotten an email from a volunteer group that a private shelter in Park Slope was looking for women to mentor its residents. I wrote the director, Rose, to say I'd like to report rather than mentor. To my surprise, she immediately agreed to meet with me. And so I found myself sitting in her cluttered office off the soup kitchen one spring afternoon. She needed someone to help manage the weekly residents meeting, she said, held from six to eight every Wednesday evening. She had one volunteer who'd been running the meeting for a few months, but she couldn't be there every week, and there were some issues with her showing up to the shelter stinking drunk. At the meeting, I'd need to ask the women about their weeks, introduce a weekly speaker, and make sure everyone showed up. If I was willing to do that, I could do whatever else I wanted there—didn't matter to her, she said.

I'm not certain why she was so blasé about inviting a reporter into her small shelter. Perhaps her need for a new volunteer outweighed any trepidation she may have felt, or she thought such attention would help the shelter with fundraising. Perhaps she was proud of the work she was doing and craved some attention for it after so many years in the field and thought that if she gave me access, her generosity would be reflected in a flattering portrayal. Perhaps she felt isolated there and thought I might be a like-minded person to talk to about the mothers in her charge, the broken system, the broken city, to be a witness to the mess she lived with every day. This was New York: Systems may have been closed, but instinct and mutual benefit led people to open doors.

It was an offer many journalists would have refused, citing common professional standards. I would be working in service to my possible subjects and, while not officially on staff, in a stafflike position. That crossed a pretty clear professional boundary. And that boundary was ringed with more ethical barbed wire. In the most rigorously defined situation, my privilege as an educated white woman with familial, class, and relative financial stability would already present a quagmire. In this one, in which I had a role in the organization, the power differential between us wouldn't be just a question of identity but of my being seen as having administrative authority over them. But, honestly, I thought I'd feel more comfortable at the shelter if I was able to be useful in some small way. And providing a modicum of service wouldn't solve anyone's problems, minute or systemic. It was a cost of entry that I was happy to pay.

The day I met Camila, she told me she'd always wanted to tell her story. She hadn't had her baby yet, but she would soon. For Camila, for now, the shelter was the best option in a bad scenario. But it was no real solution. She needed somewhere permanent, someplace hers, where she could build a stable life and be a stable parent. Her name was in more affordable-housing lotteries than she could keep track of and had been on the public-housing wait list since she was in her teens. Something would come through soon, she insisted, telling herself as much as me. The shelter on Fourth Avenue might be Alonso's first home, but it wouldn't remain his home for long.

3

HOMECOMING

Camila came home, homeless, from the hospital, eager to present Alonso to her shelter mates, and to me. A few hours before the weekly residents meeting, I climbed the stairs to sit on her bed, holding Alonso as he slept, while she washed her hair and scrunched it into curls with Herbal Essences mousse. She offered me an organic apple and then bit into one herself, walking over to the closet to select a tiny madras shirt for Alonso to wear, coordinated with a similar blouse for herself that matched her pale-pink shorts. Just a few days after her C-section, she hardly looked as though she'd ever been pregnant.

It was six o'clock, time to go downstairs to the meeting in the common room. She slipped a gold band and a cubic zirconia solitaire onto her ring finger. She said the rings had been a gift from Kevin, to remind her of him as she walked the streets of New York. "This is a symbol to show you're mine. Every time you wear it you're representing me," she told me he'd said. She wore another ring, too, on her middle finger, that she'd bought herself when she graduated high school. Her promise ring, she called it. The promise was to respect herself, be a good woman, and finish college. Camila didn't think that promise applied any less now that she had a baby on her own; the plan was the same whether she was a single mother or not. After all, most of the women she'd known were single mothers.

She beckoned me into the bathroom to hang out while she put on her makeup. We talked to each other's reflection in the mirror above the sink. As she carefully applied foundation, she told me that if a mother couldn't live a life of value, raising a kid while making something of herself, then what was the value of life, anyway. It was a statement, not a philosophical question. I asked her if it might be more complicated than that. She raised her eyebrows dismissively at my reflection and began to brush mascara on her long lashes. When she was satisfied with how she looked, she finally replied: She was going to make it in America without bitching about the system, like she'd heard the welfare mothers do her whole life. That was her refrain in those early days of motherhood, demonstrating her own strength and, by implication, deriding anyone else's weakness. I was learning that homelessness has a hierarchy, at least to the women I was beginning to know, of those on the street, then those in a city shelter, then those in a private shelter (so long as it was a desirable one), then those who were on their way out of homelessness altogether. Similar categories existed for welfare, for paternal involvement, for education, for work—a class system of the underclass, like all else.

Powdered and ready, Camila hoisted up Alonso, still sleeping, and followed the sound of young women and newborn babies down the stairwell. The shelter's common room was a long, narrow space lined with squared-off wooden couches that looked like they'd spent a previous life in a dormitory lounge. Baby bouncers and a few rocking chairs were jammed in among the couches. On an end table, a dusty bouquet of polyester roses leaned precariously in a plastic vase. A blocky PC, which hadn't worked in some time, hulked atop a dining table that had been shoved awkwardly into a corner.

The walls, painted lemon yellow, were decorated with magazine cutouts of babies and flowers pasted between hand-drawn flamingos, a tiger, a stag, and a stork. Near the ceiling, metal peel-off letters, the kind that serve as cheap signage or house numbers, spelled out A LIFE'S JOURNEY on an uneven line. Adverse childhood experiences—to use a clinical term for a range of instability, abandonment, and various other traumas—statistically predict homelessness. Every infant who passed through this room had been born into such a childhood of adverse experience, such a life's journey. Most every mother had been, too.

"You had the baby!" Susan, who had been running the weekly meetings, approached Camila with her long hands outstretched. She was tall, even in her Tevas. Curtains of dark hair and the scent of alcohol on her breath amplified what her pallor suggested. When she was sober, Susan was courteous and professional. But the suspicion that she wasn't kept the residents on edge, especially when she reached for their newborns.

Camila smiled politely and took a seat, cradling Alonso in her skinny arms. Meetings began with the residents going around in a circle to report on their week. Camila offered to speak first.

"Tell us about the father," Susan said too eagerly.

Camila explained that he was a good friend who lived in Buffalo. A football player with an agent, about to get signed. "It works great. He has his goals, I have mine," she said, her voice casual, her smile confident. "He'll play professional ball, I'll have a career in criminal justice, and we'll both be involved in our son's life." Then she changed the subject to childcare. "I want a nanny for him," she said. "I don't want to put him in a daycare. Nannies teach them, they learn sooner, they walk sooner. I'm concerned about putting him in a place that's not teaching him."

Nannies were for another kind of Park Slope parent. It always seemed, though, that Camila didn't carry the feeling that the other women did, that privileges afforded to others were unthinkable for themselves. I'd noticed how that distinction often intimidated and distanced women from Camila, women who were mystified that she didn't know that such things weren't for her, who were perplexed by her elegance and her ability to fit in anywhere—which made her belong nowhere. The room was quiet, as it often would be after Camila spoke, as the women looked away from her toward their babies or stared, bored, at the floor.

Sherice was the one resident who never seemed intimidated by Camila. She was sitting on the next couch, in a Minnie Mouse sweatshirt and leggings, bouncing her son, Tyrese, on her lap. Tyrese had tiny braids sprouting from his scalp that Sherice fussed over when she was nervous. He was almost one. That meant Sherice only had a couple of months to find a new place to live—her year at the shelter was almost up.

"I know a place that is pretty good for daycare," Sherice said, tucking her weave back behind an ear, unfazed by Camila's high-class preferences. She worked day shifts at Applebee's. Days paid much less money than nights, but between daycare hours and the shelter curfew, she had no choice.

Alonso let out a cry. Camila rocked him in her arms and changed the subject again. "I didn't want him to be a Gemini," she said, her smile still fixed, looking down at his face. "Gemini men are so two-faced. I'm just bummed Alonso wasn't born a couple of weeks sooner."

"You're a Capricorn, right? That's so Capricorn, so headstrong you think you can control when your baby's born." Sherice grinned and shook her head.

"That's me." Camila smiled even bigger, her white teeth gleaming.

Near her feet, another baby rocked in a bouncer. His eyes, as black as his hair, were glazed over, staring unfocused at the ceiling. He began to wail. His mother, Tina, ignored his cries from a few seats away. She was a pale, stocky brunette with eyes only slightly less vacant than her son's. Despite the early-summer heat, she was wearing a thick hoodie and lace-up winter boots.

"I'm worried about running out of diaper wipes," Tina said, when Susan called upon her to talk about her week. "I've been trying to conserve them by ripping them in half, but they don't work as well that way."

"I'm sure we can find you some more donated wipes in the office," Susan said.

"I'm worried they're going to run out." Her baby had begun to shriek.

"I think he might be uncomfortable," Camila said.

Tina turned on her, suddenly frantic, her eyes wild. "Why? Why would you say that to me?"

"He's crying. That's all."

"Why would you say that to me?" she shouted again. "And his name is Jayden, not 'he'!"

Sherice looked at Tina and then just shook her head.

No one ever seemed to remember his name. People had a hard enough time remembering hers. Their sentences would just trail off when they began to refer to her. Or they'd call her "the crazy one." Rose had admitted Tina despite her personal rule against offering a room to anyone with pronounced mental instability. Tina had promised she'd take her medication, meet with her psychologist, her psychiatrist, and the two social workers who'd been assigned her case. But once she had Jayden, she stopped. No more meds, no more sessions, nothing. Social services sent in a parenting coach to meet with her at the shelter. Tina said she didn't like the coach or her accent. She wouldn't talk to her. Now it was as though she had two settings: absence or eruption.

Sitting beside her was Irina, who told me she prayed for Tina every night in her room—the one across from Camila's. In the past month, Irina had graduated from Bible college and given birth to Dima, the blue-eyed, towheaded baby she held in her arms. She'd admitted that her Bible college certificate would do about as much for her prospects as her law degree from Russia. But the church had become the only stable thing in her life, other than her husband's face on the screen of her tablet when he called from his military base in Kiev. "He is a soldier," she'd explain to each new resident who arrived. "He jumps out of airplanes. He needs to keep the land safe."

Irina got pregnant the last time she saw her husband. Who knew when she'd see him again. A lot had happened since that time. Not just Dima, but the tragedy. That's what she called it, when she mentioned it at all. She wouldn't describe it to anyone, not even Camila in the weeks since their friendship had developed. I only knew about it at first because Rose told me it had been in all the newspapers for a week and on the local nightly news.

That spring, Irina had been living with her brother and father on the second floor of a walk-up off Ocean Avenue in Brighton Beach. She was concerned about her brother, who had become morose and withdrawn. They were only a year apart and had been raised together by their grandparents in Russia. When they were young children, their parents had left them there to look for better work in the States. After finishing their studies, they joined their parents in Brooklyn.

A typical Eastern European immigrant story. Until one night, when Irina woke to hear a struggle in the next room. She rushed in to find her brother repeatedly plunging a knife into their father's neck. When she lunged at him, her brother sliced her forehead and wrist. She turned from him to protect Dima, growing inside her. He stabbed her in the back. Then he threw himself through a window to the pavement. Irina ran screaming out of the building for two blocks before she collected herself enough to call the police. Irina's father was dead. Her brother was dead. And she was homeless and alone in America. Her husband couldn't leave the army, not even for a week. She sometimes said she'd go back to Russia, where her mother had returned, if it got safer. But she found it hard to imagine it would.

It was Irina's turn to tell the room about her week. Dima had hardly slept, and the exhaustion was breaking her down. "When I cry, Dima hears me and cries, too, so I try not to be sad in front of him," she said. "But I only have one room. Where else could I go?" She sighed and gazed down at her son in her arms. "I pray and try to stay positive. God will take care of us."

The pregnant woman sitting next to her, Anselma, hadn't spoken yet during the meeting. She sat with her hands folded in her lap under her huge belly, in elaborate makeup, her cheekbones highlighted and contoured, her eyebrows carefully drawn. She wore a thin T-shirt, pajama pants covered in hearts, and slipper socks designed to look like cats. Anselma was new, and nervous.

Camila sensed her anxiety. She offered a bright look of encouragement, looped an arm inside hers, and scooted closer on the couch. The weekend before Alonso's birth, they had gone to Manhattan Beach together. They took selfies in the white Memorial Day sunlight, both enormously pregnant in their bikinis. Camila told me she was excited to have a new friend, well put together and Dominican like her. They'd become mothers together, she said.

Anselma had been working as a bartender at a midtown hotel, where her extravagant lips and curves yielded ample tips. But nobody wanted to see a pregnant woman shaking a martini. For the first time since she dropped out of high school, intending to make it in the fashion world, Anselma was out of a job. She couldn't pay rent. Her boyfriend, a single father, could barely house and feed the kid he already had. At first he told her he'd be there for her. Then he changed his mind.

Now she spent sleepless nights and anxious days in a near-constant state of terror about her coming childbirth. That week, her eyes had frequently brimmed with tears, anticipating what was certain to come, fear squeezing her voice into a whisper. She had seen deliveries before, many of them. Her grandmother was an obstetrician in Santiago and had her own clinic at her house. Throughout her childhood, until she moved to New York, Anselma would watch her grandmother deliver babies, silently peering into the clinic room. She was frightened by, rather than inured to, what she'd seen.

The prior week at the meeting, she and Camila had sat side by side, comparing sunburns from their day at the beach, each marveling at the kicking in the other's womb. They promised they'd tell each other when their labor began. And yet when Camila had gone to the hospital, she hadn't said a word to Anselma. Nor did she reach out when she returned. Anselma told me she had thought they were friends. She didn't understand why Camila would exclude her from something so important and then switch on the charm at the meeting. She played along, cozying up to Camila on the couch, but she didn't trust her anymore.

It seemed, as it often did with Camila, that jealousy was to blame. It was one thing for Camila when Anselma talked about her baby's father breaking her heart; Camila could feel solidarity with someone similarly beautiful and refined, homeless and alone. But that week, Anselma had said her man might be coming back to her after all. The connection severed. It was intolerable that Anselma might have that possibility when, despite Camila's attempts to convince herself otherwise, Kevin wasn't coming back to her. Not even now that Camila had a baby.

During the meeting that night, Rose's old friend Michelle was minding the desk. She looked like a wizened doll in white Capri leggings and a matching ruffled tank top, her hair sprayed in a French twist, her nails painted in a French manicure. An inventory of tinny necklaces and stacks of bangles chimed her departure down the stairs for cigarette breaks. Her smile was easy, but under it she was a bulldog. She liked to say, "You don't want to see the Brooklyn come out of me." Rose had trusted Michelle with the responsibility of the shelter in the evenings, and she wasn't going to mess it up. That meant enforcing regulations.

As the meeting ended, an immaculate woman in a black blouse rang the buzzer downstairs. Beside her stood an equally immaculate five-year-old girl. The woman said she was Camila's sister, here to take the baby out for a walk. Michelle buzzed her in. She'd thought Camila had no family to look after her. Rose had told Michelle that she thought Camila was probably a con artist. Michelle could see why: Camila's preppy clothes? And a doula? "Who has a doula?" she'd said to me, incredulous. She smelled a rat.

The woman entered with her daughter and smiled nervously at Michelle.

"Camila! You have a visitor here!" Michelle rasped, annoyed, from behind the desk.

Camila came out from the common room holding Alonso and kissed her sister Teresa on the cheek.

"They're going to take the baby for a walk," she told Michelle. "Can she just go up to my room to get the car seat and the Snap-N-Go?"

"No one goes upstairs. Those are the rules."

Camila stiffened. She was exhausted and in pain. She just wanted her sister—a little help, a little sense that someone was there to do something as simple as fetch a stroller for her. She wanted a little peace. Instead, she got this woman barking rules at her.

"They just need to get the car seat and the Snap-N-Go," she repeated politely. "That's all. I'm really not supposed to be walking up and down stairs or lifting anything five days after my C-section."

"You want it, you get it yourself."

Teresa and her daughter stood immobilized, frightened.

"Please," Camila said. Her eyes pooled with tears.

"No visitors. You know the rules. He shouldn't be going outside anyway." She pointed her sharp chin at Alonso. "He's too young."

Camila warned herself not to let the ghetto come out of her. She felt her temper rising. "He's all cooped up in here! He needs fresh air!"

Teresa shifted her weight awkwardly. "I don't want to cause any problems," she said, reticent.

"It's a liability!" Camila raised her voice. "You need to make accommodations!"

Michelle was unbending. And she was furious that this girl would speak to her this way. Wait till she told Rose.

Rose didn't need any troublemakers, anyone who'd be less than respectful of the rules and of the people she employed; she didn't need anyone who wouldn't be grateful for a room in Park Slope for less than three hundred bucks a month. Rose had a hunch Camila had talked her way in to take advantage of the cheap rent—a con artist, she told me, like she'd told Michelle. Rose said that she'd already heard from a pro bono lawyer who called to advocate for Camila soon after she moved in. And if she could find resources like that, she didn't need the room as badly as the other girls who came here. Rose thought she was playing me, too, trying to fool me into helping her. She warned me to watch out.

But in the short time I'd known Camila, I'd come to believe she didn't have any other options. Neither of her parents would take her in. Her sister said she couldn't, either. I'd seen her C-section dressing, held her mewling newborn. Camila would only survive if she pushed back, but pushing back branded her as unworthy of charity. Her best hope for future stability lay in her ability to seek out resources and put them to use, to avail herself of all the social services and pro bono help the world could offer her. Yet would doing so mark her as a con artist? She was only worthy of help if she was otherwise completely helpless? Camila's shrewdness and tenacity in grasping for any resources available wouldn't do much good without a safe place to sleep.

There was more money than ever in the city, but it was hardly padding state budgets. The New York City Housing Authority was essentially bankrupt. The emergency-shelter system was flooded, with an overflow that couldn't be stanched. The richer city residents became, the more housing cost, stranding anyone in need. Those rich residents relied on a massive service class, people to scrape the food from tasting-menu plates, the filth from toilets in renovated brownstones and towering condos, the crusted white faces of toddlers and the elderly. Their pay barely afforded shared bedrooms in overcrowded apartments past the end of subway lines. And Camila didn't even have that kind of cash.

There was a class up from those workers, a professional class, mainly of color, still struggling: social workers, nursing staff, TSA agents. It took a degree to rise up into that class, which meant days spent in school and at the library, not tending to the refuse and progeny of the wealthy. A degree in criminal justice, Camila determined for herself; that was a growth field. She'd have a job on the border patrol at the airport, or as a cop, working her way up through the department. Without a living wage, the life Camila led now— and the only one she'd seen modeled, albeit in a time of housing vouchers and turnover in the projects—was the only future she'd ever see. Shelters. Evictions. A life of no control.

Camila had another vision. A plan. But she needed a stable place for herself and Alonso to stay while she put it in motion. She knew she was lucky to get this room. She knew she couldn't find another.

Not with a newborn. Not while she was still healing from her surgery. Not with no one there to help her.

The next morning Camila received a text from the woman who was in charge of the soup kitchen downstairs. Rose had asked her to write Camila to inform her that she was to be evicted from the shelter. Camila knew she should have kept her mouth shut.

4

GERALDINE

Camila was fifteen when she had sex for the first time. She'd been hanging out with a friend of Teresa's, an older guy who was into her. They weren't *together* together, but they had a thing. A thing Camila's mother found out about. Geraldine called the cops on the guy for statutory rape. Then she kicked Camila out of the house.

When Geraldine was Camila's age, her parents had shipped her off from Queens to the Dominican Republic, where an arranged marriage awaited her. Geraldine's parents believed that becoming a wife would cage her teenage desires. They believed, as well, that becoming a mother, only three days after her sixteenth birthday, would render her an honorable woman. Compared to such a sentence, the lesson Geraldine was teaching Camila by kicking her out of the house seemed moderate. But Geraldine's interests weren't merely, or even mainly, disciplinarian. She saw that she could rid herself of the only one of her kids who fought back, and still cash in Camila's food stamps without even occasionally feeding her.

Plus, Camila's Supplemental Security Income would continue to arrive every month. Geraldine had secured those SSI checks a couple of years earlier when she wrung Camila's arms purple with bruises, brought her to Bellevue, and informed doctors that Camila had been harming herself. Camila had been abusive with the smaller kids in the house, too, Geraldine told them. So began a process of labeling Camila as disabled so Geraldine could obtain federal disability benefits on her behalf. By assaulting and maligning her daughter, Geraldine had augmented her income. It worked so well that she performed the same ruse with Camila's younger sister, to similar results. All this I heard in cold, flat tones from both Camila and her sister.

Before she was even in high school, Camila worked in the hardware store her dad managed, making forty bucks a day. Geraldine would usually claim the money as soon as Camila got home. Sometimes, though, Camila spent it before her mother could take it away from her. She bought herself clothes and Air Jordans so kids at school would stop teasing her about being poor. Or she went shopping for food—usually just rice, really—so she and her siblings wouldn't go hungry. Often, if she didn't, there would only be her mother's takeout in the fridge. If one of the kids ate it, Geraldine would give them a beating. Camila was the only one who would speak up against their mother's abuse. It never made things any better, but silence was an insufferable alternative.

Soon after Camila returned to the shelter from the hospital, she heard a pounding on the door to her room. Wearing only her nursing bra and the postsurgery underwear the hospital had given her, Camila pulled on a bathrobe, freed a breast for Alonso's hungry mouth, and answered the door. Unexpectedly, her mother stood on the other side. Apparently, Teresa had given her Camila's address. And whoever was staffing the desk downstairs had decided to let her come up to meet the baby.

Geraldine gave her a withering once-over. "Get dressed," she said. "No one told me you were in a shelter. This is a shelter, right? Why are you breastfeeding? Your baby's father must have smoked a lot of weed if he's that hungry." She raised a penciled eyebrow.

Her painted face uncannily mirrored her daughter's. The same round eyes, so opaque and dark brown they looked black in the shaded room. The same high cheekbones, lifting every expression into a vague haughtiness. The same defiant chin. Camila always insisted that she looked nothing like her mother, but when I met Geraldine myself, I was stunned by the resemblance.

Geraldine marched over to the cabinets above the counter in the kitchenette and flung them open. Seeing no food, she demanded Camila's food-stamp card, snatched it from her daughter's hand, and left.

Camila climbed back into bed. Still in the lingering anesthesia fog from her C-section, she slept soundly. Until she heard a cabinet door slam. She heard her mother snap, "You don't have any of the right seasonings. I hate cooking at other people's houses."

When Camila woke again after a few hours, the room was quiet. The dishes were done, she told me, and the food was gone. Geraldine had evidently cooked a meal, and instead of sharing it with her daughter or leaving it for her to eat after she woke, she'd just vanished and taken every scrap with her.

All she'd left behind was her name on the guest log. That was enough to convince Rose that Camila had tried to pull one over on her during their intake interview, when she'd said she had no relationship with her mother. If that was the case, then why was she visiting? Rose said she'd met slicksters like Camila before. And she wasn't having it.

If you had a mother, you had a mother, people thought. You had someone to take care of you, somewhere to go. It was rarely that simple for anyone, and it certainly wasn't for Camila. Her only choice was to define herself as utterly motherless. But to Rose, and probably to most people, such larger truths were no better than lies.

5

HOW TO BECOME A
HOMELESS SINGLE MOTHER

Late one night at the shelter, Camila wrote down the twenty-nine places she'd lived. The length of the list didn't strike her as all that unusual, nor did the constant instability it represented. Perhaps it wasn't. One in ten Americans in her age group had also experienced homelessness: three and a half million young adults, age eighteen to twenty-five. Like most of those young Americans, she'd never slept on the street, not yet.

Camila's experience of homelessness had begun in early childhood. Among that ever-growing number of homeless Americans under twenty-five, young parents—especially single mothers—were at three times the risk of finding themselves without shelter. Camila, just a few days into motherhood, was about to find out why.

Her mother, of course, had discovered this truth before her, albeit in a time of lower rents and greater social services. Camila had lived in her mother's apartments, paid for by a government check, with a shelter in Harlem keeping them off the street between leases, back when Camila was ten. One eviction had come when a landlord decided that he didn't want her mom's rent to come from the welfare office anymore—though maybe he had just used that as an excuse to get rid of the Dominican woman with the violent temper and the unsupervised kids. He blamed her poverty instead of her explosive personality, though one certainly set fire to the other.

Things were always tough with her mom, and ultimately untenable. Camila's mom kicked her out of the house. She landed briefly at her dad's, but he didn't want her there either. Foster care in a group home came next. When that proved unbearable to Camila, she rented a room in an apartment on the Lower East Side with the money she earned working in the hardware store. After high school graduation, a college dorm at the University of Buffalo promised stability, but the rest of her life didn't: She had sued her parents for child support, and the expensive and disruptive trips back and forth to court appearances in Queens were more than she could manage, so she dropped out. There's more to all of this, of course. Back in Corona, she found a job with a harassing boss who offered her a place to crash, though she knew she could only hold him off for so long. When she met a woman at church with a spare room in the projects, she moved right in. There's more to this, too; we'll get to that. For now, know that she found herself in a succession of Craigslist rentals, paid for with jobs at a deli and a pharmacy. In between she'd crash with her cousin in the projects in Manhattan. Until she found herself pregnant.

Back in September, when Camila was crashing at her cousin's place in the projects in Chelsea, she'd taken a trip to Buffalo to visit Kevin. They'd met when Camila was a freshman at the University of Buffalo and he was becoming a star on the football team. Like hers, his father had been absent at best. Football had saved him, but it hadn't made him cold or cocky. Camila was as taken with his humility as she was with his wide shoulders and high profile on campus. When she left school, he was what she missed. Shortly after she returned from her trip, she missed her period. She took a home pregnancy test. It was negative. Then she missed her next period and took another. Negative again. After her third month without a cycle, she made an appointment with her ob-gyn in Flushing, whom she'd been seeing since she started having sex.

Later that day, her doctor called her with the test results. After she hung up the phone, she cried. She couldn't go to her mom; that was out of the question. Nor did she feel she could tell her older sister. Teresa had become devoutly religious after an evangelist from the World Mission Society Church of God made a more compelling case about the purpose and meaning of life than anyone else had. Now Teresa spent her weekends in church, day and night, and her evenings after work abstaining from anything but her own motherhood. Though they were in touch, Camila felt she hardly knew her sister anymore.

Back in Corona, Teresa had been the closest thing Camila had to a parent—she had looked after her, taking her to school, making sure she had something to eat, even if it was just rice. Later on, it was Camila who made the rice, as Teresa spent more time at her boyfriend's place. Teresa still looked out for her, though. As Camila became a woman, they got closer, talking about guys, one especially—a friend of Teresa's boyfriend, who had a thing for the flirtatious, quick-witted little sister who'd show up at parties, her gawkiness quickly blooming into gorgeousness. He was seven years older than Camila and already defaulting on child-support payments. Camila was titillated by his attention, attracted to his desire.

Teresa worried about Camila back then, clucking over her with sisterly concern, but these days it seemed she only paid attention to her cultish church's teaching that God was alive in the body of a Korean woman, whose death would bring about the end of the world. Camila decided to keep her predicament to herself.

When she was in high school, Camila had gone to a storefront fortune-teller to have her palm read. The fortune-teller said she was going to be successful, meet someone in the medical field, and have three boys. She figured this baby would be the first.

Weeks passed. December 30, the date for her follow-up appointment, arrived. She lay on the vinyl-covered table, her feet in the stirrups, and saw a heartbeat inside her. She thought about how she didn't have anyone at all. A baby could help her get public housing. A baby could help her feel less alone.

When she called her father to tell him the news, he told her not to go through with it. He was the only one in her family who seemed bothered by the pregnancy. Most of her cousins had their first babies when they were sixteen, like their mothers before them. At twenty-two, Camila seemed like a late bloomer.

Different afternoons with Camila provoked different themes. Sometimes furious narratives would emerge about her parents, triggering questions about mine. Often she delivered treatises, dropping her g's, snapping her head, raising her eyebrows, or jutting her jaw to make a point: on personal style and self-respect, on living with unsatisfied sexual desire, on the frustrations of sisterhood. One particular afternoon she fixated on old friendships. Walking through Corona as Alonso dozed in the stroller, Camila gave me a graveyard tour of where she'd buried her intimacies, like at a laundromat where she told her best friend at the time, a girl named Erika, that she was pregnant.

"I'm taking you for an abortion," Erika told her. "Camila, I won't speak to you ever again if you have that baby."

"You just want to feel better about your own choice," Camila snapped back. She'd been there through both of Erika's abortions.

It was the last time they would see each other. Camila had no truck with any friend who couldn't support her. Plus, she said Erika had kept her boyfriend a secret from her Dominican parents because he was black. If she had a black baby, they'd disown her. That's what she said, at least, but Camila had always thought she was a coward for it.

Not that her mother would have accepted a black baby, either, Camila said. As we kept walking, she told me about when she'd received a dark-skinned Barbie doll as a birthday present. Her mom threw it away. She didn't want her daughter to play with a black doll, she said; that was how you learned to have sex, and she didn't want Camila associating sex with anyone looking like that.

A few years later, when Camila was nine, Geraldine humiliated and punished her for a crush—her first—on a black boy down the hall at the Harlem shelter. Camila wrote him a love note, but her mother intercepted it and used it to mortify her. Geraldine told everyone at the shelter that no daughter of hers was going to get pregnant with a black guy. Camila was still years away from her period, but such logic was irrelevant to her mother. It was the same thinking that barred Camila from watching *Pretty Woman,* out of certainty it would make her a prostitute. She found a way to see it anyway. It instantly became her favorite movie.

It was no wonder Camila developed an arch sense of irony at an early age: not only because of the magical thinking behind such totalitarian rules but because they were written and enforced by a woman who'd had four children with four men, none of whom stuck around to raise their kid. Mauricio had at least announced Camila's birth over the loudspeaker at the hardware store where he worked when Geraldine called him from the hospital. Camila was proud of that story; she was the only one of her mother's children who knew her father, as far as she knew. Geraldine had girl after girl after girl after girl, none of them planned, none of them the boy that she wanted. A few years later, Teresa made her a grandmother. As soon as Teresa's daughter learned to talk, Geraldine insisted that she never call her Grandma in front of anyone.

Back when Camila was little, her grandparents would send her down Forty-fifth Avenue to get sandwiches at the bodega. She would linger there while the cashier ran her mother's Electronic Benefits Transfer card, listening to people talk about her mom, about how she'd go to bed with anyone, about which guy she'd slept with the night before. Geraldine had met Mauricio, Camila's dad, at that very bodega. He'd picked her up one morning when she'd gone out to get the papers for her dad. Mauricio lived just seven blocks away from the apartment Geraldine shared with her siblings and parents. His girlfriend lived even closer. Soon both women would be pregnant.

Camila told me that when Mauricio found out she was having a baby, he didn't even ask who the father was.

"You'll be on welfare," he said, "like all the Mexican moms with five kids."

"I'm never going to be on welfare," Camila said. She didn't bother to comment on the fact that Mauricio had seven kids, or more. She didn't actually know how many. She suspected he didn't, either.

The last week arrived when she could legally get an abortion. Camila made an appointment at Planned Parenthood. She told her cousin Nikki about the appointment. "I've regretted every abortion I've had, every day of my life," her cousin said.

Camila didn't show up for the appointment.

Despite her advice, Nikki had no intention of letting Camila go into labor in her apartment, where she was crashing, much less live there with a newborn.

Camila had no place to go but a shelter. She found two in New York that accepted pregnant women, one in Brooklyn and another way up in the Bronx. But each required the applicant to be in her last trimester. That was months away. She took the bus back to Buffalo to stay with Kevin for a week, but she needed to find a more permanent solution, or at least a more stable temporary one.

The only place she could find that would accept her was in Sussex County, New Jersey, over two hours away on the bus, which offered young expecting mothers an attic room lined with cots and a shared bathroom in an old Victorian house. Camila packed her bags, took the subway to Port Authority, and boarded a bus. She lugged her bags up the hill from the quaint but largely abandoned historic town center toward the shelter. In the open attic, she unpacked her things. She realized she wouldn't be able to return to the city to see anyone—the round trip on the occasional buses couldn't get her back by curfew. Her shelter mates would sit around all day eating and fighting. Camila tried to keep her temper under control and stay out of the house. She enrolled in community college there, the only pregnant student at the school. She got a job in the registrar's office and wrote term papers on the Black Panthers and the relationship between single parenthood and incarceration.

While she was living at the shelter, she had a dream. She was in a cavernous lobby hung with chandeliers. In the center of the room was a fountain that pumped liquid gold instead of water. She and Kevin rode an escalator upward together, holding hands. When she woke up, she searched online for what escalators signified. Dream-Dictionary online said they represented success. She thought it was a sign that she and Kevin would be a family and achieve their goals. She barely noted that in the dream she wasn't pregnant.

In that shelter, Camila began planning her baby shower. Over five pages of a spiral notebook, she carefully wrote down the addresses for the sixty-odd people she planned to invite: aunts, cousins, former co-workers, all the people whose lives she tracked on Facebook. She'd have to rent tables, chairs, hire a DJ. Camila designed invitations with stickers she made that said, *My belly is too big, My luggage is too tight, So a gift certificate is just right.* She sent them out to all the names in her notebook. Other than her sisters, none of them knew she was in a shelter. She didn't want to see these people unless she had something to celebrate. Some replied to the invitation, some didn't. A couple of weeks before the date arrived, Camila canceled the shower. She told everyone she wasn't feeling well, but it was just an excuse. She didn't have the money to pay for it. And, she thought, most of them weren't going to show up anyway.

6

THE DECIDER

A few days after she got the eviction text, Camila took a seat in the chair wedged between Rose's desk and the door to the soup kitchen. While Rose wrapped up a phone call, Camila stared at a wall calendar. She'd been here barely a full month. Alonso was a week old; Kevin had told her he was going to train outside Chicago after his graduation that week. Teresa's apartment was overcrowded.

Rose hung up and turned to look at her. "So, what's the problem, Camila? I heard you had a problem with Michelle."

"Michelle isn't polite," she said.

"Where'd you grow up?" Rose asked her, as if she was just making conversation.

"New York," Camila said.

"In a private home? With a family?"

"In a foster home, as a ward of the state." That was stretching it a bit, as Camila was with her mother until high school.

"And everyone was polite?"

Camila just stared at her. How many times had she heard this order of logic before? Because you were born with nothing, you deserve nothing. Because your family had no respect, you deserve no respect. Because you can't afford what's decent in the world, you deserve indecency.

Rose was exasperated. Since Camila had received her eviction text, she'd gotten calls from an attorney, from Camila's high school mentor, even from the executive director of the shelter's board. Rose told me she saw it as just more proof that Camila was trying to con her—if she had all these resources at her disposal, why was she in a shelter? All these people calling, asking why Camila was being kicked out without notice, all telling her that Camila felt unsafe.

"If you and your baby feel unsafe, you shouldn't be here," Rose said to Camila. "I'll put you in a cab. You won't have to take the train."

"I think you should fire Michelle," Camila said.

"When you sit in this chair, you can make those decisions."

Camila stared back. She'd been recording conversations, saving emails, making notes everywhere she went for as long as she could remember. No matter what place she was in, she knew how to protect herself. Legal action provided her the only form of power or control in her life, and legal action required evidence—evidence that could only be gathered proactively.

"The manual says that the shelter has a three-warning policy before eviction," said Camila.

"Well, then you obviously have the wrong manual."

Camila tried to contain her anger in silence.

"You had a number of visitors after the baby was born," Rose said.

"I had family come to visit my son."

"Your mother came to visit. In the intake session, you said you had no contact with your mother."

"I haven't for a long time, but she wanted to meet the baby," Camila said.

Rose studied Camila's face in silence. "I'll give you another chance," she finally said.

Camila thanked her, carried Alonso upstairs, set him down on the bed, and opened her laptop to search for housing. She had planned to do whatever it took to get a place in the projects, but that would still take time. Now she didn't have time. They had to get out of this place as quickly as possible, while she could still control the situation.

7

MAURICIO

The following weekend was Father's Day. Camila wanted her dad to meet her son, his grandson. Alonso was already gripping Camila's curls in his tiny fists; ahead of the developmental curve, she noted. His Cupid's-bow mouth expressed hunger, pleasure, curiosity; his broad nostrils flared to inhale the world around him. Mauricio would see his own face looking right back up at him, she said, all that Alvarez intelligence glinting in Alonso's round eyes, his irises as black as brown could get. Today was the day for Alonso's first big trip, taking the train to the B84 bus to East New York, Camila decided, to meet his grandfather at work.

On the bus, she called Kevin to wish him a happy holiday, his first Father's Day. He didn't have a dad himself, but now, she said, he was one. Camila found her father at the hardware store where he worked off the books. She knew the job didn't pay for his new white Porsche Cayenne. She suspected he was still dealing. Even if it was true, it didn't seem to bother her much. People respected her father, and that was all that mattered.

She fastened Alonso's car seat into the back seat of Mauricio's car and slid in next to him. Mauricio sped down the Jackie Robinson Parkway to Corona, where Celia was preparing a holiday barbecue on their back deck with hot dogs, hamburgers, rice, and beans. Celia was his newest wife, though who knew if they were actually married or not. She likely wasn't going to be pleased with the surprise visit. Celia was yet another barrier blocking Camila from her dad, and perhaps the one Camila most resented. Celia's jealousy was legendary and burned a path straight to her stepdaughter. Not for nothing: Until Camila appeared at the funeral for Mauricio's mother, Celia didn't know that he had fathered any children other than her two kids.

Back when Geraldine had discovered that Camila was having sex and kicked her out, Mauricio and Celia's apartment was the only place she had to stay. When she'd shown up with her bags, Mauricio immediately confiscated her phone. He didn't trust that she wouldn't just use it for booty calls. She was her mother's daughter, after all. Camila had almost no sexual past of her own, and yet her mother's carnal history soiled her reputation, sowing disgust and distrust in her own father.

Unless she had a shift at her dad's hardware store, Camila had to come home immediately after school each day. While she lived there, Mauricio took her weekly paycheck. He said he was depositing it into a savings account for her. Celia said it was her rent payment. Either way, she never saw a cent of it again. In fact, later on, when Camila was pregnant and homeless and borrowed one hundred dollars, Mauricio and Celia harangued her to repay the debt. They'd ask for the money back during her rare visits, in front of their big-screen TV, or in texts sent from his Porsche.

In high school, when Camila complained to the woman who did payroll about her father taking her paychecks, the woman just said, "He's the boss. I can't get involved." Camila figured she was afraid of him. Everyone was. She remembered the night when he broke down the door at her grandparents' apartment and charged into the bedroom looking for Geraldine, waving a shotgun. Camila would tell me occasionally that people only respected him because they feared him.

Mauricio never lived with Geraldine. She wanted him to, Camila said, but he refused. Camila would hear gossip, like about the time Geraldine was hanging out in the park and Mauricio came up behind her and dragged her down the street. After such episodes, Camila would usually overhear Geraldine tell one of her sisters, "That's what love is. If he doesn't abuse you, he doesn't feel for you." But Mauricio never laid a hand on Camila. He bought her Christmas presents, he took her to Six Flags. And when she got a little older, he gave her that job at the hardware store so she could have some independence, he told her.

Camila lasted just over four months at her dad's. One bitterly cold day in January, Mauricio told her it would be best if she went back to Geraldine's place. He gave her a set of keys to Geraldine's apartment. Camila had never had her own keys before. She assumed they were offered with her mother's approval. She packed her bags and returned to the white aluminum-sided row house just down the block from the grounds of the 1964 World's Fair in Queens. For the first time in her life, she let herself into her own home, or what she believed was her home. But when Geraldine returned to find Camila there, her bags unpacked, she screamed, "You can't be here, he has to take you!" Camila realized her father had simply tossed her away.

No matter how she conformed to Mauricio's rules, or turned on all her charisma, or showed off all the street smarts she believed she'd inherited directly from him, it never seemed to work out with him. Not when Geraldine kicked her out after she found out she was sleeping with that guy, when Camila had nowhere to go but her dad's place. Not the one other time, either, when she was younger. In third grade, Geraldine sent Camila to stay with Mauricio, saying she was too much of a troublemaker to have around. "You have to come get this girl!" Geraldine had yelled into the phone.

It was a long-distance call. Back then, Mauricio had taken up residence with a white girlfriend in Illinois, about an hour and a half from Chicago. He flew Camila out. Suddenly she was living in a big suburban house at the end of a road, with a backyard and a dishwasher and a washer-dryer. A red Ferrari, a black Escalade, and an orange Prowler were parked in the garage. When Camila was snooping around one day, she found bags of cocaine taped inside the front wheels of the Ferrari.

Mauricio would have different girls at the house while the white girlfriend was at work. When Camila came home from school, he'd make her give them back massages. Then the white girlfriend would come home and she and Mauricio would fight—not just argue, but violently brawl. One afternoon Camila called the police. They sent a car with sirens to the house.

Mauricio had to flee the state. He told Camila to get into the back seat of the Escalade and sped all the way from Illinois to Corona without saying a word to her. Camila told me that after the day her call forced him to flee the state, her father never liked her again. She never knew what happened to the girlfriend.

She said that she hoped he'd feel differently now that she'd had a boy to make him proud. That perhaps the sight of his grandson, with his very surname, would recalibrate her father's paternity. Maybe it could even help her find a home.

It didn't.

On Father's Day, Mauricio lit a Romeo y Julieta cigar as soon as Camila walked into his apartment with Alonso.

"Dad, you need to wash your hands if you want to hold the baby."

He wasn't interested. "Let me finish my cigar."

Camila and Alonso left a few hours later, without provoking her father's interest in her son, or herself, and without telling him about her need to get out of the shelter. In fact, she didn't mention the shelter at all. Why would she, when he couldn't even express interest in his own grandson, she said; why would he care if Alonso was out on the street any more than he cared that she'd spent her pregnancy moving from shelter to shelter? It would be all right, she told me. She didn't need her father's help, not that she ever expected it. She'd get public housing. She'd do it on her own.

8

LEGITIMACY

The following week Kevin told Camila he wanted her to take a DNA test and that he would pay for it. She had known this was coming. His mother had insisted on the test as soon as she'd learned Camila was pregnant. I asked her if she was worried. I asked her if she had a reason to be.

She was quiet for a long time before she admitted there was a good chance that Kevin wasn't actually Alonso's father.

That morning, we'd escaped from the first broiling pavements of summer down into a vacant air-conditioned subway car. Sitting beside me, close, she told this missing part of her story. She had been dating a guy named Jeremiah that past summer—though she didn't really want to call it dating, more like they'd hang out and have sex. Camila was lonesome with Kevin up in Buffalo, and Jeremiah was attentive. He was in his thirties, smart, a potential asset to affordable-housing applications with a job that paid him fifteen dollars an hour as a dentist's assistant in Corona. But she was suspicious of his temperament, and his intelligence was the only refined thing about him. Camila had invited him to her cousin's sweet-sixteen party at a rented hall. All the men there knew to dress up in suits, but Jeremiah showed up in a thermal and low-slung pants. She was horrified by how he presented himself to her family, she said, and never looked at him the same way again. Then there was his jealousy, which was unremitting. One night after she told him she was pregnant, Camila went to a movie with a friend. Jeremiah, thinking she was out with a guy, texted to say that he hoped she fell and had a miscarriage. That was it—she was done with him.

Character was what Camila loved most about Kevin, who coached kids from his old neighborhood and applied his values of conduct to life on and off the field. Jeremiah had no character, not as far as she was concerned. All she felt for him was distaste. She decided the baby couldn't be Jeremiah's. It had to be Kevin's. If it was Kevin's, she'd have a family with the right man. The one whose possible football contract could pay the bills. It didn't matter that they hadn't been in a real relationship for a while; he was the one whose body and heart she wanted. She needed the DNA test to bind him to her. If it didn't, she'd lose him forever, and Alonso would lose him as a father. She'd be the kind of single mother she never wanted to be.

Maybe that was why she didn't tell me about the test earlier: because she simply couldn't admit the possibility of an outcome she found unendurable. Camila gripped hope in her fists so tightly it was like she was trying to transform it into reality by pure pressure. Oftentimes, she walked the world as a veteran realist, brutally assessing people and circumstances, a defense mechanism against ever being fooled. And yet her blind spots were almost always caused by her relentless hope, by using it to deflect realities she couldn't accommodate.

During Wednesday-night residents meetings, when the shelter residents would update everyone in the room on the status of their employment and housing searches, hope tended to warp most accounts. Tina—who spent most meetings locked away in her own mind, until she erupted in a fit—would talk about how she was finishing up her master's degree in the fall and getting her old job at the Gap back, with a better title or a higher wage. Anselma would talk about starting a new career in nursing once her baby was three months old, though she didn't have a high school diploma or any plans to get one. Irina's hope was trained on God, who she'd say was going to provide her a nice apartment near her church in Brighton Beach, paid for by the city. Sherice kept her dreams to herself, feeling resigned to their fictiveness, shaking her head at what she regarded as the other residents' naïve nonsense. She wasn't going to get blinded by anything, she told me, even if it meant a life waiting tables, just so long as she could find an apartment her Applebee's tips could afford—a hope that felt as impossible as any others.

It was hard to see how or why any of them could wake up each morning without hope and live another day. But while hope was a necessary tool for survival, it was often a delusion. Sometimes the women's hopes were the pink tulle of fantasy—talk of working as fashion designers or landing recording contracts—to fight back the encroachment of depression. Other times they were simpler lies they told themselves to combat desperation, lies about work or childcare. Those more workaday hopes could be ultimately self-defeating. Why spend your days in waiting rooms if God was taking care of things? Why apply for a new job if you convinced yourself the old one was coming back, this time with a bigger check at the end of the week? When hope was connected to action, it could be both buoy and motor. But when it wasn't, hope was a paradox, threatening to sink these young women while they needed it to stay afloat.

Camila asked Irina to join her for a La Leche League nursing circle that met weekly in Bedford-Stuyvesant. "I know it's the hood, but at least it's at a yoga studio," she told her. Camila dressed the part wherever she went; today she was playing a gentrifying lactivist in a hand-lettered T-shirt that said YOU ARE WHAT YOU EAT, long khaki shorts, and a loose ponytail. After hoisting and heaving their babies in huge car-seat strollers up the steps at the Bedford-Nostrand stop, they found themselves on a block of brownstones under renovation, Anita Diamant and Curtis Sittenfeld paperbacks stacked in a box of trash on the sidewalk. On the corner of Clifton Place was a new building with a café on the first floor. It had all the Brooklyn hallmarks: Edison bulbs, Marais stools, direct-trade coffee, and heirloom grain bowls. A few doors down, the yoga studio beckoned with central air in the early-summer heat.

An auburn-haired woman in her forties introduced herself as a lactation consultant still proudly nursing her four-year-old. She invited the mothers to sit in a circle with their babies. A trim black woman laid out a blanket and placed her fifteen-week-old son on his stomach. He arched his back to look up at a redheaded baby in a mod-printed cloth diaper cover.

"Those cloth diapers are the ones I wanted," Irina whispered to Camila. "They are so hard to find." Setting Dima on the mat in front of her, in his pilled blue onesie, she seemed to withdraw, self-conscious of her cheap knockoff watch and even cheaper flare jeans.

Camila bounced Alonso in his secondhand Nike T-shirt, hoping he'd stop crying already. It felt like he'd been crying nonstop for days. The doctor had said the term "colic" didn't mean much; he was just a kid who had reflux, was uncomfortable, and expressed it whenever he wasn't sleeping. Managing his constant crying was exhausting. She loved him and felt her chest swell with each of his minuscule developments, but she felt debilitated by her ragged sleeplessness paired with her ineffectual attempts to soothe him.

A petite young Russian woman joined the circle, carrying a newborn in an elaborate sling and nibbling a delicate pastry. Camila reached into the black plastic bag in the bottom of Alonso's stroller and rooted around for the bodega donut she'd bought earlier.

The mothers introduced themselves. Irina was silent when it was her turn. Camila quickly spoke up for her, her smile luminous, her eyes wide and inviting. "I'm Camila and this is my friend Irina," she said. "We live in the same building."

"When do you go back to work?" the lactation consultant asked Camila.

"September," she responded without pause, holding her smile.

The lactation consultant let out a deep yogic exhalation. "Enjoy every second of your summer with your baby," she said. "Just savor your time. It's great that you have so much time off. Not everyone gets to have that, you know."

Camila solemnly nodded as though she was accepting the great weight of her privilege, like she should be grateful for a job with paid parental leave covering her expenses. As though these months were to be spent luxuriously communing with her baby, rather than establishing paternity, filing for child support, applying for a child-care voucher, finding a caregiver who would accept that voucher, gathering all the necessary transcripts and grant information to transfer schools and find work-study, and finding stable, permanent housing when there was none she could afford. All while she was caring for an infant utterly alone, with only food stamps and the little money she'd saved to support her. She gazed at her hands, her face composed.

Irina, meanwhile, had gathered the courage to ask the redheaded baby's mother, a heavyset brunette, about the diapers.

"They're from Diaperkind," the brunette replied.

Irina looked puzzled.

The Russian mother interjected. "You do the service, yes?"

Irina just smiled awkwardly.

"They wash them for you," she explained.

Irina asked the brunette, "You buy one or two?"

The brunette raised her eyebrows. "You need at least twenty."

"It's cheaper than buying regular diapers, right?"

"Uh, it's not cheaper," she said, cocking her head.

Camila discharged a look of warning in Irina's direction. Irina couldn't let them know Dima's diapers were donated to the shelter.

When the meeting ended, Irina couldn't get out of there fast enough. "What a waste of time," she muttered on the sidewalk. "All they did was talk about how great they were for breastfeeding their babies. I thought we were going to learn something."

The subway screeched out of the station. Camila was visibly annoyed. She'd taken Irina to this supportive gathering, with successful women, and Irina had embarrassed her, she complained later. She was the one with the law degree, with the husband. Why couldn't she have more class? Did she want to be in the shelter forever? Camila thought Irina just wanted to be taken care of, by a man, by a handout, by whatever she could get. She had no respect for that. But it's not like she had anyone else to talk to.

To avoid eye contact with Irina, Camila looked down at Alonso sleeping deeply in his stroller, his long eyelashes fluttering as he dreamed. Then she said, "I took a DNA test yesterday."

Irina's eyes popped in surprise at such a confession. Camila made her nervous, but she had to ask. "Why did you take the test?"

"Kevin called and said I had to go. But it has to be his. Look at him."

Irina examined Alonso's face.

"I was dating someone before, but that guy was Spanish," Camila continued. "Alonso is obviously black, like Kevin."

Silently, Irina nodded again.

"It was embarrassing," Camila admitted. She grimaced and shook her head. "I won't get the results for a while."

Irina nodded sympathetically; she figured this was the most Camila had exposed herself to anyone in the shelter. But what could she say? Irina was married to her son's father. She'd told me she thought life was complicated enough without the way some girls got pregnant.

"I don't even know where Kevin is. He may have gone back home to New Mexico, where he's from. Or he could be training in Chicago. I texted him last week two times. He didn't write back." Camila set her jaw against her admission.

Irina just nodded again. She wanted to believe in Camila. She cared about her. After Camila had received the eviction text, Irina used her influence with Rose—who considered her saintly after all she'd survived—to make Camila's case, to beg for leniency and trust for her friend. She hadn't told Camila this; she did it for moral reasons, she said, not for credit. But she could see something darkly self-protecting in Camila's eyes ever since Rose had threatened to kick her out. "That was the first time," she told me, "but now I keep seeing it."

Since then she'd noticed that Camila was recording everything that happened with the staff, like she was always preparing to defend herself in a fight for her own survival. "I know it's because she's young and only does what she can to help herself, because she's been abused in some way," Irina told me. "But look where we live, where bums off the street come to eat. What does she expect." There wasn't much to buoy either of them, or anyone in their straits. Judgment was often all they had, so they judged one another harshly: for choices they could disdain, for unequal advantages, for being stuck in situations they felt they wouldn't tolerate. Any opportunity to feel superior to one another elevated them from the bottom of the heap, bolstering their dignity.

For another subway stop, neither Camila nor Irina said a word, about the DNA test or anything else. Alonso woke suddenly with a cough, spitting up a little milk. Camila wiped it from his mouth with a diaper wipe, since she didn't have a burp cloth. She didn't have a baby blanket, either, and it was cold in the air-conditioned subway car. Camila asked Irina if she had one she could borrow. Irina pulled off the plaid shirt she was wearing over a tank top and handed it to Camila, who wrapped it around Alonso and laid him in his car seat. Camila thanked her quietly.

Irina nodded in return. Both women were silent for a while, until Irina made an effort. "My church said they'd pay me seventy-five dollars a week to clean," she said. "It won't be enough to pay someone to watch Dima, though, and I can't work with the baby there. I thought I could clean houses, maybe, but there's some issue with the 1099. Before the baby, I tried to do legal work with the Russians in Brighton Beach, but they wouldn't teach me anything about law here."

The women were quiet again for another couple of stops. Irina broke the silence once more. "Anselma had the baby, you know. She's been back a few days."

Camila didn't say anything in reply. As she told me later, she didn't need to know about Anselma's life—they weren't really friends anyway.

9

SCHEDULE B

Here's a very different immigrant story than Camila's family would ever know. Harry Ratowczer was one of eight siblings who left the then-Russian city of Bialystok in 1921, looking to build a better life in the United States. The family settled in Cleveland and Americanized their name to Ratner. Harry made his money carrying water to construction workers, until his siblings founded a hardware-and-lumber business, which in the thirties began to purchase lots for commercial development. Wartime arrived as a business boon for the Ratners, delivering great opportunities to construct military housing, then strip malls.

Harry's son Bruce was born during the final months of the Second World War into radically different circumstances than his father and came of age to graduate from Harvard, then Columbia Law School. In New York, the young attorney took a job with the city, eventually working as Mayor Ed Koch's consumer affairs commissioner, chasing down corrupt businesses. In the bright lights of the eighties, he turned to real estate development. Ratner made his name with MetroTech, the first billion-dollar complex in Brooklyn, built on ten largely forgotten blocks where frame houses once stood.

MetroTech was merely a precursor to what Ratner had in mind for the borough: a million-square-foot development proposal for a plot of land down Flatbush Avenue. The project was announced in 2003 and would take three thousand days to complete. Its financing would rely on $100 million in tax breaks. Furthermore, it would require taking advantage of the state's power of eminent domain. Fifty-one community organizations opposed the development, claiming it could displace nearly three thousand residents. The centerpiece of the project, and the first building to be constructed, was the Barclays Center, which would house the Nets basketball franchise. Its Brooklyn industrial chic would be expressed in a façade of quick-rusting steel, its roof planted with enough grassy sedum to carpet a large public park.

The development project cost a billion dollars. That figure didn't include the cost of the team itself. Ratner partnered with Jay-Z to buy the Nets for $300 million. The arena would be erected across an intersection from a two-bedroom apartment that was Jay-Z's former stash spot, before rap began to pay his bills. The former drug den hit the market for $1.5 million shortly after Barclays opened its doors. Later that year, Ratner declared that real estate development and investments had earned him $10.5 billion in assets.

There was another partner in the Nets deal, who'd come from Russia to America with no immigration papers needed, a man named Mikhail Prokhorov. Around the time Prokhorov was becoming a majority owner of the team representing Brooklyn, he took up residence in a penthouse apartment in the Four Seasons Hotel in Manhattan and put a deposit down on a $750 million villa in France. The villa was named for its previous owner, King Leopold II of Belgium, and required a staff of fifty to maintain its manicured gardens. Prokhorov decided he didn't want the house after all and forfeited his $68 million down payment. That loss was chump change to a man who was about to sell his $2 billion stake in a fertilizer company and almost $1 billion more in aluminum—all with an eye toward Brooklyn. Already Prokhorov owned a reported $3 billion in real estate in the borough, much of it just down the street from the shelter where Camila lived. In 2009, Prokhorov purchased his partners' interest in the team and the Barclays Center. Ratner wanted to move on to focus on the next stage of his adjoining massive development project, which years later would remain an eight-and-a-half-acre pit next to the stadium, on Atlantic Avenue.

That sinkhole of billions opened up at the front door of the underfunded, overcrowded, and collapsing last hope for permanent housing for thousands upon thousands of desperate New Yorkers. For directly across the street from that pit, one of the most expensive holes on earth, was the Brooklyn office for the New York City Housing Authority, or NYCHA, the largest public-housing program in America.

The month Alonso was born, 599,493 New Yorkers called public housing home. That was the official city number, which didn't even count the many thousands living in the projects off lease. If the New York City Housing Authority had counted as its own city that year, it would have been the thirty-first largest in the country, just bigger than Milwaukee. Some families had been praying for over a decade for an apartment in NYCHA's 2,462 buildings. To New Yorkers who could afford stable housing, the projects represented a living nightmare. But to the many who couldn't, it was an impossible dream.

That dream meant never paying more than 30 percent of one's income in rent in a city where most people paid twice that amount. Federal guidelines defined anyone paying over 30 percent to be rent-burdened, but the housing market didn't care. It was no better outside New York. Among residents of Flint, Michigan, and Hialeah, Florida, three-quarters were rent-burdened, as were two-thirds of people living in Boulder, Colorado, and Allentown, Pennsylvania. The housing crisis was a national epidemic, one NYCHA had tried to solve long before anyone could have imagined its coming magnitude.

Many of the neighborhoods encircling now-decayed housing projects had become very rich ones. Geraldine had a lease in the projects on the Lower East Side, right by new developments overlooking the Manhattan Bridge. Camila hadn't been inside that place for years, she told me. From time to time she'd crash at her cousin Nikki's place in a NYCHA project in Chelsea, built during the white flight of the sixties on what had been the industrial edge of a middle-class neighborhood. Recently, Chelsea had become New York's most expensive neighborhood for apartment rentals. The average resident's income was $140,000, a number that factored in the NYCHA tenants in the neighborhood, whose average income barely scraped $30,000. The projects' brown brick towers formed a canyon of poverty among the glass-and-steel apartments rising up over galleries and boutiques. A new private school had been established in the neighborhood, right across the street from a church's busy soup kitchen, with a base tuition equal to the median American salary. This was New York. Or, rather, this was America, but the disparate ends of our inequality spectrum lived pressed together here, the setting of a dystopian novel where real lives were lived as tourists took selfies.

Nikki's father had gotten his NYCHA apartment years before, when public housing was available to people who needed it. When he died, the lease transferred to his daughter. As far as Camila knew, Nikki had never swung open the glass door to one of the famous galleries or boutiques surrounding the building. Nor had Camila during any of her stays there. Camila didn't even know that the elevated railroad track two blocks away had been transformed into a park called the High Line. The New York City Housing Authority office around the corner was the only neighborhood feature she felt she knew at all.

While she was pregnant, Camila had spent a morning in the Chelsea NYCHA waiting room. Camila had a head cold that day, and a flaming bout of conjunctivitis, and a guy relentlessly hitting on her while she tried to focus on the paperwork. After four hours in the waiting room, she gave up and went back to Nikki's. She would register as a family after the baby was born.

Camila pushed Alonso's stroller past the Bruce Ratner–owned hole in the ground along Atlantic Avenue, on her way to the Brooklyn

NYCHA office. The asphalt shimmered in the ninety-degree heat, but Camila's foundation remained smooth, her lips perfectly glossed, every moussed curl in place, her white skinny jeans and cream peplum blouse pristine.

Camila had applied for housing as soon as she moved back to the city from Buffalo, two years ago. Since then the wait list had swelled to 270,000 names. Even with the baby, she would be just one of 147,000 families in the city waiting to raise their kids in the projects; she knew these statistics as well as her own Social Security number. But she was here with more than just her motherhood to add to her case. Everyone knew that a domestic-violence case could get you marked as high priority for public housing. And Camila had been shrewd enough to make sure she had a case on record before she came back to New York from the New Jersey shelter where she spent most of her pregnancy.

Another resident would regularly materialize in the bathroom when Camila was getting out of the shower, she told me. When Camila told her to stop staring, the other resident became fiercely belligerent. Everyone in the shelter fought with one another like feral cats, Camila said; belligerence was the norm there. But this young woman's hostility amplified, and her voyeuristic bathroom appearances became even more frequent. Camila did what she'd taught herself to do when she felt her rights were being threatened, especially if she might use it to her advantage: She began to record each provocation.

One evening, Camila started a load of laundry. Her adversary decided she wanted to do her laundry first. They argued. Camila left the room. She returned to move her wet clothes into the dryer. The woman followed her and began shoving her laundry into the machine as Camila was pulling her clothes out. Their bodies collided. It was enough for Camila to feel like she could get somewhere with the police; she immediately called 911 and filed a report. The police didn't want to call it domestic violence, but she argued the law right back at them and supported her case with the pattern she'd recorded. The police allowed it and wrote up a restraining order.

Camila now had the supplementary documentation she believed

she needed to catapult herself ahead on the waiting list. A domestic-violence record was one of the only ways to get public housing anymore; she didn't know anyone who got NYCHA without it. She'd safely guarded the paperwork she brought with her from New Jersey to prove she'd been a woman at risk. It had made moving back to New York a possibility for her, she thought, especially now that she had a baby. NYCHA wasn't going to make her raise him in shelters, where she could be at risk again, she rationalized, nor would they need to know the particulars of the case. So what if she wasn't brutalized; it was still considered abuse according to the law, as it should be, she said. Her whole body would stiffen with rage when she'd tell the story of that girl walking in on her while she was showering, but all those miserable months in that miserable shelter would be worth it, she told me, if it got her a place in the projects, a place like her mom's. All she had to do was file the right paperwork.

At the Brooklyn NYCHA office, she pushed the building's door open with her back and swiveled the stroller into the startling cool of the air-conditioned lobby. Upstairs, fifty women were seated in lines of red plastic chairs that stretched the width of the building. Among them sat only two men, each accompanying a hugely pregnant woman. Except for mine, Camila's face was the palest in the waiting room. Considering the number of people there, the quiet was discomfiting, just a hum of low nervous voices, clacking computer keys, and the central-air vents, until Alonso's wail ripped through the stillness. Eyes tracked Camila as she pushed him past the lines of chairs and a long counter where workers sat, bored and exhausted, to the two computer terminals at the far end of the room. A woman held a baby on her hip with one hand and pecked at the keyboard with another. Humiliated by the other baby's calm silence, Camila tried to ignore Alonso's shrieks as she lifted her chin and peered at the other screen. Feeling so many pairs of eyes trained on her, she reached down into the car seat for his pacifier, pushed it into his mouth, and held it there with her left hand while she rocked the stroller back and forth with her right. He stared up at the fluorescent lights overhead, punching the air with his tiny fists, fighting sleep.

Alonso's screams took on a fearsome guttural vibrato. She pleaded with him, "Can you let me finish the application on the computer? Please? Please?"

He was wet. She noticed an empty chair and wondered aloud if she could change him on it. Then she caught sight of a security guard coldly staring at her. If she tried to change him, someone would say something and then she'd say something back, she muttered to me, and that wouldn't go well. Camila tried to focus on the computer monitor. For easily the hundredth time in her twenty-two years, she estimated, she typed her Social Security number and date of birth into a public computer. In the time it took the woman beside her to figure out the first page, Camila had raced through the main portion of the application.

Any priority case required multiple copies on file, the application said. Where was she going to get copies? Camila pushed the stroller past the lines of chairs to the counter. She clenched her jaw and waited for acknowledgment from the employee ignoring her on the other side.

After a minute she straightened her spine and spoke up. "Excuse me. Excuse me?"

No response.

"Excuse me?" she said again.

The woman behind the counter slowly raised her eyes with a barely tolerant look of inquiry.

"Do you have a copy machine?"

The woman didn't blink.

"Can I make copies here?"

Almost imperceptibly, the woman shook her head once before lowering her eyes.

"Do you know where I can make copies nearby?"

"Nope."

"Thank you."

Camila fled the office, back into the broiling heat. Across the street there was nothing but that billion-dollar pit in the ground. Down the block was a mall with a Target, worth a try. She searched for an entrance along the windowless walls. There were no storefronts alongside this urban thoroughfare; all commerce was hidden away inside. Finally, a door and an elevator behind it painted Target red. Holding Alonso's pacifier in his mouth to calm his cries, she tried her best to steer the bulky stroller one-handed to the photo-processing center. Perhaps they'd have a photocopier. They didn't.

Next she found her way to OfficeMax and searched the cavern-ous, windowless box of a store, Alonso now screaming as loudly as his tiny lungs could muster. Where was the photocopier? She scooped Alonso out of the stroller, sat herself on a huge block of spiral notebooks, opened her woven peplum shirt by its side zipper, twisted the entire garment until her nipple appeared through the opening, and gave Alonso the only thing in the world that could soothe him. Camila closed her eyes and exhaled into the sudden quiet.

After a moment of calm, with Alonso still on her breast, she found the folder of documents jammed into the stroller's bassinet and began laying out her paperwork beside her on the stack of note-books for sale. She needed to affix the police report and restraining order. No problem—she'd been holding on to it since last March. Camila double-checked the tiny print that formed a border around the edge of the document. Schedule A asked for a report from within the past twelve months. Schedule B asked for a second report from within the past twenty-four months. She didn't have a second report.

Camila handed me the sheet of paper, blinded by anxiety, unable to decipher it. It was the first and only time I was able to grasp the meaning of legalese she couldn't crack. I had to recite the words aloud a few times, turning the paper to read the minuscule words wrapped around the margins, before I understood: She needed two reports from two incidents over two years, with the same abuser. But she only had one report. Just one incident.

"I'm not going to get public housing," she whispered, perhaps to herself as much as to me, her eyes gleaming in fear. Then she went silent for a long time. Frozen by the terror of her circumstances, not a muscle shifted in her face. Only her eyes changed, like a dark filter dropped down over her pupils. I laid my hand on her shoulder. She was cold and still as granite. Finally, her voice rasped out frantically, wondering aloud if she could get a letter from a social worker and then appeal. But she knew it was hopeless, she said.

Still holding Alonso against her breast, she read through the documents a few more times before sliding them back into the red paper folder where she stored her documents. The folder was getting shabbier by the day.

10

WELFARE

In 1976, a few years after Geraldine was born, Ronald Reagan gave a campaign speech during which he told a story about a woman in Chicago who had gamed the system out of $150,000 a year, collecting checks under eighty fake names. A headline writer slapped the words WELFARE QUEEN on his article about the speech. The reality is that the woman had used four aliases, not eighty, and had defrauded the government of $8,000, not $150,000. But the moniker would remain to humiliate generations of American women to come.

Geraldine was the closest thing to a welfare queen that Camila had known. But all the checks Geraldine cashed—even the SSI payments she'd abused her daughters to receive—amounted to a grim living. Benefits were shrinking for the poorest Americans every year. In 1970, while Camila's grandparents were preparing to move to Queens from the Dominican Republic, the average public-assistance check was about $1,100 a month, in today's dollars. By 2015, when Camila began collecting welfare, the average monthly check was barely more than two hundred bucks.

Half of all single mothers tried to survive with the help of government assistance programs. And most of them worked: Almost half of home-healthcare and childcare givers collected welfare; more than half of fast-food workers did. The more likely you were to have a college degree, the more likely you were to stay off welfare. Camila knew this well, of course.

She didn't want to go on welfare. There was great shame in it for her: not just the dependency, but perpetuating her mother's legacy. Furthermore, she thought it was barely worth the hassle and the humiliation. She knew they'd just tell her that she shouldn't be in school, that she should be working some dead-end job instead, and she'd probably still need the check to supplement her income. Most people on welfare worked and still needed the supplementary check. She'd still be homeless even if she was working full-time with a job like that. Plenty of people were.

Welfare offices had been renamed "job centers" during the Clinton years and under the oversight of Mayor Rudy Giuliani, whose focus on reducing the welfare rolls took a brutal toll on poor families. At the Waverly Job Center in Manhattan, on Fourteenth Street, the only nod to employment that Camila saw was an empty bulletin board with the word JOBS tacked on it, dangling askew. It was a gulag block of a building, its midcentury teal panels streaked with age. The city had changed, the neighborhood had changed, but this block remained one of the few where people of color crowded the gum-spotted pavement outside, queuing to be admitted into waiting rooms. Purgatory in the form of vinyl chairs, Venetian blinds, fluorescent lights. She hated it.

Camila had to make five trips to the job center on Fourteenth Street before the paperwork for her rent payment went through. Though Rose ran a shelter, because it wasn't in the city system, she was paid in checks from the job center, as if she was a landlord accepting housing assistance. And though Camila had applied for those checks in April, just before she moved to Fourth Avenue, the shelter had yet to receive a single check. That's what Rose told her, at least.

The first time she went to the job center, just a few weeks after Alonso was born, Camila waited for a few hours to speak to a worker, who had failed to add the shelter to her case file.

The second time, a couple of days later, she waited for a few hours, and a different worker succeeded in adding the shelter to her file. She verified this by asking for a printout of the file, but the worker had failed to add her to the rent-payment list.

The third time, the next week, she waited for a few hours and was told that she had to follow up with the worker she'd spoken to before, but he was on vacation.

The fourth time, a week later, she waited for a few hours and was told he was still on vacation.

The fifth time, her wait wasn't as long. He was back from vacation. She watched him click a single button on his keyboard to add "rent payment" to her case. Then he hit PRINT when she asked for a document to verify her case status. It took about ten seconds.

A week later, Camila got a note under her door saying she owed back rent from May, right after she'd moved in. The shelter still hadn't received a rent check from public assistance.

Camila was given three days to come up with the eight hundred dollars she owed. If she couldn't, she'd get a formal eviction notice this time.

She explained to Rose that she'd gone to the job center multiple times to resolve the issue. The check should have gone through weeks before. It made no sense, Camila said.

But it made sense to Rose: She believed Camila was lying about trying to get a check for her rent. She told me she'd seen more girls than she could count lie to her face about going to the welfare office. They just didn't want to bother with the hassle, she said. It was her duty, and her pride, to make sure no one pulled one over on her. This was a shelter, not a way to get a cheap studio apartment in Park Slope.

Rose wanted her out and told her so.

Camila showed Rose the documents from the job center. And she said she'd fight the shelter in court if they put her and her baby out on the street. The issue wasn't with her, she told Rose, it was with the ineptitude of the system. They were the ones who had committed to pay her rent. Camila believed a court order would be required to evict her; she knew the New York tenants' rights booklet front to back. Unfortunately, those rights usually didn't extend to shelter residents, whether a rent check paid for their bed or not.

So that week she returned again to the job center. Humidity was thick on the already steaming day, the summer stench of garbage and urine sickly sweet in the air. The twisted form of a man slept on a torn length of cardboard, his head on a filthy navy duffel bag. The United States and New York flags hung limp in the air over the line of twenty-odd people waiting for a guard to unlock the office doors. Camila pushed Alonso's stroller down the sidewalk as the doors opened. Rather than feeling dread, she anticipated the pleasure of accomplishing something, of skillfully navigating the opaque and labyrinthine system that left others paralyzed. Today, she vowed, she wouldn't leave the premises until she'd gotten what she came here for.

While she waited upstairs, she opened her broken compact and covered up the dark circles under her eyes with foundation. Alonso wasn't sleeping at night. He wasn't sleeping much during the day, either. The reality of caring for a sleepless, crying baby all alone was chipping away at her composure, and it was beginning to show. At night she sang to him and kissed him, and she nursed him when he was hungry, but she needed to take care of business, too, she said. She'd often tell him, like a firm schoolmarm, that he needed to learn that she wouldn't cave to his every demand.

Ignoring his whimpers from the stroller, she snapped her compact shut and flipped open her phone. Camila used waiting rooms as her office suite. As long as she had Wi-Fi, every moment she spent sitting in the city's rows of plastic chairs could be productive. Diligence in a vacuum offers few rewards, for anyone, but especially for someone as unseen as Camila. My presence offered her someone to report her daily endeavors to, finally, someone who would be a witness to her persistence. I didn't hide how impressed I was with how she kept her life organized in a single folder, every application deadline in her head, every address for every appointment memorized, internally quieting the noise around her. Today, in the next chair, her office mate was an ashy man humming tunelessly as he thumbed through a yellowed copy of *Men Are from Mars, Women Are from Venus,* his eyes on Camila's slim figure instead of the pages in front of him.

Ignoring him, Camila called the Manhattan child-support office. She needed to begin her registration process, no matter who the father might be. No one was going to do it for Alonso but her, she muttered to me. A voice on the phone informed her that a paternity hearing had just been scheduled. In Queens. She was residing in Brooklyn. Her case was based in Manhattan. It made no sense.

"Who scheduled the hearing?" she asked.

"Jeremiah Cole," said the voice. The guy she'd been dating that prior summer, the only other possible contender for her son's other chromosome, the one she couldn't bear the idea of being tethered to through parenthood.

The night before, Jeremiah had written her a message on Facebook. He said he needed the baby's last name, his Social Security number, her Social Security number, her address. In his new profile picture, braids were woven tight against his scalp and hanging down his neck. Camila felt repelled by them, by him.

After Alonso's birth, Camila had posted pictures of Kevin in the hospital, holding Alonso in his arms. Jeremiah saw the pictures, but he didn't reach out to Camila. Instead, she learned, he wrote Kevin to say the baby was his. Kevin didn't challenge him. He just asked Jeremiah if he wanted Camila back, if he wanted to raise Alonso, like it was a simple exchange, an elegant solution. Then Kevin told Jeremiah he was getting a paternity test.

As Camila stared at the empty bulletin board in the waiting room, she recalled how when they were together, Jeremiah stopped showing up to his job as a dentistry assistant. He was a smart guy, but all he wanted to do was hang out and smoke weed with his friends. She couldn't fathom raising a son with someone who was in his mid-thirties and living on his sister's couch.

She'd been with Kevin in September. Alonso was conceived at the end of August. She knew it didn't look good.

Whatever. She didn't need either of these men, she mumbled, to herself as much as to me. Alonso didn't need them, either. How many people did she even know who were raised by their fathers?

Camila checked the time. She had to pee. The only bathroom was on the first floor. If she left the waiting room to go downstairs, she might miss it when her number came up to meet with a worker. She was used to holding it for hours in rooms like this.

Alonso began howling for attention, beating his tiny fists against the stale air. As she tried to quiet him, her number was called. She was ushered behind a door into a warren of cubicles, past a sign that said HOMELESSNESS DIVERSION. Camila sat in a chair as directed. Alonso continued crying; he needed to eat. She took out her nursing cover and began to feed him as she waited to explain her case to a new worker. The man she'd spoken to before was no longer there; this time it was a petite Russian woman with short gray hair. She wore a wool cardigan over a thin flowered dress to protect her from the frigid air-conditioning.

The worker looked askance at Alonso. "You shouldn't have him here," she said. "Not a good place for him at that age. A lot of germs."

Without taking Alonso off her breast, Camila reached for her folder of documents tucked into Alonso's stroller and explained the nonpayment issue. The worker pulled up her case on a monitor that dated back to the mid-nineties, which slowly presented Camila's life in blocky white letters and numbers on a black screen.

"They paid July," she said.

"They paid July?"

"Yes. The shelter must know this."

Could they? Camila wondered. Was the shelter lying to her? Or was someone covering for a fuckup at the welfare office? She didn't trust anyone in this invisible chain. But she also knew she couldn't ask Rose about it—it was too risky to open her mouth about anything at the shelter, not since the eviction notice. She'd have to resolve it on her own and accept whatever circumstances she encountered without indicating a single flash of her fury.

Camila smiled politely at the worker. "Can you verify this with a payment document, please?"

The worker sighed. "In this place, not enough workers. Everyone has several responsibilities. Today it is a little slower. I do not know why. So perhaps I can actually help today."

She wandered off behind the cubicle wall and returned with a copy of the payment record and sat back down at her desk. That was all it took.

"That was fast, thank you," Camila said.

"The supervisor is out today, so I could just do it myself without asking anyone. Too few people, too many rules here." She shook her head. "If you do not have work, you need to find work," she said brusquely, examining Camila's case file.

"I'm going to school full-time."

The worker turned to look Camila in the eye. "Good," she said. Then she leaned forward. "They will tell you to go pick up cans in the park instead of school," she said very seriously, lowering her voice. "Do not listen to them."

The worker held Camila's look intensely for another moment and then turned back to her computer. Camila thanked the back of her head. She gathered up Alonso, set him in the stroller, and was silent in the elevator down to the street.

Someone had seen her as worth more than minimum wage and a dead-end life. Someone employed by the city had seen her value. She'd been starving for such encouragement. It was so rare that someone would validate Camila's stubborn commitment to a path forward, set by her personal compass, charted at great risk. Such moments sustained her confidence and momentum through months of darkness, when the only substantiating voice she heard was her own ever-quieting inner whisper.

As she left the office, a beatific smile spread across her face. It was the first time I'd encountered this smile. It seemed to release itself from deep inside her body. Her skin glowed as her cheeks lifted her lips into a curve that was both broad and relaxed. Then, in a rare moment of reverence, her eyes looked upward, shining. In total, I witnessed this smile, this skyward glance, only a few times. Each time, I found myself stunned by the magnitude of its radiance, like it was something holy, an aura surrounding a miracle.

11

AMBITION

Camila wasn't bullshitting when she said she was going to school. At least, that was the plan.

The other women at the shelter mainly seemed to try to make it day by day; the extent of their ambition was to establish stability. Camila felt she was born for more than that. Whenever Irina would suggest she take one of the city jobs often offered to welfare recipients, Camila would privately scoff later that she wasn't going to waste her intelligence picking up cans in the park. Whenever Sherice would mention a new chain restaurant moving into Downtown Brooklyn and looking for workers, Camila would nod politely but later tell me she wasn't going to spend her life taking people's orders and cleaning up after them.

August had crept up quickly, which meant Alonso was already eight weeks old. If she couldn't prove that she was in school instead of working by the time Alonso was three months old, she'd lose her benefits. She'd also lose the room she'd managed to hang on to at the shelter. Policy was policy. Plus, classes started up in a few weeks anyway. She needed an acceptance letter or she needed a job.

Weekdays, most of the shelter residents would drop their babies at childcare to clock in at one of the city's far-flung work-placement offices. There they'd spend the entire day in a waiting room alongside hundreds of other welfare recipients, all listening for their names to be called for one of the few jobs available that day. Eight hours later, they'd clock out, pick up their babies at childcare, get back to the shelter by curfew, and then repeat the day again. Possibly a part-time home-healthcare job would come through the office, or a temporary cleaning position. Mostly, though, the "working" hours they'd report to the welfare office involved sitting on lines of chairs, squandering the precious hours of precious lives in spirit-crushing boredom, while other people cared for their babies. It was like a Beckett play, in which the waiting was the work.

Irina had begun spending her days in a work-placement waiting room, though all she'd contracted thus far was pneumonia. She'd told the intake worker that she had a law degree, which meant she was overqualified for anything that came through the office. Rose was furious at Irina for not keeping her degree to herself. "You need to get any job you can, however you can," she scolded her. "No one cares about your law degree—you're homeless!" Irina hadn't imagined that her education could possibly be a hindrance. But she never mentioned her law degree in a public employment office again.

Camila saw college, and perhaps even graduate school, as the only way forward for herself and her son. A degree linked to a career was the only way she thought she could break the cycle of her family's multigenerational poverty and reliance on a system that offered less support each year. Just getting by was no goal at all.

Her plan was to continue her studies in criminal justice, a good match for her skills. She identified these skills as being smart, being fluent in Spanish, and being a badass. Occasionally she'd allow herself to look toward the distant gleam of law school. The law was the way out for her, she believed, the path to certain independence. It was a highly professionalized form of claiming and dispatching power, of getting on the right side of the game, the one that called the shots. She'd be the one throwing down, she'd often say. Instead of getting thrown. Instead of the one being thrown away.

As long as she had a roof and a bed for herself and her new tiny son, plus a childcare voucher to cover her classroom hours, Camila thought she'd be working border patrol before Alonso's second birthday. Before giving birth, she'd already downloaded the requisite exam study manuals for the patrol, which offered a starting salary of over $40,000 a year. That was a life. What life could ten bucks an hour offer? Or shaking her ass for tips? she'd ask me derisively.

It wasn't like having a job prevented homelessness, not in this America. Half of the country's homeless population worked. Plus, seven in ten housed Americans believed they were just one paycheck away from a shelter or the streets. Working mothers had the most reason to feel they tiptoed on an infinite tightrope: Families were the fastest-growing homeless population. And in poor, nonwhite America, families usually meant women raising children alone. The experience of managing and supporting a household alone never makes it onto a résumé, but you can bet it prepares you for something far more formidable than picking up cans in the street.

When Camila was eighteen, someone she barely knew suggested she become a cop. Television had told her that uncompromising, attractive Latinas had a place in law enforcement; plus, life in uniform was the only professional model her family offered, and she had to reach back a generation and across the Caribbean Sea to find it. None of Camila's elders had ever modeled career ambition or signaled that she might have talents that could advance her life beyond the financial and emotional insecurity they had offered her. But in the Dominican Republic, Camila's grandfather had been revered for his work as a police officer. Not that her grandfather was a hero, she told me, her voice sharp, at least not as a father: He never claimed Mauricio as his son.

Her interest in law enforcement was cerebral, as well. She'd talk to me about articles she'd read on gender and the use of appropriate force. The key to justice in law enforcement, she said, could be found in how rarely women officers reached for their guns or nightsticks—not that she wouldn't if she had to. Her ambitions steered her to enrollment at John Jay College of Criminal Justice in Manhattan. It was the best program in the country, and right here in New York. After high school, she had been awarded funding for tuition and work-study at any university in the state system—that was how she got to the University of Buffalo. Her College Discovery grant would cover a few more years' tuition at any New York public institution, including John Jay.

She had a plan and was going to attack it methodically each day: The admissions officer had her transfer application; he was just waiting, impatiently, on a transcript from the community college in New Jersey that she had attended while living in the shelter there. But what she somehow didn't know was that John Jay's reputation for excellence meant it was highly competitive. Applying to transfer didn't guarantee admission, just as sheer will could only carry one so far in a life as unstable as hers. But since her will was all she had, she couldn't afford to doubt.

Plus, the myth of America raised her to believe that if she was determined enough, she could achieve anything. Camila knew she had a very strong and able mind; her teachers had always told her so. And she saw its effects, how people would either be magnetized to her or put up their defenses when they encountered it. She was writing the narrative of her life from scratch, without conventions—of course it veered into fantasy, but the alternative was to imagine that every door was closed to her. That would mean a life without ambition or progress, a life like her mother's. Her survival depended on seeing those dreams as possibility.

Camila's ambitions were hardly fantasies of glamour, like the way Anselma wanted to be a famous fashion designer or Sherice wanted to be a renowned photographer. She didn't even hold fast to hopes of having an active father for Alonso. Other than stable housing, her immediate aspiration was simple: a degree in her chosen field from a reputable institution. She'd always been told she just needed to apply herself. She had the grants in place. She'd made her way back to New York. She only needed to get the transcripts and do the paperwork. Then she'd be ready to start classes.

She didn't seem to realize that by banking on John Jay, she was risking everything. If Camila wasn't admitted by the end of August, she would find herself, Alonso, and her clothes in garbage bags on the sidewalk of Fourth Avenue, with no welfare benefits to keep her going. I asked her frequently if she had another plan in place or if she thought that she should, just as a backup. She would look at me like I was questioning her capacity and not say a word. Backup plans were a form of doubt, anathema to the single-mindedness that powered her unceasing will. Like how, perhaps, she couldn't fathom that Kevin wasn't the father, that she even had to take a DNA test, until she had no choice but to let a nurse draw blood from her arm. Narrowing her vision may have been naïve, but it was necessary for her mental survival—an unspoken, and perhaps unconscious, strategy.

Camila had marked August 4 on her calendar before she gave birth. She'd been invited to participate in a focus-group meeting about working with volunteer doulas. Showing up would earn her twenty-five dollars and a MetroCard, but the real reason it was worth her time, she said, was that she might make some good connections there with like-minded ambitious women. She'd anticipated a formal meeting in a conference room and planned an outfit in advance.

As she walked up Fourth Avenue on the way to the meeting, Alonso suddenly needed to be fed. Camila stopped to nurse on the edge of the sidewalk, as she assuredly told me about the letter she had to write to the John Jay admissions department that afternoon, asking them to waive the seventy-dollar transfer-application fee because she was enrolling as a homeless single mother. It was rare to hear her refer to herself that way.

Camila was hunched by lingering C-section pain; her recovery was taking far longer than her doctor had anticipated. She pulled Alonso off her breast and made her way down Atlantic Avenue, ignoring the pain of each step, rattling off her first-semester plans. She'd already examined the course catalog and was anxious about seminars filling up quickly; classes started in just a couple of weeks. She needed to make sure they knew she was coming, even though she was still waiting on that transcript. While she was talking, I noticed a blush-pink price tag tied to a set of mid-century lawn chairs on the sidewalk outside a vintage-furniture store. The rusting chairs were on sale for $2,500. The Brooklyn that Camila occupied may have shared the same sidewalks with such a bizarre parallel economy, but she acted as though it was an unseen dimension to her. Perhaps she was simply complying with what was required of all people who didn't share in the increasing—and increasingly concentrated—wealth in the city and far beyond: to cope with the barricade between haves and have-nots by pretending it didn't exist at all.

Jaywalking with a stroller, like a true New Yorker, Camila crossed the street to the RAICES senior center, the stout four-story building where the focus group was being held. Over the past five years, the building's value had more than doubled, now estimated at $5.8 million. But unlike the lawn chairs proudly announcing their inflated worth, the hodgepodge of plastic Catholic wall decorations and chipped linoleum inside the building still reflected Camila's dimension.

A dreadlocked fifty-something woman in a leopard-print tunic and a rubber wristband that said STRONG FATHERS welcomed Camila to a wood-veneer conference table and informed her that the meeting's facilitator had the wrong date. Not to worry, the facilitator would be joining via speakerphone, she said. Camila nodded once in response, immediately hardening in disappointment. She'd been fastidious with her hair and makeup, buttoned up a pristine blouse over leggings, and wriggled Alonso into a onesie that looked like a tuxedo, all just to talk into a telephone.

None of the other mothers had brought babies with them. Camila noted resentfully that they all must have had people to take care of their kids at home. At the table, a woman just out of girlhood poked at a smartphone. Her bleached hair with long dark roots hung limply over a faded V-neck T-shirt that exposed a neck splotched with yellowing bruises. Camila sized up her chipped nails and sallow skin, then stiffly turned away to load a plastic plate with fruit and a muffin, swatting at the flies that formed a buzzing halo over the catering tray. At least she'd get breakfast out of this waste of time. At least Alonso had finally fallen asleep.

The dreadlocked woman's phone rang. A millennial- and white-sounding voice spoke through the speaker, asking the women at the table to talk about their doula experiences.

The room was silent. Camila gathered her poise to speak first. "I was scared and by myself. I didn't have any family," she said, her voice measured. "But I had my doula. Though at my hospital in Queens they said they'd never had a doula come to a birth."

"Interesting," said the voice.

The validation spurred Camila to continue. "I didn't know how I was going to take care of myself and my baby after my C-section. My doula brought food to my house." She poked at her muffin. "Well, my shelter. I live in a shelter," she corrected softly. "I don't have my mom in my life, so having a female to give me advice, keep me on the path, that's important." She folded her hands to compose herself. Her voice grew strong again. "My labor and delivery—none of my family showed up. My doula showed up and respected me. All I wanted was someone to respect me, to continue a relationship with me." Camila so rarely revealed herself in this way. She nodded once to signify the end of her speech.

The young woman with the bruised neck spoke next. She couldn't remember her doula's name, she said. She lived in public housing in Bushwick with her husband and two kids, and now she was pregnant with twins. She addressed a question to Camila. "They cut you open and take out your whole stomach, right? What's it that they're in? The stomach?"

"The uterus," Camila answered, her voice firm with expertise.

"Yeah, the uterus or whatever it's called. I don't want that to happen to me."

With clinical precision, Camila advised her about reasons to prefer noninvasive procedures and articulated the importance of filling out all her HIPAA forms in advance. Everyone around the table stared at Camila like she was a species they'd never encountered. She kept on, unruffled by their looks, explaining how she toured three hospitals and, after selecting one, scheduled a meeting with the manager of the maternity department.

"Did your doula go with you to do that?" the voice on the phone asked.

"No, I did it on my own."

"I'm not on my own," the young woman with the bruised neck said proudly. "It's going to be my husband, my two sons, my two daughters, and me. I'm happy. I've got my team."

Camila glared at her for a moment. The young woman became self-conscious at Camila's visible resentment. She looked down at her plate and ruefully began to pick at the wrapper on her muffin.

"My oldest son is three," the young woman continued. "I'm going to be twenty-one when he's five."

The room was quiet, except for the flies droning over the food. Camila pressed her lips together. While the imbalance between wealth and poverty seemed almost invisible to Camila, inequalities within her own economic and cultural bracket punctured her deeply. Like this girl, who was about to have four kids before she was nineteen and didn't know what a uterus was, who couldn't even bother to remove her cracked nail polish or run a brush through her hair before coming to a meeting with a professional organization. But she had housing she could afford. And she had a father to her kids. Camila ran her tongue over her teeth in contempt.

Outside the meeting, sudden sheets of heavy midsummer rain pounded the pavement. Alonso woke, his cries competing with the thrum of the downpour. Camila leaned down over the stroller and sniffed the air, squinting against the torrent. He needed a diaper change. She ducked into the entrance of a mosque on the first floor of a tenement building and smiled at a bearded man in an embroidered dishdasha. Then, as though she'd been in this unfamiliar space many times before, she set about changing Alonso in his stroller. When she finished, she pushed the stroller back into the pouring rain; she had errands to do, and she had a fee-waiver request to write. Time was running out. As she soldiered on ahead, I noticed a run snaking its way up the back of her leggings.

12

RENUNCIATIONS

There was no end, it seemed, to the to-do list Camila carried in her mind. One item gave her pleasure, though: planning for Alonso's baptism. Camila had been obsessively anticipating the ceremony. She'd reminded me of the date every several days since June. *You sure you'll be there?* she'd text me late at night from the shelter. Weeks before, she'd carefully selected her outfit of an aqua sleeveless dress with a white lace yoke, stiletto sandals, and a long strand of pearls that looked almost real. The baptism was less about faith, as Camila saw it, than an overdue celebration of her motherhood.

For weeks she'd been talking about how I'd get to meet her whole family there, as though they'd simply show up for her. While she hardly knew Mauricio's cousin, she asked him to be Alonso's godfather, hoping her choice would strengthen a connection between her dad and her son. She told me she expected Mauricio to come, to finally exhibit some pride in his daughter. All these Alvarez men welcoming the newest member, she said, triumphant, placing her hand on her heart. There weren't many women who Camila deemed competent for the role of Alonso's godmother. She'd chosen Dorcas, the Corona girl Mauricio had gotten pregnant soon after Geraldine. Camila had her own relationship with Dorcas. In the rare moments when people would see them together, she'd refer to Dorcas as her "mother," partly to simplify their relationship but mainly out of wishful thinking. It was Dorcas who'd lent her Alonso's baptism gown and a pair of tiny white booties; plus, she would have to come to the baptism if she was the godmother, which meant her son Michael, Camila's favorite half sibling, might be there, too. Camila's sisters all said they'd be there. Geraldine wouldn't come, surely. Still, Camila couldn't help but hope, in spite of herself.

It was hard to imagine her son's life with no grandmother at all. But at least someone she called an abuela would be there, even though they'd met only recently, the week Camila moved into the shelter. She had been just a few weeks from her due date and hoped to start the baby moving by taking a walk near the park, along the streets of stately townhouses where the other residents didn't venture. On her stroll, she passed a brownstone Catholic church. She paused to admire it. An aging Haitian woman sat outside.

"I see the baby waving at me from inside your belly!" the woman hollered.

Camila turned on her smile. She introduced herself.

The woman was named Odette. She chattered excitedly about Camila's pregnancy and led her inside to see the Gothic ornamentation, the rotunda of stained glass, the oriental rugs thrown over mosaic tiled floors. Surveying the magnificent sanctuary, Camila knew it was where she wanted to have Alonso baptized. He had to be blessed somewhere beautiful, she said. As they toured the church, Camila talked to Odette about her childhood church in Corona.

"Where are you delivering?" Odette asked.

Camila told her about her doctor in Queens.

"All the way out there? You'll have to take a taxi."

Odette brought Camila back to her apartment and gave her an envelope of cash to cover the car service to the hospital. Her granddaughter was home and was planning to go to a party that night. She insisted Camila join her. The party was pretty lame, though Camila had done her best to make it worth her while, flirting, charming the room. When she didn't hear from Odette's grand-daughter the next day, Camila figured she probably hadn't expected a pregnant girl to get all the attention that night.

Out of all of Geraldine's kids, Camila was the only one who'd been forced to go to church every Sunday with her grandmother. That was because she was always in trouble for mouthing off or for sneaking out to play with the neighborhood kids. She would fume about the hypocrisy of faith in her family, about how her mother would run around with guys and then take the bread and wine whenever it suited her, like she'd been living a virtuous life. I don't think a week went by that year without Camila bringing up how her mother would dress in belly shirts and high heels every time she left the house, how it mortified her seeing Geraldine teeter to the bo-dega in the morning sun, dressed in what Camila called "hoochie clothes." By the time Camila was eight, she figured she had to act like the martinet parent.

"Why do you have to be such a whore?" she yelled at her mother.

Geraldine replied by punching her square in the mouth. Then she ordered Camila's grandmother to take her to church. That's how Camila began her life as a Catholic.

Once her grandmother turned *carismático,* church became al-most as scary as her mother's beatings. Camila would sit in the pew, watching her grandmother roll on the floor, speaking in tongues. Her grandmother's piety seemed to take the place of actual feeling for her family. Camila couldn't recall a single kiss or hug from her, yet she'd watch her be overcome by passion every Sunday in church. But people had told her faith might brighten her prospects, so she managed her skepticism. She packed holy water in her hospital bag to keep Alonso's delivery room safe from trouble, and, moments after he was born, she anointed him with the water to shield him against any evil forces that might set him on the wrong path. She didn't want him to have her mother's mental instability—"touched," as she put it. Anything that might help, she'd try. Every day, for luck, she wore a bracelet woven from a red nylon cord she'd bought from a Chinese woman on the subway platform in Flushing. Alonso wore one, too, tied around his tiny wrist, with a medallion that dangled wildly when he waved his arms.

Some nights in the shelter, when she felt incapable of summoning any more solutions, Camila would stand in front of her Bible, which was on the dresser. She'd ask a question, close her eyes, open up the Bible, and press her fingertip onto the page before opening her eyes. She hoped that her finger would land on a line of scripture that would offer her the answer. But lately, as faith hadn't secured her school transfer or delivered the results of the DNA test, she was doing this less often.

Camila had met Odette at the church every Sunday before the baptism; she wanted to make sure she'd belong when the day came. When it did, Odette was readily awaiting them inside the heavy wooden doors.

"Abuelita!" Camila cried, hugging her.

She introduced Irina, who'd joined her. The minutes passed. Camila kept her eyes on the marble-arched entrance, waiting to see if anyone else would show up for her.

The church offered communal baptism services to simultaneously anoint the babies of multiple families. A couple of dozen people had streamed into the cavernous sanctuary, but so far none of them were there to celebrate Alonso. Two women with cropped hair, man-tailored vests, and bow ties, one of them carrying their infant son, entered the church with a gregarious pack of friends, trading throaty laughs and fist bumps. Another family began trickling in, the men and boys in capacious suits, the women and girls in yards of pastel rayon. They were pasty and pious, cowed by the religious tableaux glowing in the stained-glass windows. Then came a crowd of Dominicans. Camila smiled at three small girls in frilly white confirmation dresses and elaborate braids, but they weren't her people.

Camouflaged at the back of that crowd, Mauricio's cousin shuffled in alone, wearing a dark jacket and a wide-collared white shirt. Nobody joined him. He pecked Camila on both cheeks and then withdrew. Then Dorcas appeared in tight white pants and a bright-yellow blouse, her tinted hair flowing to her waist, her young twins following distractedly behind. Camila kissed her and tried to hide her disappointment that Michael hadn't joined them.

The priest said it was time to start the ceremony. Camila wasn't expecting her father any longer and felt naïve to have thought he might come. For a moment she considered asking his cousin if he'd sent word, but it was too mortifying. It was fine, it was fine, she told me, trying to convince herself. Her sisters were surely still coming, she said. She didn't need him.

Camila politely asked the priest to wait just a few more minutes for her sisters, trying to hide her desperation. As the families gathered around the baptismal font under the gaze of wooden-inlaid saints, Alonso began to howl, filling the hall with his colicky wails. Bouncing him to calm his cries, Camila stood in the front of the congregation, flanked by her few guests. The priest told Camila gently that it was time to begin.

"Stand over here," he instructed, gesturing to the side. "Your group is so much smaller."

Camila shyly scuttled to the margins of the big white family, which had grown impatient for the service to begin. Except for Alonso's cries, the church fell quiet.

"Baptisms are a very special way to turn to God and give thanks for the children in your lives and to thank God for our families," the priest said.

Camila smiled respectfully, her lips apologizing for Alonso's continuing wails. The congregation stared at her, some irritated, some charitable. She hunched her shoulders around Alonso, shushing him, trying to jam the pacifier in his mouth. He refused it. Slowly, Camila stepped backward, disappearing into the large family like a fugitive escaping into a crowd. The four other parents smiled in the front row, standing reverently in front of the priest. She had become a bystander at her own child's baptism.

How she wished Kevin was here. She'd whispered to me that morning that his presence would make her absentee family bearable. Everyone here would see his strength and grace, she said. She'd stand tall beside him. Adjusting her plastic pearls, she tried to pay attention to the prayers. The renunciations began: six questions, posed by the priest. Speaking clearly over her son's cries, Camila offered the answer to each one.

"I do. I do. I do. I do. I do. I do."

These were the words she wanted to say in a different church ceremony to someone who wasn't here. She'd begun to fear he'd never be.

After the ceremony, the other parents and godparents held their newly baptized babies and posed for pictures on the altar with the priest. Then he invited everyone for a luncheon in the rectory.

"Before we go for lunch, can we have our picture, too?" she asked, as the priest was leaving to remove his vestments. He stood beside Camila and Alonso's godparents as Odette took a picture with Camila's phone. None of them would bother to attend Alonso's first birthday party. She wouldn't get so much as an inquiry about Alonso from his godfather that year, and it was the last time she'd see the abuela, but for that moment they were her family.

In the rectory, dark wood and dark paintings filled the fusty rooms under high parlor ceilings. While Odette and Dorcas politely chatted with the priest over salad and pizza, and Alonso finally slept in his car seat, Camila perched on a high-backed chair away from the dining table. She checked her phone. Her sister had texted that she'd overslept. Michael had texted that he was working. Teresa had texted that she needed to go to her own church for a meeting.

Then Kevin's name appeared on the screen.

We should go our own ways, his text said.

Camila read his one simple sentence over and over.

She realized what it meant: that he got a verdict from a lab that was grounds for her dismissal from his life and from her only desired future.

At least Alonso had that time with him in the hospital. She insisted, that day, as she would frequently in the future, that those hours in the maternity ward would be the foundational memory of her son's life, something he'd always be able to hold on to, as though he'd been baptized in that hospital room by his rightful father. I was never sure if she truly believed this, but she adopted it, in the dining room of this rectory, as a new faith.

She clenched her teeth so no one in the room would sense that she was feeling anything but gratitude and penitence.

What now? she tapped into the phone.

Do as you wish, he wrote.

Like her wishes were options.

After the luncheon, on the way back to the shelter, Camila stopped into the bodega for a juice. On her way out, a panhandler asked her for money.

Devoured by rejection, she felt vicious. "I'm a single mother," she barked. "Why are you asking me for money? I hope you don't have kids."

"Yeah," he said sadly. "I've got kids."

13

SOCIAL WORK

Another seven days closer to the three-month mark, when she had to be enrolled in school full-time. Classes were starting soon, but she still hadn't heard from John Jay about her acceptance. Nor did she have a place for Alonso to go during the day, though a voucher finally came through the welfare office that would cover Alonso's daycare. Now she had to find someone who would accept it, which, she'd heard from the other mothers at the shelter, was not easy to do. She just needed somewhere safe, somewhere with decent hours so she could drop him off in time to get to morning classes and pick him up after late-afternoon ones. Evening classes were out—not only because it would be impossible to find childcare but because the inflexible shelter curfew of nine o'clock sharp wouldn't permit such a schedule. That meant she couldn't work at night, either. She'd have to count on a work-study position to fill in what money public assistance couldn't provide.

Nursing Alonso, who was increasingly unsatisfied by what her body could produce to feed him, Camila flipped through her red folder for the list of area daycare centers she'd found that would take her childcare voucher. Not many would. She chose the one she thought Sherice had mentioned during the Wednesday-night meeting. It was in the same building as her pediatrician: Hanson Place.

The daycare was in the old Williamsburgh Savings Bank Tower, just down Fourth Avenue by the Barclays Center. Until the recent surge of development, its four-sided clock tower had been the most iconic stack of brick and mortar on this side of the Brooklyn Bridge. When the tower was built, in the 1920s, its clockfaces were the largest in the world. Etched into the building's cornerstone was a dedication to those who had *swept aside the petty distinctions of class and birth and so maintained the true spirit of American democracy.* The bank tower's chief architect said he'd designed the building to be "a cathedral dedicated to the furtherance of thrift and prosperity." Prosperity won out: In 2006 the building became luxury condos.

Camila dialed the phone number for the Hanson Place daycare center.

"Good afternoon," she said. "I'm calling to inquire about childcare for my son."

"There's a two-year wait list," a chirpy voice replied. "You're welcome to put your name on the list. Shall I sign you up for a tour?"

Two years? Two years ago she had no idea she'd be having a baby. Camila politely declined the tour and hung up. Alonso had finally drifted off on her breast. Camila held him there for a long time after she hung up, her eyes focused on her son's sleeping face. She called another number she'd written down. It was out of service.

It was worth ignoring the day's heat advisory to get out of her room and get something to eat. She wanted some Dominican food from Lisa's, the bodega on Fourth Avenue. A bowl of rice with pink salami, yellow egg, and white cheese, called mangú, was hearty enough to feed Camila for a day or two. Lisa's egg-and-cheese sandwich was only three bucks, but it wouldn't carry her as far as an eight-dollar mangú. Food stamps didn't cover hot food, but mangú was one of Camila's only comforting indulgences. She'd eat exactly half when she got home and save the other half for the next day. She didn't need to eat much anyway, she'd tell me, even breastfeeding; she'd just drink a lot of water if she got hungry.

The mangú didn't grant her just sustenance but also access to Lisa, the bodega's owner, and her relatives who worked there. Everywhere she went, Camila found temporary kin among the Dominicans scattered throughout the city. At the bodega, Lisa would lavish attention on Camila while her sister fried up the salami on the industrial griddle. And if I was there, she'd silently check in with me to see how Camila was doing, looking into my eyes, reading my face. She knew the three-month mark was coming up for Camila. She knew to worry.

Camila pulled open the door and backed in with the stroller, careful not to wake Alonso. Lisa's was crammed with junk food. Pork rinds and off-brand chips filled the shelves; refrigerators glowed like church windows with the bright liquid hues of Jarritos bottles. Lisa was ringing up a bag of Hot Fries. She was dressed for success as always, in a black blazer with matching slacks. Camila smiled expectantly as she waited for her to hand back some change to a kid standing at the counter.

"Here you go, papi," Lisa said. She looked around the stack of individually wrapped Dominican cake slices to see who had come in the door. "Camila!" she exclaimed, coming around to kiss her on each cheek.

Hearing Camila's name, Lisa's daughter emerged from behind a shelf she'd been restocking. She worked at an eye doctor's office in the Bronx near the apartment the whole family shared, but there were no after-school options for her son, so she had to pick him up at school and bring him to the bodega in Brooklyn every day, where he'd bide his time until the family rolled down the gates at midnight. The boy wasn't sitting on his usual stool behind the counter, Camila noticed. She kissed Lisa's daughter on both cheeks and asked after him.

"Whenever he's not there and he's quiet, you know he's gotten into the chips again," Lisa said. Camila peered around a rack of shelving to see the boy with his hand plunged into a foil bag. "How are you?" Lisa asked, squeezing Camila's arm.

"I'm good. Trying to get housing. Childcare. You know how it is."

"I do, I do." She nodded solemnly for a moment and then forcibly brightened. "You want something to eat, baby? Mangú? Steak and rice?"

"Mangú, please."

Two college-age white kids came in through the door and stared at the shelving under the counter.

"Do you have Kind bars?" one asked.

"No, honey. Not here," Lisa said sympathetically.

While Lisa's sister prepared the mangú, Camila asked about Lisa's mother, who was slowly dying back in the Dominican Republic. Lisa's siblings had been flying down in six-week shifts, and her turn was coming up. Camila offered to work in the bodega while she was gone.

"I want to help you guys out however I can," she said. "You don't have to pay me."

Camila was genuinely sympathetic about what the family was struggling with. She also saw a family that she might be able to belong to, if she could demonstrate her value. Lisa just smiled. She was distracted by an African American man in filthy baggy pants and ragged dreadlocks crossing the street toward the bodega. She watched him stumble toward the glass door and then collapse to the pavement outside.

"One moment, honey," she said to Camila. She gently pushed open the door and spoke to him quietly for a minute. He stood, nodded respectfully, and moved on.

The mangú was ready. Camila lingered for a few minutes, but she didn't want it to get cold. She kissed Lisa and her daughter goodbye and took the aluminum takeout dish back to her room, where she ate exactly half the rice and egg, one piece of salami, and one piece of cheese.

Camila was beginning to fear that there was no option for her and Alonso outside of an emergency shelter run by the city. She was just days shy of the three-month mark, and John Jay still hadn't admitted her. Her welfare check and the roof over their heads were in jeopardy. She'd gotten no traction in her housing search, and things hadn't grown any cozier for her on Fourth Avenue. Meanwhile, no one at the shelter had offered help beyond a weekly check-in to see how her housing search was going. She wondered to me, bitterly, if Rose thought the barriers to getting a permanent place to stay would be lifted if she simply committed herself more.

Since the shelter wasn't going to provide a social worker, Camila had to find a volunteer one herself, and not just one who'd tell her to get a job instead of going to school, like the one who'd come to the last residents meeting. She'd heard about a woman who was seeing clients out in East New York, who said she could help with a housing search. It was a long trek to the address the volunteer social worker had given her over the phone.

Inside a brutalist concrete building, tinted windows filtered out the sunlight. The lobby was completely empty, sepulchral, lined with unoccupied waiting-room chairs. Camila found her way upstairs and wandered a silent beige labyrinth of abandoned cubicles until she saw an office door standing open. Above a desk hung a calendar from a Caribbean bakery and a picture of Sojourner Truth. She smoothed her seersucker skirt and tried to quiet Alonso's cries.

"Who's that crying?" said a jovial, lilting voice.

The desk chair swiveled and a dark woman in large glasses and a thick-braided updo reached out her arms. Understanding the gesture, Camila lifted Alonso out of the carrier and passed him to the woman.

"Miss Angie?" Camila asked.

"That's me! Now, come here, baby," the woman said to Alonso, "and stop your crying. Welcome, welcome!" Miss Angie gestured to a chair near the desk.

Camila took a seat. "Thank you for taking the time to see me today."

"First things first," said Miss Angie. "We're going to help you move forward, not only for yourself but for him. A better future for him. That's the focus I want you to have. What do you need? Today we're going to talk it into existence!"

Camila grinned. She hadn't encountered this much spirit in a long time. "I think they're going to kick me out of my shelter," she said. "Can you help me figure out what to do? On the phone, you mentioned contacting someone at another shelter on my behalf?"

Instead of looking up at Camila, Miss Angie studied Alonso's face. "I didn't get ahold of Mr. Graham, the director of the other shelter," she said. She coughed, loudly and for a long time. "If you have to move, you're moving the way you're supposed to move."

Camila looked at her quizzically.

Miss Angie's phone rang.

"Will you quit calling me?" she yelled toward the phone. "I have no money! Every minute they're calling me! It's student loans." She shook her head and laughed.

Camila forced a smile.

"Depending on your case, they will offer you Section 8," Miss Angie said. "But it has to be an emergency."

Camila gently corrected her. "They don't offer Section 8 anymore." The New York City Housing Authority hadn't accepted applications for Section 8, the federal housing subsidy program, since 2008. She continued her correction. "Also, Miss Angie, they will only give me emergency housing if it's a domestic-violence case," she added.

"You have a restraining order?" Miss Angie asked.

Camila shook her head.

"No? You've got none of that? So it's not a special case," Miss Angie said. "Like if you were to witness a murder, that would work. They'd get you in priority and put you somewhere." Miss Angie's voice suddenly became clipped and schoolmarmish. "Now, you need to get involved in his school. Every time a boy fails the SAT test, they build another jail. He can't be part of those statistics. You need to get involved in every step of his education. Don't give his teachers the opportunity to label him."

Camila knit her brows together. Her baby was two months old. She needed shelter. Why was this social worker talking to her about SAT tests?

Alonso began to wail louder.

"Okay, okay, Mommy going to feed the baby," Miss Angie said.

She passed Alonso over to Camila. "Feed that boy right now," she ordered.

Camila pulled down her tank top and bandeau bra and lifted him into position. He quieted.

"See? We just solved a problem!"

While Camila nursed Alonso, she ran through her prepared list of questions about housing vouchers and what other shelters might take a homeless woman with a baby.

"I don't know about that, honey," Miss Angie said, waving her fingers in the air. "But I know this: You've got to try to keep as stress-free as possible so you're feeding him stress-free milk. Okay? That's the most important thing. He's got to get stress-free milk. So don't fret about those things when you're nursing him."

As soon as Alonso was satisfied, Camila thanked Miss Angie politely and found her way into the glaring sun outside, waiting until she was on the sidewalk to allow frustration to twist her mouth into a grimace. She told me she knew people who had been cheated by fake Section 8 registration websites, which charged a fee and stole personal information—probably fed by the utter cluelessness of so-called aid workers like this one. She wasn't going to get fooled like that, she grumbled, making her way back to the subway, another afternoon squandered, another hope smashed.

I wondered when her composure would break with someone who misguided her through a system that ostensibly existed for her support. How many appointments she'd summon her nerve to schedule, only to find herself more discouraged than she was before. If she would become like some of the mothers at the shelter, who could barely shuffle out of bed. And when the last of her hope would be wrung out of her.

14

WHO BY FIRE, WHO BY WATER

The only reason Camila spent most of her childhood in apartments rather than homeless shelters was because of Geraldine's Section 8 vouchers. Until her mother scored a place in the projects, those vouchers paid the family's rent. But that was a story of poor single motherhood from a different era, one that had quickly vanished. It had kept Camila and her sisters not only housed but attending school consistently in Queens. In the years since, there had been record demand for housing assistance, while budget cuts shut out almost anyone who found themselves newly in need. When new vouchers became available, rarely and unpredictably, they went to the top of a wait list that had been capped at ten thousand names. Over one hundred thousand families waited for their chance to compete in a lottery for one of those few wait-list spots. Camila had heard the wait list opened once in those seven years, for only five days.

Section 8 had come about in the 1970s, when the high cost of housing was identified as a national blight, and when researchers declared that housing subsidies were the single most effective way to prevent widespread homelessness. That thinking hadn't changed among people who studied housing insecurity, despite funding shrinking to the point where New York could accept no new applicants. While Camila was searching for a place to live that summer, the Department of Housing and Urban Development released new research to support that long-standing conclusion: Long-term housing subsidies were the only solution to the homelessness crisis, and programs like Section 8 would save the country a fortune.

Only one-quarter of Americans in poverty received government rent support. Meanwhile, emergency housing was costing taxpayers more than four times as much as long-term vouchers would if anyone sleeping in a public-shelter bed could count on a rent check, or a permanent apartment, instead. Mortgage deductions for the wealthiest property owners had reached stratospheric highs, and yet not a single county in the entire country could offer enough affordable housing to keep those most at risk from homelessness.

Occasionally, small programs would try to make small differences. Rose had heard about a city voucher program designed to get long-term shelter residents into permanent housing. One person could apply from each shelter, but it had to be the resident who had been there the longest. That August, the senior resident was Sherice, whose year at the shelter was now up.

The voucher program was only open to residents in the city's network of homeless shelters, Rose had heard, but she encouraged Sherice to apply for it anyway. Rose saw her as a model resident, she told me. Sherice followed the rules without complaint; she showed up at Applebee's every day. "She does everything she's supposed to do," Rose said. Sherice applied but was rejected, deemed ineligible because she'd chosen to stay at a private shelter. Once she became the longest-residing person at an emergency city shelter, she could apply again.

Rose was furious. Her yells in the office carried all the way up the stairs. "Do they really want to pay a fortune to have her sit in a shelter—just so she could qualify for a program like this? They're going to deny her because our shelter doesn't take money from taxpayers? They are going to disqualify this kid because she refuses to milk the city? Shame on them." She told me she was going to take her outrage straight to city hall and sent an email directly to the mayor's office. She knew him from way back when.

Having worked with the homeless for decades, Rose had contacts all over the city. She could potentially change a life with a phone call. But despite her longtime exposure to the progressive brutality of life under the poverty line and her immersion in the structural inequality that produced it, she still believed that hard work and determination were the answer. Neither Sherice nor anyone else should rely on her professional affiliations to find their way out, she said. Not everyone was equipped to escape it, though. This she knew well. She made another couple of calls and secured the voucher for Sherice. Regardless, Sherice and Tyrese would have to go soon. Everyone had to go, somehow, whether they had a place to go or not.

The week before, Tina, the shelter resident with the vacant stare and erratic temperament, the one Rose had thought twice about admitting, had pushed Jayden's stroller through the thick night air up Fourth Avenue. When she reached the massive five-way intersection near the Barclays Center, she rolled the stroller off the curb and stepped down behind it. Cars sped around the corner, taking a right off Atlantic Avenue.

Tina was blind to their headlights, deaf to their horns, nor did she notice a crossing guard in a reflective vest yelling at her to stop. As she kept pushing her way into traffic, a crowd quickly assembled and formed a chorus of yells to halt her. She kept moving farther into the street. The crossing guard ran out to block her way. Police arrived to restrain her, before she or her baby got hit. An ambulance quickly followed, to bring her to the psychiatric ward at Methodist Hospital. She hadn't returned to the shelter since.

That's what Rose told me had happened. Camila said she heard Tina was hit by a car. Anselma thought she moved in with her parents in Queens, embroidering the story with hope about her returning to her family. When I asked Sherice what she knew about Tina's disappearance, she just shook her head, reticent. It was none of their business, they figured. Women went missing all the time. They'd all seen drugs, boyfriends, and evictions cause women to vanish, from shelters most of all. It was a transient short-term world. Better not to try to put down roots. You never knew who would be gone tomorrow.

15

LETTERS AND NUMBERS

Classes were starting in days, and Camila was still waiting on her transcript. She'd been calling the registrar daily. The John Jay admissions office granted her an extension, but once the semester started, time would be up. The television in the empty common room at the shelter blared the upcoming Labor Day weekend weather report. Upstairs, Irina looked after Alonso while Camila took the subway alone to the admissions office at John Jay. It always served Camila well to show up in person, where she could present herself with charm and elegance. She couldn't show up with a crying baby.

An admissions officer welcomed her and took interest in her circumstances. He was sympathetic and wanted to help and said that as long as her transcript arrived with the grade point average she anticipated, she just had to sign up for classes. He promised to shepherd her through the process himself.

Camila's ability to attract such notice in people—whether it was the cashier at the hardware store or someone with the institutional power to redraw her future—was an unusual force. This was her spark, illuminating her, drawing people to her intelligence, her presence. But while it produced and strengthened quick intimacies, it often failed to help her set expectations around the limits of what institutions could promise, when policy rather than personalities made the rules. She'd never been taught about the gatekeeping of elite institutions like John Jay.

The next day, the transcript arrived. She had expected to see a run of high grades and a few incompletes from the prior semester, when she had moved back to New York to have the baby. But the incompletes were listed as Fs.

John Jay would not accept her with failing grades on her transcript. Plus, with that grade point average, she'd lose the grant money she was counting on to support her through any public university in the state. She had asked her professors if she could take her exams remotely or write papers instead. They'd refused. She'd addressed this in her transfer application, to explain the courses she thought would appear without final grades, credits she'd make up with new classes. But it didn't matter.

No matter the potential of Camila's agile mind or the resources she could hunt and gather to help herself survive, she was always only the sum of her paperwork. Her shelter application, her welfare case, her NYCHA file, and more. Now this transcript. The facts were immutable and inescapable. She couldn't protect herself from them. She couldn't will a different narrative. These letters and numbers, stored in hard drives and file cabinets, often divorced from who she knew herself to be, were what determined the shape of her life, her very subsistence. Her professors didn't know that an F would mean she'd lose her welfare check or her room on Fourth Avenue.

And if they did, what difference would it make? Not everyone could bend the rules for her. Rose certainly wasn't going to. And in the system, she was nothing but a case number, no different than any other. There were no exceptions to be made. She wouldn't be going to John Jay to embark on her plan for the future. She wasn't going to school at all. She was going to lose shelter, public assistance, childcare—everything she relied on. Alonso's three-month mark was just days away, rendering the cascade of consequences even more tidal. And she had no backup plan whatsoever.

FALL

1

ADMISSIONS

Fewer things are harder to live with than uncertainty, and Camila's life was perpetually uncertain, from where she'd live to whom she'd become. She'd managed it alone for years. Now she was facing that uncertainty attached to a tiny new person, who was utterly dependent upon her. There was no afternoon to wallow in bed, anchored by depression and frustration, no mental space to surrender to hopelessness.

Camila knew what she was doing when she'd left Alonso with Irina to go to the John Jay admissions office herself. The guy she'd met in the admissions office might not have been able to admit her, but she'd impressed him with her intelligence and drive and kindled his compassion with her story; he couldn't just let her slip away because of a few incompletes. He promised he'd make a few calls, see what he could do. The first call was to a friend in the admissions office at Bronx Community College. She could spend a year there, the admissions officer told her, get her GPA up, and then transfer—the criminal-justice program there fed students directly into John Jay once they'd completed an associate's degree. She wouldn't even have to go through the admissions process.

She mapped the subway commute on her phone and examined

the course listings, ignoring the academics, scrutinizing only the times that classes met. It was impossible. If she didn't have Alonso, or the shelter didn't have a curfew, it could have worked. But Camila couldn't drop Alonso off at daycare, commute up to the Bronx, get back from class to pick him up by the end of the day, and be back at the shelter in time. She told the guy in admissions that she'd try to find a place to rent in the Bronx.

Classes started the next week, so she had to get moving, he warned her; within minutes she'd applied for a studio up in Mott Haven, in the South Bronx. Or she'd tried to. She didn't make the minimum-income requirement. For five days straight, she called and emailed the rental office to see if they could be flexible about the income. No reply.

Meanwhile, she scoured Craigslist. The only listed room she could afford was in an apartment with four guys. She sent an email inquiring about the room, the first she'd had to send that said she was clean, quiet, and seeking a room not just for herself but for her baby. She checked her email every few minutes. Again, no reply. "What four guys would want to live with a baby?" she scoffed, more to herself than to me, admonishing herself for getting her hopes up. I was holding Alonso, bouncing him to try to stop his crying, which was only getting louder as his lungs grew. I wondered why anyone would want to live with a stranger's baby. Or most anyone else's baby. If they weren't raising that child, if they didn't have to.

I kept my thoughts to myself. Camila clenched her jaw and stared darkly into the space between herself and the locked door of her room. She didn't say what was roiling under that stare. But I hazarded that she was thinking back to her choice to skip her Planned Parenthood appointment. It had seemed less of a choice than a reaction on her part, and a familiar one at that. One where, in a moment of defensiveness, she'd been unwilling to consider the myriad complications that would result from a reaction. In the past months she'd confronted that tendency, learned to suppress what swelled up in a moment if it could threaten her dangling stability. But she hadn't envisioned the extent of the complications on the afternoon of her scheduled abortion.

What on that afternoon had seemed as passive as not showing up entirely changed the math of what she could will into existence. No longer was she a perfect roommate—clean, quiet, respectful—if she could just make the rent each month. It was hard enough to be homeless without a baby, but there were rooms to rent in other people's apartments, stopgap couches to crash on. Now her wits, determination, and elegance could not obscure this mewling creature she'd saddled herself with as she moved from shelter to shelter.

Camila called the admissions officer to say she was grateful, but she couldn't make it work.

He told her to hold on.

By the end of the day he called her again. He'd reached out to another friend, this time in the admissions office at Kingsborough Community College out in Manhattan Beach. It was a long commute, but at least it was still in Brooklyn; it was doable. Kingsborough was part of the same Justice Academy network that would allow her to transfer directly into John Jay. If she did as well there as she did her first semester in New Jersey, she said to herself, she'd be a John Jay student by Alonso's first birthday. She just needed to register for all the criminal-justice courses she could. Classes were starting next week.

Flatbush Avenue was still a dividing line between the ghetto-gold nameplates of the Fulton pedestrian mall and the fourteen-karat minimalist pendants of Fort Greene. The Applebee's where Sherice worked the lunch shift was right off Flatbush. A few blocks away, near Fort Greene Park, was the brownstone where a decade before I was outbid on a one-and-a-half-bedroom apartment; it had since doubled in value. On the far side of Flatbush, towering cranes lifted steel beams into place for skyscraping luxury-apartment buildings; the clanging rhythm of construction had replaced boom-box bass as the soundtrack of the neighborhood. On the near side, the season's big ribbon-cutting was for an IHOP, where I never saw a white customer. One Hanson Place, the renovated historic bank tower that now housed jewel-box condos and the daycare with the two-year waiting list, was on the far side. A few blocks and a massive income drop away was a very different daycare.

This daycare was not what Camila had imagined when she was researching childcare before she had Alonso. Instead of the one-on-one nanny arrangement she thought might be best, or a small group that would encourage early socialization with arts and music and developmentally focused play in a small nursery school, Alonso's first classroom was to be a ring of fifteen cribs around a square of industrial carpet littered with plastic toys and bouncers. But they had room immediately, which Camila needed. And, furthermore, they accepted her public-assistance voucher. Here, most parents—most mothers, to be more accurate—paid their daycare bill with a check from the state. Sherice did. She'd told Camila that when she picked Tyrese up last week, he had marks on him, marks that didn't look like they'd come from other kids. Camila didn't say a word about this, though, when she brought Alonso for his first morning there. She couldn't be choosy. Her classes wouldn't wait for her to see if another family gave up their spot at a better daycare. She'd been with Alonso every day for the first season of his tiny life. Now, on that steaming August morning, it was time to move forward with her own.

She carefully pointed out everything in the room to Alonso: the alphabet chart along the ceiling; the pictures of animals; the cabinets; the other babies' food, labeled in unevenly round handwriting. A dark-skinned woman, her straightened hair pulled back in a ponytail, her teeth rimmed with gold, watched Camila's explications like she was crazy, like she was a bum talking to a burning trash can. Then she just shook her head and put on a record of Solange Knowles's songs for children to drown out the cries from the cribs.

Camila kissed Alonso goodbye.

"Don't cry, mami," the caregiver instructed.

She didn't. She told me it would never occur to her to cry. That wasn't how she approached her motherhood. She was going to school; that was the most important thing for him, she said. The rest would just have to do.

2

COLLEGE LIFE

Her first hike out to Kingsborough. It was almost Labor Day. She rode the halting B train for over an hour, anticipating what lay ahead. At the end of the line, the subway doors slid open. The salted breeze off the ocean, just blocks away, chased away the last stinking steam of summer. Seagulls barked overhead. There was no sound of construction here, she noted, no drilling that rattled the pavement.

The elevated train platform lined a block of crumbling brick buildings; a delicate green fern frond sprouted from a crack in one, pushing its way to the light. She found the B1 bus across the street from the subway and took it past blocks of similar bricks to the very last stop.

Camila said the buildings reminded her of an old apartment at the end of the A line in Ozone Park where Section 8 checks had paid the rent until her mother got public housing. Before that, they'd been in a shelter in Washington Heights. But Section 8 had given them the ability to move somewhere stable. Camila said she couldn't believe how lucky her mother was to get that check, to have that apartment. And then once she was offered a place in the projects, she was set for life. Camila said she thought anyone who complained about the conditions was an ingrate, her mother most of all.

Still, the place in Ozone Park seemed inhumane at the time, she said. Her youngest sister had turned one in that apartment. Her mom slept in one room, though often not alone. All the kids slept in the other. She'd spent fourth to eighth grade in that room. But the overcrowding wasn't the worst part of life there. At the time, Geraldine had a boyfriend, a retired cop, who usually crashed at the apartment. He used to drink a lot, Camila said. She told me a story about one afternoon when she was in fourth grade. She'd just brought home her school portraits and was sitting at the kitchen table, cutting the photos along the white lines that separated the larger pictures from the wallet-sized ones. The boyfriend was sitting on Geraldine's bed, staring at her through the open door. Then suddenly he charged toward Camila and snatched the scissors from her hand.

He pressed the blade against her neck. "You're not behaving," he said. "You're not obeying your mom."

Camila just stared at him, paralyzed. After a very long time of staring back, hard and cruel, he dropped the scissors.

She told her mother what had happened. The boyfriend said that Camila was lying. Geraldine chose to believe the boyfriend. That afternoon was always the first thing she thought about when she remembered her years in Ozone Park.

The bus pulled up to the Kingsborough campus at the edge of Manhattan Beach's promontory, ringed by Sheepshead Bay and Rockaway Inlet. Ribbons of pathways wound through pristine stretches of grass—like a real college, she commented with a pleased smile. Poised, eyes forward, Camila sought out a building called the Marine Academic Center, where registration was being held. Among the tank tops and short shorts and hijabs, she looked like Jackie O. She'd dressed in white capris, her white camisole, a pale-pink sweater, and faux-pearl earrings; sunglasses held her tight waves off her face. The forest-green-and-white tote bag that she used to carry her breast pump was slung over a proud shoulder. Dominican by way of Vineyard Vines. She lifted her chin and strode up to a young security guard, who deferentially gave her directions through the maze of connected buildings.

The college was founded during the sixties' golden age of investment in public good, and its main buildings had been largely untouched since then, fixed in the Pop Art design movement of the era. Red egg-shaped phone booths, long defunct, sprouted through the halls like tulips. Enormous orange plastic Verner Panton–style lights hung from high concrete ceilings. But the campus wasn't decrepit, at least not in these quarters. Camila remarked that she'd never seen a bathroom as pristine as the one in the administration building and took a selfie of herself standing by the stalls, so she could show everyone how clean it was.

The Marine Center, the main axis of the campus, where the college's maritime program was housed, was filled with giant aquariums that gave the air a slight funk of algae. Camila stared in wonder at the tropical-fish tank, her eyes fixed on a small electric-blue damselfish. The damselfish would become aggressive and solitary as it matured, or so said the wall text next to the tank. In another tank, with a sandy floor and gray-tinged water, swam the fish of New York Bay. A summer fluke shimmied into the sand and appeared to vanish. The wall text said the fish was known as the "chameleon of the sea" for its ability to disappear entirely into its surroundings. The bay itself beckoned through double glass doors. Camila stepped out into the cool ocean air, marveling at how quiet it was.

She took a seat on a bench by the seawall to feel the breeze for just a few seconds before getting in line to register for classes, allowing herself a rare moment of arrival, or at least a moment to breathe. She'd already released herself from unrealized plans. There was a new plan now, a good one. Enough class and homework hours to keep her welfare checks and childcare benefits and to remain at the shelter. The threat of eviction had passed. She had time to find a place, a good place, for her and Alonso to live. Maybe she'd even meet a guy here at school; she'd noticed some fine-looking men in the hallways. They'd noticed her, too. But she'd only make time for a man if he respected her as a mother, she said, as a serious person. If he wouldn't be too distracting. She felt normal, considering normal things, like who she could imagine dating, what her professors would be like. The ticking clock had hushed.

A seagull swooped down and landed on the railing in front of her. Camila and the seagull gazed together at the water. She began to talk about the time her grandfather caught a seagull with his bare hands and kept it as a pet in their bathroom. The bird didn't survive long, and when it died, her grandfather had explained it wasn't the right climate. And when her grandfather died, she told me, she got a tattoo of an aquamarine heart scrawled with his nickname. She missed him always wearing his hat, smoking his funny little pipe, singing in Spanish. Geraldine wouldn't speak Spanish with him and wouldn't teach it to the girls, as if the language was a source of shame.

Camila was proud of her Spanish, though, and curious. She'd become fluent as a speaker, talking to her grandparents at first and later with any Dominican who still had an accent, but she hadn't learned to write it. There was a huge demand for fully bilingual cops, she'd heard. She wanted to study it here at Kingsborough. Excited by the idea, she sprang up from the bench and went inside to find registration.

The hushed clock was a figment. Camila joined a line of students waiting to register, which stretched through a vast auditorium and into the hall beyond. By the time she moved up to the registration tables, every criminal-justice class was already filled. She registered for the few classes that were left, barely noticing the subjects: art history, constitutional law . . . at least there was space in a Spanish class. Not one of these classes would get her closer to John Jay or even her major. And worse: Three of her classes began at eight-thirty in the morning. Which meant she'd have to drop Alonso off by seven at the latest to make it in time, and that was if the subways and buses weren't delayed. But even that timing was a fiction, since his daycare didn't open its doors until eight. She'd figure it out, she said. What else could she do?

Furthermore, textbooks for these classes would run her three hundred dollars, even if she bought them used. She didn't have that kind of money. Her College Discovery grant would help. The College Discovery program was part of the Educational Opportunity Program at New York's state and city schools, for which she had qualified out of high school. It provided grants and most books for ten semesters. She'd only used up two, at the University of Buffalo. Two more semesters of tuition would be gone by the end of the year at Kingsborough. Still, the grant could cover John Jay, if she got there, and a master's degree, or the first half of law school. She just had to register for College Discovery here—but today was the deadline.

The College Discovery office was tucked away on the top floor of the library. It took Camila about a half hour to find it; most of the campus was in a series of connected buildings, a maze of startlingly long corridors. The director would be in a meeting for another half hour, she was told. She sat waiting awkwardly by the stacks. An hour and a half later, there still was no sign of the director. She checked the time. It was four o'clock already. She had to leave soon to pick up Alonso and get back to the shelter by six for the Wednesday-night meeting. And there was much more she had to get done on campus before the day was over—it was also the deadline to formalize her work-study agreement. After another half hour of searching the corridors, she found the human-resources office. She waited ten minutes to speak to someone, who told her she needed to go to financial aid first.

Camila knew she needed to run, but she was faint with hunger. A few days earlier, she'd run out of her EBT food stamps. She only had freezer waffles left at home, so it was waffles and water until her new stamp ration kicked in. In her search for the financial-aid office, she passed the cafeteria. Even though she didn't have any EBT left that month, she realized she needed to know if she would be able to eat on campus. She marched up to the bagel counter, where a guy in a visor was filling up a cream cheese tub.

"Do you take food stamps?" she asked without hesitation, too anxious and pressed for time to bother feeling shame at her question.

His mouth cracked into a leering smile. "No. But I bet I can fix you something nice."

Camila turned on her heel and walked a straight line to the cashier, a Chinese woman in a red apron, who was counting bills.

"Do you take food stamps?"

The cashier didn't understand her.

She said it again, slower.

The cashier just looked at her, puzzled.

Camila took her EBT card out of her wallet and showed it to the cashier.

"No EBT," the cashier said. She laughed nervously and turned back to her counting.

Camila pressed her lips together and nodded. She muttered that she was going to have to cook and bring the food she'd eat all day. When was she going to do that? She didn't even have Tupperware. But no time to think about that now.

It took another fifteen minutes to find the hall where financial-aid registration was being held that day, in a cavernous space with water-stained industrial drop ceilings. She scanned the queue. There was no way she could pick up Alonso in time if she waited in that line; she was already late. She walked up to one of the folding conference tables at the far end of the hall, where staff members were registering students. A middle-aged white woman peered from behind a pair of large glasses.

"Have you filled out your high school information sheet?" the woman droned.

Camila hadn't, because she'd been at two prior colleges. The sheet was irrelevant to her incoming status. But she didn't know how to explain this without explaining everything. She just stood there, her eyes cast down, unable to conjure a response. Exasperated, the woman asked Camila for her college identification card. But she could only get a college identification card once she enrolled. And she couldn't enroll until she submitted a dependency letter from public assistance, which the job center hadn't sent yet. Again, how to explain this without explaining everything. She just shook her head. The woman groaned with irritation and directed her to another line.

Camila took her place behind twenty-five other students, all clutching their identification cards or their inked-up yellow high school information sheets. Her breasts ached. She had to pee. She bounced on her heels. The line was barely moving. She couldn't come back again the next day. There were appointments: with Alonso's pediatrician, for her public-assistance case, her weekly review at the shelter. She checked the time and realized she couldn't wait any longer. She had to get to daycare in time for pickup. Then she had to get back to the shelter in time for the weekly meeting. But this all needed to be resolved today—classes were about to start.

Her enrollment depended on her financial status. Her financial status depended on her enrollment. Everything keeping her fed and sheltered and educated depended on everything else. Her place at the shelter, payment for her room, her public-assistance check and childcare voucher—all depended on a certain number of hours of class and work on campus. Which was what she needed to confirm and finalize today. Here. Before the hour-plus trip to the daycare. And the fifteen-minute walk to the shelter. And somehow pumping and accounting for subway delays in between.

Eventually, the front of the line.

There was a problem with her financial aid.

"You have to wait."

There was a form they needed her to submit, but no one seemed to know where.

Finally: "You have to go to the registrar's office."

Another line.

Camila ignored the guy who was trying to get her number.

Her breasts felt like they were going to burst.

She waited.

They didn't have her dependency letter.

"You need to go to another office."

Another line.

She simply didn't have time. Everything was a fight, it seemed, an exercise in Sisyphean futility every hour of every day. Her determination and focus couldn't make more minutes in the day any more than it could shrink subway tracks or eliminate paperwork. It would be so much easier to quit. To just get a job. To end up like her mother's eleven siblings, who didn't have a college degree among them. She was hardly alone in her lonely struggle—14 percent of community college students in America were homeless, and over 20 percent were single mothers. But to be both, and so truly on her own, was perhaps more than even she could manage.

Camila sprinted down Fulton Street to the daycare. Six o'clock. Outside the door, she wiped the slim moons of melted mascara from under her eyes, molded her face into a smile, and walked into the crib-lined room.

The caregiver sat slumped in a chair. She glanced up impassively at Camila. "You had stuff to do today, mami?" she said.

Camila stiffened and nodded politely.

"He was expecting you earlier. You threw him off his schedule."

What schedule? He was a baby. He was new to daycare. And she was right on time.

"Sorry to be so late," she said calmly.

Camila bundled Alonso into his carrier, gathered his bottles, and raced back to the shelter.

She was late, but she was still the first resident in the common room. To calm herself before the others arrived, she cradled Alonso in one arm while she used her free hand to pull up Kevin's highlights reel on YouTube. She relaxed for the first time all day.

Sherice shuffled into the meeting with Tyrese on her hip. Her weave was long gone. Tyrese's braids had grown quickly. They stuck out, unruly. He stomped around the room, eyes glinting, cackling with the pleasures of each loud footfall. It was one month past her official move-out date. Rose, the rule-maker, had decided to let her stay on. She was working, doing her best, Rose said; she deserved some more time to find a place to land.

The Wednesday volunteer, Susan, arrived with a guest, a nutritionist who came to the shelter a few times a year. Today she was planning to make smoothies with the group. Susan had brought blenders from home, toting them in a takeout bag from Nobu, the Tribeca restaurant that lured celebrities and bond-trading gentrifiers to once-neglected warehouse blocks. Susan set a Bullet juicer on the coffee table. The nutritionist asked if she liked using it.

Susan chuckled. "I wish I could tell you. My husband does everything in the kitchen. I don't touch a thing."

Tyrese dropped his container of Cheerios on the ground, scattering them everywhere. Sherice, exhausted, remained stone-still where she sat on the couch. Tyrese began stamping the Cheerios into the floor. Sherice finally leaned down to gather them. Expertly, she swept them into a small pile.

As Camila watched her, she whispered to me that all she could think about was how she had to figure out how to go back to Kingsborough the next day. She couldn't work at Applebee's. She was going to get her degree in criminal justice, maybe even go to law school, no matter what classes she just registered for. Returning to the shelter had restored her ambitions. She wouldn't be defeated like the rest of these women. Alonso would know what a badass his mother was, she murmured. She'd just have to return tomorrow. At least she had a new folder now, from her registration package. On the cover was a photo of the campus. That night, after the meeting, Camila proudly transferred her public-assistance forms, birth certificate, letters from past colleges, childcare vouchers, and housing applications from the beat-up red folder she'd carried everywhere with her since Alonso was born into this glossy white one.

Camila worked her Camila magic: Via email and at campus the next afternoon, she convinced various administrators to give her deadline extensions, sorted out her registration details, and explained to the professors that taught her eight-thirty courses why she'd be late. The quarterly schedule meant more exams, but hopefully more breaks that would allow her to catch her breath. She was beginning to see the shape of the year come together.

———

She made it through the first day of classes. It went well. She was excited about art history, psychology, and American political history; her Spanish professor was handsome and charming; and she'd even managed to talk her way into a criminal-law course.

And she'd met someone.

It was like the movie *Hitch*, she told me the next day, grinning with delight. She'd been lost in the maze of campus hallways, searching for the financial-aid office. There was a guy in a crisp shirt, really clean, she said. He was dark and had a pigmentation disorder that mottled his hands and neck with white splotches. Somehow this didn't detract from his looks, she told me. It added a certain sophistication. She felt him admire how fine she looked in her dress, a clinging striped column of red, blue, and white cotton and spandex.

Camila asked him where the financial-aid office was located. He said that he just happened to be walking there himself. Not only did he walk her to the door, but he waited until she was done. Everyone in the office had greeted him by name. Amare. She gave him her number. School was off to a promising start, she said, that grin still fixed on her face.

3

TWENTY-TWO

The next Wednesday, the residents appeared gradually with their babies and takeout containers for the meeting. As soon as Camila sat down on one of the wood-frame couches, her smartphone buzzed. It was Jeremiah. Her eyes narrowed when she saw his name. She tipped the phone toward me so I could read his name, cocking her head and pursing her lips in silent dismissal. No part of her lit up, or even felt curious, to hear from him. She'd known that Jeremiah was Alonso's father since Kevin got the DNA results and texted her during the baptism lunch. But she never mentioned him. He asked if he could FaceTime with her, or meet her in person soon.

Camila couldn't stand that she was scheduling time to talk to Jeremiah, not Kevin. A few days earlier Kevin had written, but only to ask her to send him a hundred bucks. He said it was an emergency. He was broke. She said no, even though her refusal might mean she wouldn't hear from him again. Despite her heartbreak, denying him was the only power she had left in their otherwise-extinct relationship. Broke, he was far less appealing anyway. Just another man to fail her.

She longed for a real man, she'd tell me often. Someone who

could respect her independence but still take control in bed. Someone who was a little bit dangerous but made her feel safe when she needed to. Like her dad, she'd say. I didn't know if Camila thought that the only reason Geraldine gave birth to her was to hold on to Mauricio. If she did, it didn't work, not for a year, not for a week, even. I didn't know if Camila thought she'd have better luck keeping Kevin if she had Alonso. Her sly self-protectiveness, that utter unwillingness to get fooled, had toughened her in so many respects—it would seem that she'd be cynical about men most of all. And yet, despite her disgust at her own mother's cautionary tale, and the likelihood that she'd seen the last of the man she'd thought was her true love—in the maternity ward, no less—her heart remained open, hopeful, yearning. She was a twenty-two-year-old who dreamed of her own love story, like anyone else. That she turned heads on campus, like she did anywhere, was not lost on her. She felt alive walking through that world. I watched her stride lengthen with confidence, her shoulders roll back, her eyes pretend not to catch the desire on her periphery. She wanted sex, and sex wanted her. And, best of all, she was sought by the guy who intrigued her most, the one she'd met on the first day of classes.

Amare wore fresh button-down shirts. He ran track. He played drums. He said he was a theater nerd. And he could really talk. He talked about his job at Lowe's, where he worked before afternoon classes, and about his little sister dying from brain cancer, and about the daycare his mother ran when she wasn't pastoring a church. So what if he was only eighteen. She was fascinated by him.

What impressed Camila the most, though, was that he asked her questions. Kevin never asked her questions, she said. And he always gave one-word answers to her questions. Like: "How was your day?" "Good." That was it. But Amare wanted her to tell him about her family, her goals; he even wanted to know the difference between blue-suit and green-suit border-patrol guards. His curiosity underscored how respectful she thought he was, and how caring. It matured him. That mattered to her: At Kingsborough she felt like she was a generation removed from the other students, though she was only a couple of years older. She was a mother. She had responsibilities. Amare seemed to get this, to match her. He felt like a peer. And, she said, she was dying to see what he looked like naked.

It was an unseasonably steamy weekend when Amare took Camila and Alonso to a Flatbush Avenue street fair. He'd been walking her to class every day, but this was a new level. Camila flushed when she told me about how he held her hand, carried Alonso, cracked her up. He even bought her lunch from the stands and waited while she queued for a street artist to draw a portrait of her and Alonso. A guy approached her in line and told her that she was beautiful and that he'd draw a portrait of her in pastels, right there on the spot. She told me Amare didn't even mind that she laughed and flirted with him as he captured the angles of her face, Alonso's plump cheeks. A man who could handle her flirting was a man of confidence, she said.

And then, pushing Alonso's stroller, Amare took her home. He lived in an eight-bedroom Victorian house in Flatbush, deeper into Brooklyn. Camila didn't know these kinds of houses existed in New York. His stepdad, five siblings, and various other extended family members all lived there with him and his mom. It was afternoon; the house was quiet. But Camila could still feel the presence of a big family, all living under one roof. Camila admired the carved banister, the patina of the old wood, as she mounted the stairs, carrying Alonso in his car seat.

Amare's room was on the third floor, tucked up under the eaves. Camila set Alonso down, hoping he'd stay quiet. Amare started dancing, more goofy than sexy. A teenager.

Laughing, he pulled Camila close to him. "I'm dancing like a blind man!" he cried, closing his eyes and jerking his torso. "I'm grinding like Ray Charles!"

He peeled off his T-shirt. Camila's breath caught when she saw his eight-pack.

She wondered impatiently when Alonso would fall asleep in his car seat. She didn't have to wait long.

He said he didn't want to use a condom. She didn't want to insist on it. And she didn't want to use one, either, to be honest. She was breastfeeding. You couldn't get pregnant when you were breastfeeding, she thought.

It'll be safe, she figured.

The next day they took Alonso to the beach. She felt the sun warm her skin, her hand moist in his.

"I don't want a girlfriend," he told her. "I'm not ready for that until I finish college."

Camila nodded. She stared straight ahead and gave the only reply that would hold on to him: "I'm down with being friends." But she said she knew from the fire blazing deep in her chest that she didn't want to share him with anyone.

As Alonso dozed in the sunshine in the cradle of Camila's long, bent legs, she told Amare about the shelter, her apartment search, her growing anxiety about it all. She could add his name and income to her applications, he offered, while he was living at home. "Then we'll have a place ready if we decide to live together," she told me later. But she didn't dare say it out loud to him.

Talk of Amare had turned to talk of ex-boyfriends, hers and mine, one afternoon at the shelter. I'd made myself comfortable at the foot of her bed while she nursed in her desk chair. For weeks she'd been studiously working her way through my romantic past, always making connections between my impulses and hers, triangulating our frustrations and impulses. That day, her queries and analysis were fixated on one man who'd complicated my marriage years before. He reminded her of an ex of her own, she said. She was uncharacteristically vague about him. I didn't think to wonder why.

Then she surprised me.

"Want a drink?" she offered offhandedly.

"Like, a drink?" I asked.

"Yeah. I've got some Hennessy in the freezer."

I was fairly certain that alcohol was forbidden on the premises. Sure, the rules at the shelter seemed to change constantly and were communicated by word of mouth, beginning with Rose's mouth, of course. But a bottle of Hennessy lurking in the freezer, considering the regularity of room inspections and the fragility of Camila's continued tenancy, was no doubt a loaded gun.

Camila said she didn't want any herself but that she'd love to pour me a glass if I'd like. She loved hosting and was always suggesting she go out and get steak and rice with her food stamps and cook something for us, or she'd press a piece of fruit on me when she had one. Even when she had nothing to offer, she'd present me with a glass of water like it was Evian in cut crystal. Hosting was part of adulthood, part of motherhood. So was the choice to possess a bottle of liquor. She rarely had a drink herself, and only if she was out for the evening; the only time I would see her throw back a few came on a night many months into the future, out at a dance club, where I was the one ordering our mojitos.

The lure of the Hennessy bottle wasn't the liquor inside it; it was the right to have it at all and to offer it to a guest. It was a question of agency, the sort of agency any adult responsible enough to parent a child, to hunt for an apartment, to do her own paperwork, should have. But Camila didn't have a home, and without a home, does a person still have agency? The rules on that case, written or not, were fairly universal. It was hard to imagine a shelter that would permit drugs and alcohol. It didn't matter that Camila didn't have the tendency to abuse either. It was the option to make her own decisions that she wanted.

I couldn't tell if the risk she was taking was born of hubris or if she was poking a coiled snake, testing to see if Rose would actually kick her to the curb.

4

PARENTHOOD

Jeremiah said he only had an hour, so Camila made sure she was an hour late. She wasn't going to make this convenient for him, she told me.

Not when she hadn't heard a damn word from him during her pregnancy or after Alonso's birth. Not when he hadn't come to the hospital or bought anything for the baby, she said, not even some Pampers. This was a monologue I'd heard verbatim several times and would hear many times more: Kevin wasn't sure he was the father, but he came to the hospital like a real man, all the way from Buffalo. He'd brought Alonso a present. Jeremiah thought it was his baby and he didn't do a thing.

He was waiting for her at the Starbucks outside the Barclays Center, anxiously bouncing a leg. The first thing she noticed were the impressive Nikes he was wearing. Money she needed for the baby. She looked coolly at him, lifted Alonso out of the carrier and sat.

"Why couldn't we meet in Times Square?" he complained. "I don't have any swipes left on my MetroCard. Why'd I have to come all the way over here?"

"Why do you have to be in Times Square?"

"That's near school for me."

Camila nodded. She wondered if he was really in school or if he was lying to her.

She dryly commented that he had some new ink. How much did those tattoos cost? she wondered. That was more money she needed for Alonso.

"My son's going to get tatted, too," he laughed. "He's going to get tatted at eight years old."

She was appalled by the thought.

Jeremiah said he was hungry.

"So get something to eat," she said.

"I don't have any money," he said.

Camila offered him her food-stamp card.

He shook his head.

She dug through her book bag to see what food she might have in it. Just an apple. She handed it to him and he took a large bite. As he ate it, he stared at Alonso.

"He's so small."

"Want to hold him?"

He reached for the baby, clearly apprehensive.

"Good. Now you can feed him." She reached into the bag for a bottle of pumped breast milk.

She glared at Jeremiah as he held the bottle to Alonso's lips. He looked up at her for approval. She was not impressed.

"Why doesn't he have my name? Why does he have your name?" Jeremiah asked.

"He's my baby."

"Why did you name him Alonso?" he pushed her.

Camila ignored the question.

"Do you have an apartment around here?" Jeremiah asked.

"I'm in a shelter."

He said nothing.

"You got a placc?" she asked.

"Nah," he said. "I'm staying couch to couch. In Jamaica."

"Ah. So you're going to live with me?" Camila asked, antagonistic.

He looked down, quiet. After a moment he said, "We can decide that as parents."

"Well, first you can take a DNA test. If you're the father, you're going to have to pay off my public assistance and then pay me child support."

He laughed darkly. "I don't have any money."

"You never wanted this baby. You wished a miscarriage on me."

He laughed again, nervous.

"You never followed up with me. Kevin was at the hospital. Not you. You only started chasing me when you saw the picture of Alonso and Kevin on Facebook."

"Nah," he said again.

He reached for his bag.

"I got to go to class," he said.

She walked him up to the turnstile at the subway entrance. When he swiped his card, she looked at the green digital display. It was an unlimited-ride MetroCard. So much for no more swipes.

At three A.M. he texted, *Kiss the baby from me.*

She didn't write back.

Late the next night he texted again. *Can I see you Wednesday? I want to see the baby.*

She couldn't stand that she might be tethered to this person through her son, at least while she needed child support to survive. The sooner she could establish her financial independence, the sooner she could be rid of him. But until then, she knew, she had to do whatever she could to direct the money that was going to Foot Locker and a tattoo parlor back to Alonso.

The only thing we have to discuss is Alonso. Let me know when you take the paternity test, Camila replied.

A few weeks passed. Camila got into a rhythm of dropping Alonso off, making the long commute, going to class, commuting back, picking him up, stopping at Lisa's bodega, heading home to do homework while she tried to soothe Alonso, putting him to bed, doing more homework, going to sleep in her single bed at the shelter, waking up, doing it again. Some afternoons she and Amare would go back to his house before she made the trip back to the daycare to pick up Alonso. Sometimes she'd watch a show on her phone before she went to sleep. She kept applying for apartments, searching for new listings. She avoided Rose, kept quiet in the weekly meetings.

Meanwhile, she waited for the date to arrive for her paternity hearing with Jeremiah so she could get her child-support case moving. She couldn't bear the idea that he was out there spending money while she was worrying about the weather getting cooler without a proper coat to keep their son warm. She told me she'd ask her dad to get him a snowsuit for Christmas, but she needed something in the meantime.

Anticipating a hearing in Queens County Family Court was nothing new to Camila, dating back to the time when she was fifteen and Geraldine sent her to Mauricio and Mauricio sent her back to Geraldine. After Geraldine threw all of Camila's possessions out on the street, Camila stuffed everything into garbage bags, lugged them to a friend's house in the neighborhood, and asked to sleep there for just one night. The next morning she was cornered by a couple of uniformed cops, she told me. Her mother had taken out a PINS—Persons in Need of Supervision—petition on her daughter. The cops brought Camila to the station, where someone got on the phone with the family court to schedule a hearing.

Mauricio was required by law to appear at the courthouse. He sat on the other side of the room, ignoring his daughter. Geraldine sat a few benches away, glaring at Camila. When their names were called, Camila was not permitted inside the courtroom. Not only did she not have a single family member to look out for her, she said, but she wasn't even allowed to advocate for herself.

The magistrate suggested granting kinship custody to Mauricio's mother. Mauricio said his mother was really sick—which was true—and couldn't take on the burden. Neither parent would take her, she told me. There, behind the closed door of the courtroom, in the presence of both of her parents, the court made Camila a ward of the state.

Leaving the courtroom, Geraldine didn't look at Camila once.

After Camila was made a ward, she was forbidden to leave the courthouse without a state escort. She was a prisoner.

And here is the memory Camila would repeat to me, reminding me of the hope she felt in her relationship with her father, that she might know parental love after all. While she was detained, Mauricio lingered. Camila heard him ask the bailiff if he could go in and talk to the judge about changing the ruling.

"Can we take her back?" she remembers hearing him ask.

"It's too late," the bailiff told him. "You have to schedule another hearing."

Camila watched the glass doors close behind her father as he walked out.

Mauricio turned around and stood there for a minute or two, staring at her from the other side. She saw the pain in his eyes. Then he walked away. But for that moment, behind the courthouse doors, Camila felt something she'd never known from either of her parents: remorse. If he could feel remorse, maybe it meant he loved her. Maybe it meant that someday he could be a real father to her. Maybe she just had to get through this part of her life on her own.

She had no idea where the escort was taking her until she arrived at the facility in Manhattan. It was a detention center for state wards awaiting foster homes. Camila was told to undress and remove her jewelry. She wasn't allowed to go to the bathroom without an escort walking her down the hall. No one was permitted to go outside. A common room had a single window, which let in the only natural light Camila saw for days. She was tortured by the idea that she was missing crucial days of school. Each day she felt like she'd been wrongfully incarcerated. The yoga class they offered didn't make much of a difference.

Late one night, she was called into an office. She was told it was time to go. It was pouring outside as she was led to a car. Inside the car, a driver told her she was on her way to Staten Island. She'd never been to Staten Island before. Beyond that, she had no idea where she was going. Her questions from the back seat were met with silence. The car pulled up at a group home, a former college dorm. She was issued a PIN to get into her shared room. Every day the room would be checked for weapons and drugs.

Camila commuted from that room to her high school in Manhattan every morning. Then she'd take the subway to East New York, where she'd punch in at the hardware store. She'd see her father almost every day at work. On weekends she'd wake at five A.M. to take the ferry to get to the hardware store by eight. If she was ten minutes late, Mauricio would yell at her in front of the staff. He said he was happy she was in a group home. He said it taught her to be clean and independent and organized. "What about teaching your kid by living as an example?" she wanted to say back to him, but she didn't dare.

Mauricio wanted Camila to leave high school in Manhattan to go to a state boot camp for juvenile delinquents, she said. They'd feed and house her, teach her some discipline. It didn't matter that she didn't have a record beyond a truancy count. One afternoon, without telling Camila, Mauricio walked through the metal detectors of Norman Thomas High School and handed her guidance counselor an enrollment form for the state boot camp. The counselor refused to sign it without Camila's permission. "Do not give me your approval," she told Camila. Instead, she wrote a letter of recommendation for Camila to hold on to for whenever she might need it: *Camila is a strong woman who has not allowed her personal issues ever to deter her from her goals. I am sometimes shocked how she has the ability, strength, and courage to continue.*

When she was eighteen, Camila returned to Queens family court to fight against the injustice of her parents' neglect. A freshman in college at the University of Buffalo at the time, she took the ten-hour bus ride back to New York to sue them for child support. This time she was allowed into the courtroom. Camila testified against her parents, citing their neglect in scrupulous detail, arguing her own case. She knew they wouldn't make good on the payments.

But, still, she won.

The paternity hearing was scheduled for nine o'clock. Daycare didn't open until eight. She'd have to take a car service to the courthouse in Queens if she had any hope of making it in time, which would cost fifty bucks. It was midterms already, but the court wouldn't care about that. Nothing Camila could do but hope her criminal-law professor would let her make up the test she'd have to miss. Camila dressed in her gray vest and man-tailored pants. It was cool enough outside to wear the matching blazer, as well—a late-October chill had set in over the city. She pulled her hair back in a neat bun and then got Alonso changed, fed, and dressed for the day. She dropped him off and called the Dominican car service she knew in the neighborhood.

Amare texted to wish her luck. In the back of the car, she smiled as she replied to him, then scowled as she thumbed through the court documents in her folder. Jeremiah had listed Alonso as "Unknown Child." He must have filed the paternity suit without even knowing the name of the baby he was claiming as his son. She told me just how she planned to tell him off.

The car pulled up to the courthouse. Late. She passed through the metal detectors and quickly found her way upstairs to the hearing room. Jeremiah was napping on a blond-wood bench in the waiting area. As soon as she signed in, the bailiff barked their last names. Camila didn't have time to lay into him as she'd rehearsed in the car.

A row of wooden chairs was lined up in the small office that functioned as a hearing room. Jeremiah sat and took off his hoodie, slumping down in his thermal undershirt. Camila left a chair empty between them, perching on the edge of a seat, at attention. She could have been easily mistaken for his attorney. I sat beside her. A magistrate with long dreadlocks and a Burberry-print scarf stared at a computer. They waited silently for her to look away from her screen. She set her eyes on Jeremiah.

"Baby's name?" she asked him.

He stumbled over the name, as though he was unsure how to pronounce it.

Camila answered for him. "Alonso Alvarez."

"Ms. Alvarez, have you been married?"

She nodded slowly.

Had she understood the question? Of course she had. She kept her eyes fixed on the magistrate.

Those rings she said were from Kevin to remind her of her man in Buffalo, that tattoo of the heart and the nickname, that ex she didn't want to talk about: I realized what it all was. She'd been married. Those rings were her wedding rings. And, I was to learn, that tattoo was of his name, the name she'd never told me.

"Do you have the findings and conclusions from your divorce?" the magistrate asked. "That determines whether there were children or children expected in the marriage."

"I just have what they gave me at the court," Camila said, shaking her head.

"You have to request it," the magistrate said. "We'll have to adjourn."

Jeremiah looked confused. I was, too.

"Would you be able to order the DNA test before our next meeting?" Camila asked the magistrate.

Jeremiah had told Camila weeks ago that he couldn't afford forty bucks to take the test. She'd texted him that she'd pay for it to speed up the process. He'd ignored her offer. Now the court would have to order a test, to get the state to cover the cost. These things took forever, Camila had heard. But the magistrate said she couldn't even put the order through, because of what she was reading on her computer screen.

"I see you have public assistance from the office in Manhattan. We'll have to transfer this case to New York County." She turned to Jeremiah. "Do you understand what's happening here?"

He nodded. But clearly he didn't. He'd managed to steer clear of the system's labyrinth, to crash on a couch instead of finding space in a shelter, to juggle classes and nights working while someone else nursed his son to sleep, and, as far as Camila knew, to avoid the courts and their dysfunctional, clumsy relationship to the welfare state. And now it was going to take months, Camila estimated, to even file their child-support case, since his paternity had to be established before anything moved forward. Meanwhile, she'd be solely financially responsible for their son.

Outside the courtroom, Jeremiah said quietly, "I thought it would be simple."

"Nothing in the system is simple," she snapped at him. "You see how many people are here? How nervous and tired they all look? I filed for child support from my parents in May. Two months later they called us up. It took a year to complete. You know how much I went through?"

Jeremiah just kept his eyes on the floor. Camila stared at the razor marks striping his eyebrows. She allowed him a moment to respond to what she'd said. He didn't say a word.

"My time is up at the shelter," she told him. "Alonso and I need somewhere safe to go."

He continued studying the floor.

"I'm homeless," she said.

"I hope it works out for you," he mumbled. Finally, Jeremiah looked up and straight into her eyes. He kissed her hand solemnly. "I've got to go," he said, slinking away.

5

PEDRO

After Jeremiah hustled away that day, Camila unburdened herself of the story she'd kept hidden from me. She wasn't proud of hiding it, she said.

Camila had dropped out of the University of Buffalo and was back in Queens, making some money working for a local marshal, whose duties were to carry out evictions and seize property claimed in civil court judgments. She'd book his schedule and take calls from his young girlfriend, from his wife, from his best friend, with whom he'd smoke cigars at the pizza parlor. Camila felt capable at the office. She impressed people. The marshal said he loved her like a daughter. That didn't stop him from trying to fondle her breasts whenever they were in the same room. He offered her a room in an apartment he owned, rent-free. There was another girl who was staying there, too. It was made clear to her what the other girl was doing in exchange for rent. Camila had nowhere else to go, but she knew she couldn't stay there.

One Sunday, at church, she met an older woman who was drawn to her instantly—Camila looked uncannily like her beloved late daughter. There was a spare room in the woman's apartment in the projects nearby. Camila moved in. And when the older woman traveled to Buffalo to visit her son, Pedro, on his birthday, Camila came along.

Pedro was fit. He had a goatee. He felt like a real man, she said, like someone who would watch out for her. No matter that he was living in a halfway house in Buffalo, she told me, busted for dealing years before.

They started talking on the phone and writing letters. Pedro told Camila she'd been pushed around and bullied by everyone she'd known. She'd never fully realized that about her life, she told me, never named it for herself; she figured life meant taking other people's abuse until you couldn't. She felt seen by him, valued and protected. He taught her to defend herself, she said, the first person who ever did.

Camila wasn't bothered when he told her he held an exalted position in the Trinitarios, a criminal network of fifty thousand Dominicans worldwide. He was instrumental in making it the fastest-growing gang in New York. He was far more powerful than her dad, she thought. She was drawn to that power, she told me; she felt like his power was hers, too.

Soon, she moved back up to Buffalo to be closer to him. She rented a room in an apartment filled with college students, random people she didn't know and didn't get to know. Camila desperately wanted to be a student herself again, but Pedro dismissed the idea. For a year and a half, their relationship played out in the common room of his halfway house, with a guard ensuring their total lack of privacy. Pedro wore an ankle bracelet that would track his whereabouts, and he was permitted to leave the house only to work. She was faithful to him, in her heart and with her body. Her life had emptied of all other relationships; her only communication was with him. It seemed like his explosive jealousy was a testament to his love. He'd hold the picture of his dead sister up next to Camila's face, fixate on their likeness, and say that God had sent her to him.

When Pedro said he wanted a baby, she told him she would give him anything he wanted. During visiting hours in the common room, she said, he'd masturbate into his hand, wipe the semen into her palm, and send her off to the bathroom to inseminate herself. She didn't think it would work, but he did, so she kept trying.

He said he might get out quicker if he got married.

Camila called her father with the news. Mauricio said Pedro was just using her; she'd ruin her life if she married him.

Pedro told Camila he'd set her father straight. He called Mauricio to tell him Camila was a grown woman and could make her own decisions. Camila had never known anyone to stand up to her father before, certainly not on her behalf.

After several months of requests, Pedro was given permission to go to the courthouse. His mother found rings for both of them. Jewelry was contraband in the halfway house, but Pedro wanted to wear a wedding ring. He figured that once it was on his finger inside, no one would give him a hard time about it. So he put it in a balloon, swallowed it, and fished it out later on in the bathroom. The ring was a key part of his strategy to develop the reputation of an upstanding husband.

Camila told me that, as she put it, she confused the love of a father for the love of a husband. Pedro made her feel protected in the way she'd wanted Mauricio to make her feel, loved in the way she'd yearned for her entire girlhood. As a woman, she thought that would be foundation enough for a marriage.

Pedro was thirty-seven; Camila was nineteen. It was only three years before I'd met her. But Camila's years were not like many other people's years, especially the years between eighteen and twenty-two. The lives she'd lived in that time—marriage and divorce, pregnancy and motherhood, two shelters, three colleges, myriad courtrooms, and more; all without security, all while trying to survive—meant that time moved differently for her than it did for most people her age, or any age. What Camila experienced during, say, an average sophomore year was an entire phase of life, stretched by tribulation's clock. Before Pedro, and after.

A year after they were married, Pedro was released from the halfway house, a free man, a man who had been incarcerated since puberty, a man who wanted to make up for the time he'd missed.

He and Camila moved to his mother's spare room. He wanted to tighten her leash. He wanted her to arrange threesomes. He wanted her to ignore his calls to the girl he was messing around with. But she was nobody's fool; she refused to be, not anymore, she said. It didn't matter that she had nowhere to go. She left. It wasn't like they had a baby, she told me. Or like anyone in her life had ever kept a man. But, more than that, he'd taught her to never let herself be bullied again.

In all of our hundreds of hours of talking, at the shelter, in waiting rooms, on subway commutes, she'd never mentioned this man, whose nickname was tattooed on her chest. She'd lied to me about that very tattoo, of course, and about that wedding ring. It wasn't just that she was ashamed of being divorced. She didn't want anyone to know she'd been married to a gang member. She cultivated her image to be respected by all people at all times. To be the most poised and put-together resident at the shelter, the smartest girl in class, the welfare recipient whose working knowledge of the system exceeded most social workers', the pregnant woman with the best research on birthing centers, the mother with the best commitment to breastfeeding—it was constant work to foster the respect she'd never felt as a daughter, a female, an American.

Carefully, she struck an intentional balance between the self-revelation necessary to develop intimacy and the self-protection she believed she needed to maintain that respect. Nobody needed to know her business, she'd say to me after exposing something she deemed private. And there was a lot she deemed private. When she feared someone was getting too close, she'd often shut down that intimacy so she remained in control, so respect was never endangered—like she'd shut out Anselma after their day at the beach, never even telling her she was having the baby.

But there was another risk in revealing her relationship with Pedro, one that wasn't psychological. She would never be able to manifest her intended future as a cop or a border agent—any role in the criminal-justice system, really—if it was known that her judgment had led her to marry a criminal, an active one at that, especially while he was still incarcerated. Not that there wasn't a record of their marriage. The magistrate at the Queens family court pulled up the legal story of their relationship simply by typing Camila's name into her computer. It seemed that this was yet another obstruction that Camila opted to ignore on the road her will had paved.

Furthermore, even though she so deliberately controlled what was known about her, she still chose to tell me the story of her relationship with Pedro. And once she did, she didn't stop. She talked about him openly from that day forward. She seemed to talk openly about everything else in her life, as well—about sexual desire, problematic romances, times she'd let friends and family down, her struggles with motherhood, with jealousy, and more. There was clear relief in having someone she felt she could tell anything to. I never again discovered a willful obfuscation. Which didn't mean I fully trusted her. But after that day, she gave me no concrete reason not to.

Camila was twenty-two, and stunning, and lonely, and alive. She had stories to unburden, of missteps and messiness from the past and the present. Relationships with men whose professional standing should have never led them to meet with her outside of their offices, much less in their bedrooms. Impulses one would divulge only to the most faithful of confidants.

6

WHITE CARNATIONS

Except for Sherice, everyone was accounted for at the next Wednesday meeting. Sherice wasn't usually late. We waited a few minutes longer before I introduced the guest speaker—a middle-aged Latina with thick glasses and a thicker Brooklyn accent, who worked at a neighborhood advocacy organization.

"The main focus here is getting affordable housing, right? That's the biggest problem to solve?" the advocate asked.

Everyone in the room nodded.

"I'd apply for a studio," she said, like she was suggesting an easily attainable solution.

"Even a studio requires an income of eighteen thousand a year to rent," Camila said, primly crossing her legs. "Public assistance gives us only sixteen thousand."

"Then you have to get a promissory note from an employer about what you'll earn." She shrugged. Piece of cake.

"I don't have an employer. I'm in school full-time."

The advocate shrugged again. "Most affordable housing just says no to full-time students," she said. "They just automatically disqualify you. That's not changing. How successful have the other residents been at finding housing?"

Everyone shook their heads.

The advocate looked around the room. All the babies had fallen asleep in their mothers' arms. One occasionally would rub an eye with a fat little hand or nestle into a mother's breast.

"Apply everywhere," she said. "Don't give up. That's my advice. Don't give up."

At seven-thirty, Sherice snuck into the room quietly, carrying a bouquet of white carnations. A white headband adorned with lace flowers, coordinated with a white lace tank top, held back her treated and curled hair. Aside from her stonewashed capris, she appeared to be dressed for her own wedding. She lifted Tyrese onto her lap. He was wearing a T-shirt that said KISS ME I'M IRISH.

"Sherice?" asked the advocate. "We spoke on the phone, right? How's it going?"

Sherice's eyes filled with tears under her false eyelashes. She just shook her head in reply.

"What have you tried?"

"Everything," she whispered.

The advocate listed everything she could think of: the New York City Housing Authority, landlords that had listed with city agencies, affordable-housing lotteries, Craigslist.

Sherice nodded after each, wiping away tears with a white-varnished fingernail. "Nobody will take the city voucher Rose requested for me," she said. "I've been calling everywhere."

The room was silent. Sherice stared at the floor. She didn't move as Tyrese leapt off her lap.

Finally, she said quietly, "They said I have to go. Time's up. They say they let me stay here and I've done nothing. It's not true. I've been working to find an apartment every single day. I've got no place to go. I've been trying. Every day. No one will take us." Sherice wiped away a new stream of tears. "I left my cake at my sister's," she whispered. "I didn't even notice. She had to text to tell me."

It was her twenty-second birthday.

A week later, Sherice vanished. Fourteen months living in that shelter, in that small group of new mothers. Tyrese's whole first year. One day, they were simply gone. She'd packed and moved out without a word to anyone.

Everybody had a different story about where Sherice went. Camila had heard she'd found a really nice place that took the city voucher and her sister moved in with her to help with Tyrese. Anselma had heard she'd gone to a city shelter.

Rose told me she thought she was staying with her mom. "She was given the keys to the city with that voucher," she said dismissively, "and never did a damn thing with it. Everyone just drags here." She added, "Camila is the only one who seems to know she needs to hustle to find a place. She has goals. She has abilities. Even though she's a little slickster."

We talked about how Camila was putting her name into every affordable-housing lottery she could find, scouring the Internet and the Kingsborough bulletin boards for apartments, reaching out to any advocacy group that might help. Rose commented that if Camila had applied her skills to hoisting herself out of poverty, she'd be in a very different place now. She admitted that in her long career she'd almost never seen a young woman as versed in policy and adept at piloting her way through the system.

Her admiration, and what remaining stability Camila had because of it, was to be short-lived.

7

THE BOTTLE

wasn't there when it went down, a few days later. Both Rose and Camila told me the same story.

Camila was called into the office.

"Take a seat," Rose said, gesturing to the chair wedged next to her desk.

Camila sat with Alonso sleeping on her lap. It was tense in the office, but it was always tense in the office.

"Do you know why you're here?" Rose asked her.

Camila began to seize inside, she told me. She hated questions like that. She hated being caught in a situation where she might not be prepared to adequately defend herself—and against what, in this situation, she said she couldn't imagine.

"I figured to talk about housing and what my plans are," she said, trying to sound composed and professional.

Rose smiled. It was not a kind smile. She opened up the desk drawer, just an inch or two from Camila's seat. With a dramatic flourish, she pulled out the bottle of Hennessy.

"You're here to talk about this."

Camila froze. Then she felt a surge of rage. Her impulse, she said, was to get up in Rose's face, say, "I don't need you, fuck this shit." But she told herself to just be calm and listen. She told me she feared they could call her an alcoholic, report her to the Administration for Children's Services, and take Alonso away. Now that she had a baby, she thought, she had no choice but to just take it all, no matter what might come at her.

Rose silently awaited Camila's reply.

"I brought it home from a party," Camila said. "I haven't even had a drink from it," she added.

"There's only an inch of liquor left in the bottle," Rose said.

Camila was silent. She was a grown woman, a mother. Responsible for her own life, and another's. And yet her poverty, and the choices she'd made circumscribed within that poverty, had placed her in a situation where she wasn't even permitted to have a bottle of alcohol in her room. Alcohol she was legally permitted to drink. The rules constrained her like a child: in her room by nine; her bed made for inspection in the morning; no boys. She shouldered the ultimate adult obligations with none of the freedom. That duty was all that mattered now.

"It should be an immediate expulsion," Rose said. "So the best we can say is that you have two weeks. Do your best in that time to secure another place to stay."

Camila nodded, lifted up Alonso, walked out of the office. As she carried him up the stairs to the only home they had in the world, she told herself these words, as she had so many times in her young life already: Maybe it just wasn't meant to be.

8

SALOME

When the global economy collapsed, real estate in major international cities—New York most of all—presented not just an opportunity for investment but a means to sock cash away with huge tax incentives. Shell companies sprang up to hide billions of dollars in the form of residential skyscrapers. In Midtown, a cluster of them reached insane new heights, befitting the insane amounts of money they were concealing. For one building, half of the apartments sold long before any steel was erected—over $1 billion changed hands for nothing more than floor plans.

The skyscraper at 432 Park Avenue rose quickly, an eighty-four-story middle finger extended to the stars. Its architect based its design on an Austrian trash can that had been fabricated just as fascism began to germinate there in 1905. The building was the third-tallest in the country and the highest residential structure in the Western Hemisphere. It towered over the skyline, dwarfing the Empire State Building. Full-floor apartments went on the market for $85 million, looming over the tangle of inequality hidden away below, even on the richest blocks of the world's near-richest city, second only to Tokyo—and, to Camila, about as foreign.

She'd never walked down Fifth Avenue in Midtown, not even to see the tree at Rockefeller Center or the Christmas windows at Saks and Bergdorf's. Nor had she looked in the boutique windows on the gilded stretch of Madison Avenue a block over from the Metropolitan Museum of Art. Though Camila had gone to high school just two express stops from the museum, she'd never been there, either. She had thought that it was called the Med, short for Mediterranean, where she figured all the art was from, rather than the Met, short for Metropolitan. She'd never been to the museum, that is, until her art-history professor instructed the class to go photograph twenty pieces of art made before the nineteenth century and write an analysis of five of those pieces.

Camila had dressed for the occasion in gold-tipped flats and royal-blue slacks, a white blouse peeking from the collar of her tweed coat. She proudly pushed Alonso's stroller up Madison, smiling down at him as he tugged on the jack-o'-lantern bib she'd fastened over his jacket for a little seasonal color. She examined real estate listings in a window. It seemed impossible that anyone could charge $800,000 for an apartment, she said. Then she counted the zeros again and realized she'd missed one. Next door, at Christofle, a silver caddy stocked with sterling forks, knives, and spoons gleamed under a sign challenging shoppers to radically rethink how they set the table. She had to read it twice to understand what it could possibly mean: It looked like the caddy in the soup kitchen on Fourth Avenue, she said. She stepped aside to let a man in a ragged jacket, shadowed gray with dirt, push his possessions past her in a shopping cart. A woman in an Hermès scarf laughed into a cellphone, then quickly covered her mouth once she registered his rank scent.

We carried Alonso's stroller up the grand steps of the museum and into the cavernous Great Hall. She marveled at its colossal flower arrangements, lifting Alonso up out of his carriage to better view their profusion. At the visitors' desk, she asked for a floor plan and studied it closely before heading left through the entrance to the galleries for Greek and Roman Art. She noted contrapuntal stances and chiseled drapery and explained to me the symbolism of various gestures, which ones meant victory and which meant de-

feat. And then she saw a marble torso cut like Amare's. She told me
she wanted to run her hands over it to see if it felt the same as her
hands had on his body the day before. "I think he's the one," she
told me, "I just feel it." She threw a penny in the fountain and told
Alonso to make a wish. Then she threw another penny in and made
one of her own.

She wandered the museum for hours, fascinated by the dark medieval tableaux of Bible stories, bemused by French gilded furnish-
ings, marveling at the expressive busts in the European sculpture
court. Upstairs, in Nineteenth-Century European Paintings, Camila
stood for a long time in silence before Henri Regnault's 1870 paint-
ing of Salome, provocatively posed in disarrayed golden silks, her
black curls tousled after dancing for Herod. Alonso reached a small
hand toward the leopard skin at Salome's feet as Camila made a few
notes and nodded in satisfaction.

That day, she didn't talk about her predicaments.

OTHER PEOPLE'S COUCHES

Rose had given Camila two weeks. It was the second week already. Days before, Camila had written an email to ask for an extension. No one at the shelter replied.

Camila had exhausted her options. She'd interviewed for a studio but was refused because of the baby. She'd asked classmates, the staff at the College Discovery center, the woman who ran the campus women's center, even the Dominican guys at the car service—nobody knew of anyone looking for a roommate. At least that's what people told her. Maybe it was true. Maybe it was because no one wanted a homeless single mom. She couldn't blame them, she told me. She'd asked Lisa at the bodega if she could pay her some money to stay at her apartment in the Bronx, just for a little bit. There was no space, Lisa said, not with her daughter and son and grandson there already. Camila hated asking for anything, especially when she thought the answer might be no. In this case doubly so, as her neediness tinted each query with shame. But she tried to be matter-of-fact about it all, just someone making inquiries. She didn't ask her family, though, not even her sister Teresa.

Each weekday, Teresa would wake up in her one-bedroom in Harlem, get her daughter and her boyfriend's son ready for school, rouse the friends sleeping on her couch, dress for work, drop the kids off at school, and make the trip to the Midtown office where she worked. She and her boyfriend had saved up for eight years to rent the place. Until then, they'd been crammed into his mother's overcrowded apartment. Camila would go up to Harlem to hang out. But she told me she couldn't live there; the one-bedroom was already too crowded. Teresa's boyfriend had a son who'd been abandoned by his mother; Teresa was his mother now. Plus, there was another family that would sometimes appear when they had nowhere else to go and somehow find space to crash in the already crowded living room. It's not like there was a couch for Camila to claim as her nightly bed.

Not just at Teresa's, but anywhere. It was one thing for someone to let Camila crash for a bit when it was just her, another thing entirely when she came with a baby who wailed through the night. Of course, Jeremiah wasn't responsible for the care of that baby; he had all the couches he needed, bothering nobody overnight with their son's cries. As long as Jeremiah had a couch, he wasn't homeless, not like her and Alonso.

But most people she knew didn't have that couch to spare anyway. She couldn't think of anyone she knew whose apartment wasn't already as overcrowded as Teresa's. Except maybe her own parents' places. Their couches were unoccupied, but for her needs, they may as well have not existed at all. Besides, it was harder still to think of anyone who wanted to live with even the most respectful houseguest's problems. Everyone had plenty of their own.

I own a home in Brooklyn. Well, the bank does, mostly, but because my grandfather cashed in a life-insurance policy of $300,000 and divided it between his three children, and my parents gave their share to me as a down payment, I managed to escape the rising tide of rents that sent so many of my friends to other shores. Even with that down payment, we spent years in the early 2000s trying to find a place we could afford, just a floor of a house for my husband and me to live and work in; we hadn't had our daughter yet. An apartment in a converted brownstone was the only place we made an offer on; it was on the table for just a few hours before it was contracted to another buyer for far more than the asking price. We ended up buying an asphalt-sided house with friends—they paid one-third of the price for the apartment on the top floor; we paid two-thirds for the duplex below—as a way to beat the market, since single-family homes were cheaper by the square foot than condos. Our monthly payment while I was reporting this book was $2,000 a month, which for gentrified Brooklyn was considered a steal and the reason we could continue to live in New York.

It wasn't a brownstone worth millions. Nor were we putting money down on one of the two-bedroom glass boxes rising over the city. We weren't the gut renovators or the people buying teardowns to build their dream homes or investment properties. But that didn't mean we weren't gentrifiers. Ten years after we purchased it, our house had more than doubled in value. The Italian American social clubs and butchers had all but vanished from our neighborhood since we'd moved in, replaced by a renowned tattoo studio, or a bar that sold fifteen-dollar cocktails, or a café that served only single-origin beans and vegan pastries. Our neighbor, who'd spent her entire life in an aluminum-sided house across the street, called all the other creative professionals on the street the "transients," but not us. They rented. We were here to stay, to raise a child. We were proud of this. We were also part of the new wave of homeowners who made it possible for the renovated house down the street to sell for three million dollars three years later.

And we had a couch. In a living room where no one else slept.

She needed it as much as I'd ever seen anyone I cared about need anything.

But I didn't offer it to her.

The answer was simple, I told myself: The only reason I knew Camila at all was to observe how she could, or couldn't, manage to survive as a homeless woman with a baby. If she moved in with us, even for a short while, I'd never know. And you'd never know. There was a reason that boundary was in place. And if I so much as invited her over for a dinner, I thought, it would create an irreconcilable tension in our relationship, impossible expectations. Our relationship needed to be spent in the universe of the city she inhabited, which hardly ever intersected with mine. I don't know what she imagined my home to be, though I told her exactly how much it was, how we bought it, what our monthly payment cost. I opened my privileged life to her in theory but not in practice.

My husband and I discussed what it would mean to break through that wall. He knew Camila by this point and cared about her. My daughter, then eight, adored her and was entirely taken with Alonso. She was furious when I told her they couldn't come live with us. It was so clear to her: They had nowhere to go. We had a living room. Her simple moralism wasn't wrong. I felt it, too, constantly. How could I make any other choice and try to teach her rightness, fairness, equality in society, she'd rage at me, searching for a word to encompass what she was trying to express. I explained what the word "hypocrite" meant. That was the word, she said.

She threatened to tell Camila she could move in with us, no matter what I said. She'd tell her the next time we saw her. But she didn't. Because even within her simple moralism, she understood the complex and inconvenient reality of what such an invitation would mean. Even she saw that my impetus not to interrupt Camila's narrative was not the only reason we wouldn't offer our empty couch. Like Camila had said, no one wanted to live with even the most respectful houseguest's problems, even if their lives were not defined by poverty. And that "no one" included us.

10

WHAT TO EXPECT

n art-history class on Monday, Camila said she felt like someone had wrapped an elastic band around her head that pulled tighter and tighter. Each breath was shorter than the one before. While her professor lectured, she silently packed up her book bag and slid out from behind her desk and through the door at the back of the room. She ran to the bathroom and threw up.

Dazed, she gingerly made her unsteady way to the bus and to the subway. One stop away from the shelter, she got off and aimed her stride straight for Methodist Hospital. She sat in the waiting room for three hours before she was examined by a nurse and set up with an IV. After another hour, a doctor finally opened the door and listened to her symptoms.

"It's some kind of headache," he said. "Have you been having some stress in your life? You probably had an anxiety attack. You need to cut out the stressors in your life." That should be real easy, she thought. "And you're dehydrated," he continued. "So we can fix that right away with some fluids. That and less stress should have you set." Satisfied, he left the room.

Ten minutes later a nurse entered with the intravenous-fluid sack. But Camila needed to leave. She couldn't be late to pick Alonso up at daycare. The nurse told her she had to stay longer, that the treatment had barely begun. Camila explained politely that she had to go. The nurse sighed and shook his head while he unhooked the IV from her arm.

As she walked out of the hospital, Camila's breasts ached and hung unusually heavy. It was a familiar feeling, she said. On the sidewalk, a wisp of smoke drifted from a cigarette between the fingers of a nurse on break and inflamed her nostrils. She feared she might vomit again. Every step was an effort. She admitted she'd been exhausted for days. If she didn't have to get Alonso, she would just sit in a doorway and close her eyes for a moment.

She hadn't known she could get pregnant while she was breastfeeding, she told me.

Camila bought a pregnancy test on the way home from school. That night in her bathroom, she waited for the result. A single line emerged, not a double one. That was supposed to mean she wasn't pregnant. She didn't believe it. She didn't trust those things, she said, not after her false negatives when she was pregnant with Alonso.

What she'd come to trust lately were her dreams. That week, she'd dreamed that she was at a baby shower in a rented hall. Her sister Teresa had hosted the shower, but Camila wasn't sure who was having the baby. She was rubbing the distended belly of a faceless expectant mother when she woke up. The next night, she dreamed that it was her sister who was pregnant, but it was Camila's baby in her womb.

Before the Wednesday meeting, Camila talked about her dreams to one of the other shelter residents, who was a recent arrival from the Dominican Republic. She understood these things, Camila told me. It turned out that when the new resident was pregnant with her second baby, she'd had the same dream about her own sister. Anselma joined the conversation and said there was another way to know: If the father feels symptoms, it means you're pregnant.

Amare had been saying he was feeling lethargic lately, Camila told them.

That Sunday, Camila had accompanied him to his grandmother's funeral. He seemed remote, she said. She just figured it was because he was grieving. They'd agreed that she'd ask his mother if she could stay with Amare's family for a while, until she could find something permanent, but as much as Camila's housing was feeling like an emergency, it seemed inappropriate to ask at the funeral.

Amare still wasn't calling her his girlfriend, which made her neck snap sideways whenever she talked about it. She'd been telling people he was her boyfriend so she could cut the line at the financial-aid office, where he had his work-study job, and he was pissed about it. But every new relationship had its growing pains, she said. He walked around campus with his arm around her. That's what counted.

Camila said she thought that Amare was the sort of guy who would stick around. Who she could have a family with, a real family.

But it was more than that. Camila was beginning to feel something new. Something she hadn't anticipated. Something that terrified her. She was beginning to feel that despite her own capabilities, she just couldn't manage alone. Not with a baby.

I sat beside her on her twin bed in the shelter, holding her cool hand, which had begun to clench mine. Her voice was unusually quiet. She said that Amare needed a kid of his own if he was going to stick around. That's the only way he'd take care of Alonso, she said, the only way he'd live with her. No matter how nice and responsible he might seem, no way was he going to take on someone else's son without one of his own. And without that, she'd be alone.

She couldn't, Camila said. She'd tried. She needed a new way forward.

Her pregnancy, she believed, offered more of a solution than a problem.

The only way she could find a home, and a family, as she cared for the five-month-old she already had was to have another baby. A baby with a man she barely knew, who'd offered her no commitment, who was an eighteen-year-old with a life of his own to manage.

When I met Camila, just five months before, she was committed to being the badass independent mother she would often refer to herself as, determined not to rely on a man. She was absolute about never using a baby to try to trap a man, like she'd seen her mother do over and over. (Not that she hadn't convinced herself that Alonso was Kevin's baby so he would do right by her, especially once he had his football-contract money.) Either way, she'd been fairly certain that the domestic-abuse claim from New Jersey would secure an apartment in the projects and that if it didn't, she'd get called up for one of the dozens of new affordable-housing places she'd applied for, or at least find another place to land. But she hadn't. And she was being evicted from the shelter for reasons she couldn't fight.

There was still one option left, one that she stubbornly refused to consider. Camila could go to PATH, the emergency-shelter office in the Bronx. She knew well what that meant. All of the women at the shelter did, either because they'd done it themselves or because they knew many others who had. It was a regular topic of conversation on Wednesday nights in the common room, especially since it was what most of them anticipated doing once their time was up on Fourth Avenue.

Because the city shelter system was so overcrowded, it could take weeks or more for a spot in an emergency shelter to open up. New York was one of the only cities—and the first—with a right-to-shelter mandate. While other American cities turned people away from overfull emergency shelters, taking names for a wait list instead of giving a bed for the night, the city would find a roof for anyone who was determined to be in need. This was no small effort or expense, considering that New York's shelters were crowded to capacity every night. Four thousand hotel rooms, as bleak as the shelters themselves, were offered every night to house those who couldn't fit. But it wasn't a simple revolving door of numbers: If you were a mother with a child, there were only certain shelters you could stay in. Far more people were flooding the system than were trickling out.

Until a spot opened, you had to spend your days checking in at the Bronx office. It was November. Camila was primed for the dean's list. Going to PATH would likely mean spending the last weeks of the term in a waiting room in the South Bronx, missing exams, scarring her transcripts with incompletes or Fs yet again, setting her back another semester. Which dramatically increased the likelihood that she'd never break the cycle. Even if it didn't take as long as she'd heard and she was able to make up her schoolwork, it was highly unlikely that she'd be placed in housing that would enable her to drop Alonso off at daycare and commute to the farthest reaches of Brooklyn in time for morning classes or pick him up in time when afternoon classes ended. She thought that if she went to PATH she'd have to drop out of school. All to be in a shelter where she feared she could not depend on safety or sanitary conditions and where her temper, which was hard enough to manage on Fourth Avenue, would surely get her into trouble.

She couldn't just vanish like Sherice did, she told me—and Sherice, she pointed out, even had the special city voucher and Rose's support. She needed a partner, a peer. Someone who was capable of envisioning a future, like she was. She saw that in Amare. He got good grades, like she did. He worked.

If a baby was what it took, she said, then it would be worth it.

The next day, Camila was feeling too sick to make the trip to school. After dropping Alonso off at daycare, she walked back to the shelter and went to bed. When she woke up, she texted Amare and asked him to meet her at the Atlantic Center mall after class. She said she had to talk to him about something. Here's how she described the meeting to me.

When he arrived, he was quiet and jittery. On the escalator he asked her what was going on.

She told him she thought she was pregnant.

He didn't hide the fact that he was scared. But after a few minutes, Camila finally heard the words she'd been desperately awaiting since long before she met him.

"I'm game," he said. "I'm going to step up for this."

He said he'd get his shit together so everything was in place when the baby came. He'd buy a crib for the baby. They'd save up for a place.

"I'll quit school to work full-time," he said.

"No. You can't quit school. That's a bad investment." She was firm.

Amare said he was terrified about telling his mom.

"Let me speak to her," Camila said.

He looked at her like she was crazy.

Camila shifted tactics. There was a lottery for a new one-bedroom on Cook Street available for just $600 a month. She didn't make enough for it on her own, but with the $20,000 he made at Home Depot last year, they'd qualify. As soon as she got back to the shelter, she'd send in several applications for the apartment. Applications were automatically rejected if there was more than one per family, she'd heard, but it was worth the risk.

When she applied for the apartment that evening, she put herself down as head of the household, just in case he bolted, she told me. But he wouldn't, she added, assuring herself. He was a good man. He knew how to treat women.

She rubbed her midsection and said she felt her belly button popping out.

Camila had always wanted to have more than one child. And this time she'd have one with the right man. One who said he wanted to massage her feet and take her to doctor's appointments, one who liked to cook. Who always asked how she was feeling. She said he'd told her that he didn't just want her to be his baby mama. She could see that he was approaching it seriously, taking the steps toward fatherhood. Suddenly Camila remembered her Spanish quiz and her paper due that week on Reconstruction policies. She needed to keep up her A in Spanish and continue to impress her political-science professor. If she was pregnant, she'd have even more appointments to go to, which meant rescheduled exams, extensions on papers; her professors needed to know how committed she was if she was going to ask them to be even more flexible. Then she realized that she hadn't eaten all day.

In the morning, she called her doctor. This time, he knew better than to dismiss her self-diagnosis. At his office, a nurse led her down the familiar hallway to the blood-draw station. Camila sat in the blue vinyl chair, attempting to hold Alonso in one arm while she laid the other out flat. The nurse scooped Alonso up into her arms and tried her best to soothe the baby, bouncing him, her brow furrowed, while her colleague inserted a needle into Camila's smooth, pale skin.

Camila was buoyant, singing to Alonso on the Q train. Amare had invited her to his mom's house.

She wouldn't tell Amare that the test was negative. He didn't need to know yet, she said. She'd get settled in first, become part of the family. Then she'd let them know she was wrong about the pregnancy. His mom would see by then that she was smart, organized, a good mother, like she was. They'd respect each other. By then they'd be close. She'd understand it was only a mishap.

Amare picked them up at the train station. He was jumpy but quiet, she told me later. Camila thought he had a crazy look in his eye. She told herself he was just nervous. They walked up the stoop. Amare opened the door and strode past her into the house. Camila stood awkwardly in the foyer, holding Alonso. Amare returned. His hand was hidden behind his back.

His mother descended the staircase. She peered into the bright entryway. "What's she doing here? She's not allowed in this house," she said.

Camila froze.

Amare pulled his hand from behind his back, grinning. "Take this test into the bathroom," he said to Camila.

The mother remained still on the staircase, staring her down. "I thought you were just friends. I didn't know you were having sex in my house."

Amare spoke again. "I need you to pee on this in front of my mother. I don't believe you're pregnant. You're making it up because you need a place to stay." He waved the pregnancy test at her, still grinning.

Camila's heart surged into her throat. It was all she could do to keep her limbs from shaking, her voice even. "Amare, you want to talk, you tell me. You don't need to embarrass me in front of your mother."

The mother glowered from the staircase. "Why would you want to have a kid with him? You just had a baby."

"She made it up because she needs a place to live," he told his mother. He turned to Camila. "I missed work from the stress," he said to her. "You did that to me. You want to talk, you need to pay me. My time is valuable. You already cost me."

Camila looked straight at Amare and then straight at his mom. "I'm an adult and a mother. I deserve respect," she told them. She turned and walked out of the house.

She pulled the door behind her and heard it latch, gutted by humiliation, by the feeling of being treated like a girl in the streets. Which, no matter what happened, she would never, ever, believe she was.

11

FOR NOW

To cram everything she owned into the two suitcases the city permitted. And to return to the Bronx office every day until they found a shelter placement for her and Alonso. All just to stay in a shelter that was unclean, unsafe, and uncertain. Granted, it was better than sleeping huddled with a baby on a sidewalk. Camila never seemed to consider that she could end up there—among the bums, as she called the street-sleepers of the city. She'd heard about a family that had just been murdered in a Staten Island hotel while waiting for shelter placement. She also heard that she'd be forced to drop out of school to get a job once she was given a bed. The average emergency-shelter stay in New York City stretched on for more than four hundred days. She couldn't lose a year or more of her life not progressing, not even with stable housing beckoning on the other side.

Teresa called to tell Camila she'd heard about a Hispanic roommate-matching service in East Harlem. Camila was dismissive at first. She'd spoken to various services before, and they all seemed shady. They usually wanted money up front—more than five hundred bucks. But Teresa said this place charged $150 to access their listings and that was it, and that the rents were cheap. Camila was skeptical, but she'd do anything to avoid going to PATH, and her lean savings account could handle the fee.

A Dominican couple had listed a room in their place on Sherman Avenue in the Bronx. The agent said they had a baby and were happy to have another one in the apartment. They could offer a twin bed, a dorm fridge, and a coat of fresh paint for $160 a week. That was far less than anything Camila had seen elsewhere, a price she could afford, at least for now, between welfare and savings and work-study. The apartment would be over an hour from Alonso's daycare in Brooklyn and then at least another forty-five minutes from campus, if the subway cooperated. She'd spend hours a day commuting. But she'd known plenty of people who did the same. Proximity was once a convenience of dense urban living, but it had become a luxury few could afford.

She made the trek up to the Bronx to visit the block. On the subway she tried to stop the scene at Amare's house from replaying in her head. She needed to protect herself better, to quell any thought that anyone else would be there for her, or with her. Everything added up to the same lesson, which she hated herself for having to relearn each time she allowed herself to forget it: She could only count on herself.

Other than Lisa from the bodega, Camila didn't know anyone who lived in the Bronx. It was completely unfamiliar to her. Nothing like the two-family houses of Corona or the glass-and-steel towers that had begun to creep uptown. She'd grown accustomed to seeing white people on the streets of brownstone Brooklyn, but there were none here. As always, she sought out the advantages, to convince herself of her own agency, of making a measured choice. There was a big park nearby, perfect for Alonso. The sidewalk looked freshly swept. It would do, she told herself. A fresh start.

On the spot, she handed over the first week's rent to secure the room, which they said they'd fix up in time for her to move in the following week. Camila was accustomed to making such sudden decisions. People with stable lives—people like me—reasonably labor over such an assessment, discussing at length with friends and family, deliberating its place in the larger scope of life. But when existence is a perpetual emergency, as it was for Camila, such decisions are made in a moment, in isolation. It wasn't something to thoughtfully evaluate; it was a rescue mission.

12

THE MAGIC

Packing was the only time she'd allow herself the nostalgic indulgence of examining the contents of a plastic bag she stored deep inside her camp trunk. She called the bag "the Magic." Inside was a stack of pictures, mostly of herself. In a diaper on her grandparents' plastic-covered couch. In a black leotard slipping off her shoulders, standing but not yet walking, holding tight to her father's hand, a long gold chain adorning his mustard mock turtleneck. As a toddler in her mother's arms, in front of a Dominican flag, Geraldine's hair teased and pinned up, her lips painted blackberry. With her dad at Six Flags. Her parents together, her dad in a mustache and baggy jeans, Geraldine in a skintight red minidress, holding each other in front of her mother's *Baywatch* poster on the bedroom door. Camila and her mother, both dressed in what she called hoochie denim half shirts and matching shorts—the picture she said embarrassed her most.

Under the pictures, deep in the bottom of the Magic, were gifts Pedro had made for her when he was at the halfway house. Elaborate pop-up cards he'd designed and cut for her, one with cascading layers of airbrushed hearts that said *No matter what the past has been, our future is spotless. I need you.* Handkerchiefs he'd painted with cartoon characters and romantic slogans, like Minnie and Mickey Mouse framed by a ring of thorny red roses, bearing the message *Husband and Wife II Dead Friends.* Camila explained that meant their love was forever. Sitting on her floor, Camila solemnly unfolded the handkerchiefs one at a time, absorbing the careful craftsmanship, the messages of passion and commitment. She gently held each one to her breast, folded them back into perfect squares, and delicately laid them in the bag, like an ancestral trousseau in a hope chest.

November 15. Moving day. Alonso dozed on the now-bare mattress in 3B, swaddled in Camila's gray hooded sweatshirt. Camila hummed Mariah Carey as she scrubbed the dishes in the sink.

After closing the locks on her trunk the night before, Camila had told Irina she was leaving. She hadn't mentioned her departure to anyone else at the shelter. Now she crossed the hall to say goodbye. Irina handed her a plate of Ukrainian food she'd just cooked and pressed her to eat it. Finally, they hugged in Irina's doorway, which looked directly into Camila's room, now empty of any sign of her.

"Pray," Irina whispered into her ear.

For the last time, Camila signed herself out. She carried Alonso past the empty yellow common room and down the quiet stairwell. The smell of institutional cooking, green beans and meat, wafted from the soup kitchen on the first floor. Blinking hard against the blinding sudden-winter sun, she struggled to open the glass door to the street outside and then stepped out into the chill. It was forty-three degrees, the first cold day of the year. She said she felt liberated. If she felt any nerves about leaving behind this place that gave her shelter, she didn't show it. No more room inspections, she said, deeply inhaling the bracing air, no more curfew. No more threat of eviction. Motherhood on her own terms. She felt no need to take a moment to dwell on leaving the place where she'd spent the end of her pregnancy and the beginning of Alonso's life. After a while, moving failed to signify loss, passage, reflection.

A car-service minivan, stuffed with her boxes, sped over the Brooklyn Bridge; new developments in Dumbo reflected a cloudless sky in their towering expanses of glass. Camila gazed out the tinted window as they turned onto the FDR Drive. Heading north, just past the Manhattan Bridge, she watched bulldozers crash through a Pathmark supermarket, the only place to buy inexpensive groceries near the projects by the bridge. On that parcel of land, 815 luxury apartments would soon cast a platinum shadow over their low-income neighbors next door. Camila sought out one of the brown brick towers and counted up to the thirteenth floor. It was Geraldine's apartment. No doubt she was inside on a Sunday morning, Camila said, with no idea where her daughter, or her grandson, would be living for the rest of the year.

13

SHERMAN AVENUE

The Champs-Élysées was the model for the Grand Concourse, constructed at the apex of the City Beautiful movement and completed in 1909. Seeking space and amenities, upwardly mobile families escaped congested Manhattan for the landscaped courtyards of the Bronx. By the mid-thirties, over three hundred Art Deco buildings lined the Concourse, finely gilded even through the Depression, offering central heating and private bathrooms in every apartment. But that was before the postwar dream lured new white families to the new white suburbs. And when Manhattan's decaying tenements were demolished in the name of slum clearance, nearly 175,000 New Yorkers, mainly black and of Hispanic origin, fled to the buildings lining the Concourse and its nearby streets. The buildings told the story of this diaspora: A 1927 synagogue was rebirthed as the Grand Concourse Seventh-Day Adventist Temple; the Louis Minoff apartment building changed its name to the Papaya. The southern section of the borough earned a reputation as the most dangerous place in the country in the seventies and became synonymous with urban crime during the crack epidemic of the eighties. While in 2015 the city as a whole had never been safer, the murder rate in the Bronx was quietly increasing, though the former media glare on the borough was now barely a passing glance.

Camila's new neighbors earned a median household income of $27,030—about a quarter of what Park Slope residents earned. In the Bronx, 34 percent of households, and at least 42 percent of children, lived below the federal poverty level. The most battle-scarred of boroughs ranked last of all sixty-two New York counties for health and welfare and was home to the single poorest Congressional district in the entire nation the year Alonso was born. Despite its widespread destitution, the Bronx had recently outpaced Manhattan and Brooklyn in a real estate surge, and home sales had risen 35 percent. Real estate developers saw blight as opportunity. Taxpayers had recently spent nearly a billion dollars subsidizing the new Yankee Stadium—rather than housing, health, education, or welfare—to add sheen to its $2.5 billion baseball franchise, the most valuable sports team in the country. New multilane thoroughfares that encircled the stadium did little to separate its colossus from the surrounding squalor. Just a quick walk from the ticket booth, where season tickets could run tens of thousands of dollars, was Sherman Avenue, Camila's new address.

The minivan carrying Camila, her son, and her possessions turned down Sherman, parallel to the Concourse, and slowed past the neoclassical façade of what had been Taft High School. Stanley Kubrick had graduated from Taft in 1945. The last class to receive diplomas there was in 2008, the year it was shut down as a failing school. In the neighborhood schools that remained open, less than 13 percent of kids performed at grade level. Low academic performance and lasting health issues were a common hallmark of a childhood spent in an overcrowded home. In New York, more than 280,000 apartments were overcrowded, and that number was constantly on the rise—up 18 percent from the year before. The neighborhood around the Grand Concourse was in the top five citywide for the greatest number of overcrowded units. Severely overcrowded households were usually headed by Latinos, 70 percent of whom were immigrants.

When the Art Deco buildings began to rise from the Concourse in limestone splendor, my grandfather lived just down the street, with his father and three siblings. They came from Poland—Prussia, he called it—through Ellis Island. He used to tell me stories about tuberculosis-infected kids sleeping in lines of cots in nearby fields and of roller-skating down to Midtown as an errand boy. He graduated from high school at sixteen and went straight into law school. But he was lured away from his studies by the need to make a more immediate living and began selling women's hosiery in Washington Heights, which is now heavily Dominican. The Concourse neighborhood was worse for the wear, but it had survived the battle that was the seventies, when landlords burned down blocks for insurance money. I imagined it looked both the same as and entirely different than it had when my grandfather left it long ago.

Barbed wire was tangled around the ornamental gates of an apartment building, where a young man in a black cap and sweatshirt quietly meowed like a cat. A woman in a head scarf stepped out, slipped him a bag, and walked swiftly away down the sidewalk, past a laundromat with an ATM dispensing ten-dollar bills, the windows on the floors above filled in with cinder blocks. Next door to those cinder blocks was Camila's new home.

Under a pathway of construction scaffolding, a shatterproof double door was wedged wide open to a once-grand double-height lobby with interior balconies of Spanish ironwork. Its bones were magnificent, the floor inlaid with a circle of rose-and-dark-green marble. A huge gold-filigreed medallion covered the ceiling. To me, it was beautiful. To Camila, it was dirty. She wasn't wrong—it was strewn with cigarette butts, takeout napkins, and food wrappers. What mattered most to her was that everything be clean. New. My penchant for vintage dresses bemused her. And, indeed, I'd developed an affection for old things through my privilege of growing up without hand-me-downs, in a pristine world. The grandeur I saw beneath the thick coat of gray paint failed to charm her. She stared dully at a young girl in a fake-fur-trimmed hoodie idly picking at the flaking paint and said she hoped it was lead-free.

My husband and daughter joined me that day to help Camila move. She'd asked her sisters to help, but they'd both texted that they couldn't make it. My daughter entertained Alonso as we un-loaded the van. A little kid on the sidewalk fixed his gaze upon us and loudly asked his older brother why there were white people moving in. His brother answered him with a slap across his face.

As we began to move the boxes inside to the lobby, Camila called her new landlord and roommate, Jovanka, who told her to come upstairs. Camila nervously carried a crying Alonso into a small ele-vator that reeked of urine, pulled the brown metal door shut behind them, and pushed the button. It didn't light up, but after a moment the elevator shuddered and pulled itself to the top floor. Camila searched along a hallway of worn mosaic tile and scalloped plaster-ing. A door stood ajar. Inside, a Bible program was blaring from a radio.

Camila tucked her head in and yelled over the din, "Hello?"

A woman came to the door, close to Camila's age but with the dark circles and exhausted demeanor of someone much older. Her hair was in a bun, an ornate cross clasped around her navy V-neck. She was holding a baby boy. He stared at Alonso without blinking.

"Welcome home," she said, smiling at Camila. "Come on in! I can't wait to show you your room." She shifted her baby onto her hip and reached for Alonso. "Let me hold him!"

Jovanka led Camila into the foyer. A clothesline strewn with sheets and undergarments hung overhead. Underneath, a couch was jammed against a wall, nearly invisible under all manner of clothing, shoeboxes, and baby toys. An ill-fitting cardboard accor-dion door hung open to what had been the living room and was now Jovanka's entire living quarters, a double bed and a crib stuffed beside a couch and easy chair. A big-screen TV dominated the room, the Eagles and the Dolphins competing with the Bible program.

The other room was Camila's. A new coat of pale-beige paint brightened the worn plaster walls; a twin bed was made up carefully in flowered sheets. The floor—wood parquet, which had been refin-ished in recent years—would be easy to sweep, Camila said. This was promising. Camila reached for Alonso, perched him on her hip, and matched words to each element of the room: the closet, the window. He turned his head to wherever his mother pointed.

"That one's smart," Jovanka said, smiling at Alonso. She grandly gestured to a veneer-topped table with a mismatched chair. "I have a surprise for you. We found you a desk so you can study," she said.

Camila laid a hand over her heart in gratitude.

Jovanka nodded in acknowledgment and pointed just outside Camila's doorway. "And this is the bathroom."

A bathtub leaked scalding water in the tiny, tiled space, which hadn't been properly cleaned in some time. Camila whispered to me that she was glad she'd packed her rubber gloves and her Pine-Sol. Wedged next to the running toilet was a shelf piled with hair gels, a biography of Mariano Rivera, and a bottle of cologne shaped like a bar of gold. Camila smiled and nodded politely toward the bathroom but focused instead on a pennant from Syracuse University hanging on the wall outside. She explained to Alonso that it was from a good college. He stared at the big white wool S that was stitched upon the orange fabric. Jovanka told her that she had a master's degree and worked as a case manager in Mott Haven for people with special needs. Camila raised her eyebrows, impressed. These were just the sort of people she'd been searching for, and now she got to live with them.

"Aaron! Say hello to Camila!" Jovanka yelled toward the accordion door.

A big friendly face turned from the easy chair. "Sorry if I don't get up. I take care of that kid all week. Sunday I'm glued to the game."

Camila began knowledgeably chatting about her favorite teams.

"I like this one!" Aaron said approvingly of Camila. "And these two boys, they're going to be the fraternity."

"Yes! The fraternity!" Camila exclaimed, clapping.

Jovanka grinned and dangled two keys on a ring. She pressed them into Camila's free hand. There was a key to the apartment inside, as well as one to the front door outside. Camila was stunned and moved, though she tried to hide it in the moment.

She'd never had a front door key before. Her mother never gave her one. She and her sisters would have to wait for hours after school, hungry, shivering in the cold outside. They never knew

where their mother was or when she'd be coming home. Camila
had figured Jovanka and Aaron would have to buzz her in each time
she came home, the way she'd been buzzed in at the shelter. But
here they were, her own keys. She ran a fingertip over their sharp
new teeth.

14

TIME

The alarm woke Camila at five-thirty the next morning. She was exhausted and congested with a cold. Alonso had slept in her bed, or rather barely slept, he was so fussy with teething. Every time he cried, she'd panic, nervous that he was waking Jovanka's family in the next room. She'd fallen into deep sleep just two hours before the alarm, but she needed to shower and get both of them out the door; the snooze button was not an option. It was six forty-five by the time she'd dressed and fed Alonso and prepared his bag for daycare. She'd blown ten minutes digging through boxes for his daycare bottle before she found it under a stack of pots.

The subway was delayed. Alonso wailed for milk on the platform, but it was too hard to nurse him under her parka while she was carrying bags over both of her shoulders. Once the train arrived, it was crammed with people; she couldn't nurse him jammed against other standing bodies. He screamed until she relented, setting her bags on the floor, unzipping her jacket, and pulling down the neck of her V-neck sweater to free her breast. The train halted continuously between stations, jerking her breast away from his mouth. She prepared to tell off anyone who might make a rude comment and tried not to feel the eyes on her.

It was well past eight when they arrived at the stop in Lower Manhattan where she needed to switch trains. She had to take the next subway to Downtown Brooklyn, walk Alonso to daycare, unpack his bags, talk to the caregiver, walk back to the train, wait for another subway, take the forty-five-minute trip to Brighton Beach, exit the subway, cross the street, wait for the bus, take the fifteen-minute bus ride to school, and run to her nine o'clock art-history class on the other side of campus. Didn't matter that it was impossible, she said; there was less than a month left in the semester, and she had to keep her grades up to transfer to John Jay.

"Why you rushing, mami?" the daycare worker asked, laconic, once Camila had made it through the double glass doors.

"I moved to the Bronx yesterday," she explained, as her eyes darted toward the clock on the wall.

"What do you know about the Bronx?" the daycare worker scoffed.

"I know nothing about the Bronx," Camila said, pulling a clean crib sheet from the diaper bag.

The caregiver looked at her through sleepy eyes and yawned. "When'd you last feed him?" she asked, slowly stretching out each word.

Camila explained his feeding schedule, his teething, and his sleep the night before, as she unpacked the bottles she'd filled with her pumped breast milk. She looked at the clock and excused herself. Out on the street, she felt dizzy with hunger. Knowing she was going to be late anyway, she stopped for a bottle of orange juice at the sandwich shop next door. Then back to the subway. The train was delayed—she didn't board until ten minutes after her first class had begun. Camila found a seat, pulled her ski cap low over her forehead, and let her eyelids close.

It was after nine-thirty when she slipped into the back of the lecture hall. Standing at the front of the room was a young professor with a long black beard and long black hair in a long black blazer. Camila was fascinated by his lectures and hated being late for his class. As she slid into a seat in the dim room, smiling apologetically, the professor discussed the slide behind him, *The Last Supper*.

"Da Vinci painted this to capture the moment when Jesus was told that someone at the table had sold him out," the professor said.

Camila listened as she pulled out her spiral notebook and quickly scrawled some words in her round print.

"Why is Mary Magdalene in this portrait?" she asked from the back of the room.

"She's not!" the professor exclaimed. "I think da Vinci would love that, though."

Her phone buzzed. Amare.

When are you out of class? he texted.

Why? she replied covertly under her notebook.

You want to pass by?

She ignored him to focus on the slide of the *Mona Lisa*.

"She's not Mary or someone experiencing salvation," the professor said. "She's just someone with a rich husband who hired da Vinci to paint her portrait."

Camila ran her tongue over her teeth, a slight gesture of disparagement.

"We think we know what she represents when we look at her, but we don't," he said.

Suddenly Camila was aware of the pressure in her breasts. It was at least an hour after she should have pumped. She looked at the clock. Class was ending in two minutes. She'd have ten minutes until constitutional-law class across campus, and she didn't want to miss a moment of it. If she pumped, she'd have to run to the nurse's office and take two minutes just to relieve the pressure, not even to release her supply. She'd had to pee since the Bronx, too, but there was also no time for that.

15

CHILD SUPPORT

Camila waited for the walk light on the corner of Chrystie and Rivington Streets, across from the Manhattan child-support office. The office lay tucked away in a building that was lodged between a Chinese restaurant and a tiny lumber supplier, on an increasingly anachronistic block—or, more specifically, a small section of the block—a time capsule of another Lower East Side. Just around the corner, down a dead-end alley, was the restaurant that had launched an international trend of farmhouse cuisine served by bearded, plaid-shirted waiters under the glassy watch of taxidermied deer heads. Across the street, galleries had opened in former tenements. The neighborhood's shops had once been crammed full of wares sold by Jews, then Puerto Ricans, but recently those spaces had been stripped down into minimalist white backdrops for a few garments. Since the nineties, rents here on the Lower East Side had risen more than almost anywhere else in the city.

There was a hidden map of the city, in a sense, a transparency laid over the grid familiar to privileged New Yorkers. You'd only see the hidden city—the one lined with mismatched linoleum squares, smelling of garlic and cologne—if you lived or worked in the system. Gentrification meant this schizophrenia was lived across streets, threaded through neighborhoods, blanketing vast portions of the city. Some Dominicans traveled miles of subway line to work behind the counter at the bakery on Clinton Street, where they had once lived, while white twenty-somethings in co-signed apartments upstairs went to the new café around the corner to buy their house-made vegan muffins. Others—those who still lived in the former tenements over the storefronts now converted to bistros and bars—collided with craft-cocktail-seeking millennials only when they snuck out to the stoop for a smoke. Different cities inhabited not just the same block but the same building, where invisible borders snaked up fire escapes and under drywall. The marbling was obvious from the sidewalk, if you chose to look. But it seemed rare that anyone did.

Camila used to live in one of those apartments, next to what had since been developed into a new boutique hotel, its name spelled out in faux urban-graffiti letters. During her last year in high school, after she could no longer stand the Staten Island group home, Camila had sublet a room in this neighborhood, in an apartment an older couple rented out during the months of the year they were away in the Dominican Republic. Camila paid for the room with her income from the supermarket on Columbia Street, where she worked afternoons and weekends. The couple's son had just gotten out of jail and wanted the room himself, she told me, but they preferred the hardworking, polite girl they knew from the checkout line. As soon as they boarded their regular flights to Santo Domingo, the son would break into the apartment through the fire escape. Camila would barricade herself in her room while he had big parties, hoping that none of the guys would bust through her door and that all her clothes wouldn't reek of weed the next day.

She crossed Chrystie Street, passed a gallery, and found the address on a door next to a Chinese restaurant that was holding tight to a lease from a different era. Sweet fermented air wafted from its kitchen to the child-support office on the third floor. Camila checked in with the receptionist, who sat behind a pocked panel of bullet-proof glass.

The receptionist's cold welcome was one she'd heard many times before. "Do you know your number?"

One-armed student desks lined the reception area. High up on the wall hung a video screen, with black and Latina actors presenting a child-support-hearing scenario, in which the only white performer was playing a uniformed cop. Camila wedged into a seat next to a young woman in a tube dress and flip-flops, inappropriate for the late-November chill but perfect attire for the oppressive steam heat from the office's decrepit metal pipes. Camila stretched out the neck of her gray cotton turtleneck to let some air in and pulled her hair up into a bun. At least it was better than how cold it had been last night in the apartment, she told me.

It was a long wait, which, for us, meant a long talk. Camila's excitement about life in the Bronx apartment had quickly curdled into resentment. She felt more homeless on Sherman Avenue than she had in the shelter. She was living out of cardboard boxes, Alonso's clothes in a shopping bag, no place to put anything. She couldn't even use the kitchen cabinets, they were so jammed with Jovanka and Aaron's stuff. Her supermarket cart functioned as her kitchen pantry, a giant bottle of Mazola and packets of rice piled atop her pots and pans. They were always in the kitchen anyway, she said, and never made her feel like she had a right to use it. She deliberated getting a hot plate for her room, but it would make her feel like she was living in a jail cell. A hot plate, one pot, wash it to cook the next thing—that wasn't living.

Jovanka and Aaron never offered her what they were cooking, even after asking if the smell of their cooking bothered her. She couldn't imagine not making a plate for someone if she was cooking in the same house, she said. At least Aaron would talk to her about school. She liked that, talking about goals, classes, not just bullshit. He was sociable, respectful. Maybe not entirely respectful: Once when she asked him what the Internet password was, he said it was "bitches." And there always seemed to be some drama when Aaron talked to her. Jovanka would get jealous and start texting him from the other room as soon as they started a conversation.

A large woman in a tropical-print dress shuffled over with a clipboard of paperwork. She wordlessly handed it to Camila, who began filling it out.

Emergency contact: her high school mentor.

Address: the shelter in Brooklyn, not the apartment in the Bronx. Her rental was illegal. She couldn't risk it.

Father's parents' names: She had no idea.

His place of birth: Queens?

A baby started crying in his stroller, a whimper that quickly amplified into a strangled cry. The mother tried to focus on her clipboard, but she couldn't write a word. Desperate, she started begging her child.

"Come on, just please let me do this, just let Mama do this," she pleaded.

Camila watched as the baby cried louder. The mother raised her voice to match.

"No! I'm not taking you out. You have to sit there." Anger trembled in her yells. "You have to sit there!"

Her phone began ringing. The baby cried louder still. She yanked her ski cap down over her eyes for a moment to shut it all out, then, defeated, pulled out a container of chocolate milk and an empty bottle. The baby grabbed the bottle and drank it, finally silent.

Camila asked me about the shelter, where I was still leading meetings on Wednesdays. Bitterly, she wondered who was moving into her room (no one yet) and if I'd seen Rose (I hadn't). I heard her stomach churn and asked her if she'd eaten anything. Half a bacon, egg, and cheese sandwich, really early, she said. She worried about budgeting for all the outside food that she was eating, meaning anything that food stamps didn't cover. She knew she couldn't be spending money, even the $2.50 for the sandwich she could make two meals out of, but what could she do if she couldn't use the kitchen? Exasperated, she shook her head. She didn't want to think about any of it anymore.

She wanted to think about something more pleasurable, she told me. Amare. She'd given in and gone back to his attic room after class.

"After all that?" I asked her.

She just pursed her lips, raised her eyebrows, and held my stare.

"The sex is really good," she confessed after a moment. She didn't want to talk about the rest of it.

Then she told me that right after he came, he said to her, "Don't fall in love."

"Can you fall in love just by having sex?" she asked me. The only person she ever really loved was Kevin, she said, but that wasn't about the sex. She admitted she was scared: What if she really fell for Amare and he didn't want her anymore?

The woman who'd handed Camila the clipboard waved her back into a warren of cubicles. Last time Camila was here she met with Miss Marsha, she told the woman. This time it was Miss Vernice, which meant starting over again with a new worker. Miss Vernice peered at her screen in a cubicle decorated with pictures of babies cut from magazines and newspapers.

"I'm trying to figure out why they called you in today," she said over her shoulder as she waddled off. After a long while, she returned. "Did you know there's a court date?" she asked. "There's a paternity hearing scheduled in Queens."

"I have finals that day," Camila said.

"Well, you'll have to be there. And you'll have to do all new paperwork. In the meantime, sign this."

Miss Vernice handed Camila an affidavit to attest that she'd had sex with Jeremiah.

Camila signed it and left.

She'd missed a day of classes, again, for this. Jeremiah didn't even have to bother picking up the phone when he was in class. A quarter of custodial mothers were paid no child support at all, and only 43 percent received the full amount. And those were the ones with active cases. If you were to add up unpaid support going back to 1975, you'd be looking at $114.5 billion owed to mothers raising children on their own.

Outside the office, Camila flipped open her phone and called her dad as she walked toward the subway.

Mauricio answered. "Yeah?"

"I want you to see your grandson. You haven't seen him since Father's Day. Can I come see you tomorrow?"

"Nah, I'm not feeling well." He sounded distracted. She could hear cars honking, figured he was driving around in the Porsche. "Hey, what's up with the hundred bucks you owe me?" he asked.

"I'll give it to you when I can see you."

"Celia keeps asking me if you've paid the money back."

"Just tell me when I can see you. I'll give you the money then. And you can see your grandson."

"Not a good time." He hung up.

16

COLD

Camila felt like she was running out of time every day. At least four hours of commuting, and when she got home, Alonso never wanted to fall asleep. On the way to daycare in the morning, she was so tired that she would fall asleep as soon as Alonso did, soothed by the motion and the rushing sound of the subway. She needed to be doing homework on the train, no matter how crowded it was, but she couldn't stay awake, not when he finally dozed off. Some days it seemed like the train was the only place he would sleep. She was somehow keeping up her grades, but she didn't know how long that could last, not like this. And now she worried all the time that Alonso was cold, while he was away from her at daycare, while she pushed him in his stroller down Sherman Avenue, against her chest on the subway platform.

There had barely been an autumn. For weeks, everyone in the city seemed stunned by the depth of the cold that had chased away a stifling summer.

One afternoon when Camila was on her way home from daycare, a woman without a coat made her way along the subway car, asking for help. Camila tended to Alonso, pretending not to see her.

The woman stopped in front of them. She commented on how cute the baby was and reached out a shaky hand to stroke his tiny wrist.

"Don't touch him!" Camila yelled at her.

As the woman hurried away, Camila felt deep shame at her outburst. She knew why she was exceptionally on edge. Kevin had texted the night before that he was in Westchester. And he wanted to see her. She couldn't believe it. She replied she'd come up on the bus.

Are you coming alone?

No, it's me and the baby.

Camila had stared at the phone, waiting for his response.

I don't feel like being around a kid tonight, he finally wrote. *I just want to relax.*

Camila wrote that she had motherly duties; if he couldn't accept her with Alonso, she wouldn't see him. He said she should come up on her way to class. Like he had any clue where she went to class, like that was how the New York metropolitan area even worked. She ignored him. Then he had the nerve to ask if she would give him a threesome for his birthday next week. He'd still be in town. She felt something worse than angry, she told me. She felt humiliated. How could she have believed this was the right father for her son? How could she be seen like that by the one guy she thought had true character? She was quiet the rest of the subway ride.

17

BACK ON FOURTH

Camila's room at the shelter on Fourth Avenue remained vacant. But a new resident had moved into Anselma's old room. Anselma had checked out one day and simply didn't return. For two weeks her room lay untouched, every pink onesie perfectly folded, the plastic makeup organizers stacked in her bathroom. Rose had called her repeatedly, but there was no answer. She'd left messages that her possessions would be donated if she didn't come get them. Apparently Irina had been right, she had gotten back together with her boyfriend, because they showed up together one afternoon to fetch what she'd left behind. Anselma's usual docility vanished when she couldn't find a pair of baby Air Jordans in one of the overstuffed garbage bags. She screamed about theft, threatened to call the police. Now Anselma was less than a memory; of the residents, only Irina had known her.

The new resident sat silently on one of the blocky wooden chairs. She was African American, dark-skinned, in huge thick glasses, her hair hidden under a shower cap. The residents took turns giving their weekly updates. When it was her turn to speak, she just looked around and shook her head. "I had my own place in Queens," she said.

Irina's face contorted in sympathy. "What happened?"

"The landlord didn't want kids there. I said she had to take me to court if she was going to throw me out because I was having a baby. We went to court. I had receipts that said I paid my rent fully and on time and a letter that said I intended to continue doing so. She said she didn't want my money, she didn't want a baby there. The judge gave me one month to leave. I was home watching TV when I heard a knock on my door. It was the marshal. I had to leave immediately. I went back the next day for my stuff. The landlord wouldn't let me in."

"What did you do?" asked Irina.

"I contacted the marshal, but he just said they had nothing to do with it. They gave me a date for small-claims court in August. I called her to say we don't need to go to court, I just want my stuff. She pretended she had no idea who I was. She said, 'How did you get this number?' I kept at her and she said finally that she'd thrown it all out."

Irina gasped. "You lost everything?"

She nodded. "My three-thousand-dollar bedroom set I'd just gotten one year ago from Macy's. My computer. My TV. All the stuff I'd bought for the baby."

"Where did you go?"

"I went to PATH and spent ten days at a hotel in the Bronx before they let me know I was ineligible. They said, 'You can come back ten thousand times and we'll still find you ineligible.' Because my parents have a house—but they don't want me there."

The residents all nodded quietly. It was a familiar story.

18

FINDING OF FACT

Across Thirty-fourth Street from Camila's old high school was the only permanent address she'd had since becoming a ward of the state. She opened her post office box in the main post office when she moved to the group home and had traveled back to it from every rented room, dorm, and shelter ever since. Most of the country had shifted over to email for all urgent matters since she'd opened that post office box. But the important information she received, from the legal system, the welfare system, the housing system, only came printed on paper, in letter-sized white envelopes, with no evidence of a human hand.

In her narrow, stainless-steel post office box, she found papers confirming that the court date was scheduled for the next day in Queens, which meant another day of missed classes and more bureaucracy. She didn't even know what the hearing was for. Exams were beginning that week. Exams were beginning for Jeremiah, too, but he'd lost all of one day to the life of their son, the last time they were at Queens family court. Less than one day, since it was in his neighborhood.

Alonso had a stomach flu and had been vomiting for days. Her entire life—her classes, her exams, her obligations—all slammed to a stop the moment his temperature crept over 100, no matter the consequences. But a court date was not something she could miss. She couldn't drop him off at daycare with a fever. He'd have to come with her. That she had the stomach flu as well was barely worth noting.

Camila shivered as she came up out of the subway at Jamaica, Queens. She lugged her book bag with her heavy laptop on her back, the huge diaper bag on her shoulder, and Alonso, quiet, his eyes glazed and distant, in the carrier on her chest. She was hungry but still too sick to eat, as she hustled past Wendy's, McDonald's, Burger King, Popeyes, Golden Krust, Dunkin' Donuts. A line of people huddled in the cold, stretching down the side of the Social Security Administration building, across the street from the pawnshop. As she entered the courthouse through the metal detectors, Camila doubted Jeremiah would show. But there he was, waiting outside the courtroom.

He gave her a quick hug. She gave him a once-over. New-looking Nikes. Black thermal and sweats. Those ghetto-looking braids, as she called them.

"Alonso has a fever of 100.4," she told him.

"Should he go to the hospital?"

"No, I gave him Tylenol," she said dismissively. "I got pictures for you." In her backpack was an envelope of Alonso's school pictures, taken at the daycare the week before. "You can have one of the small ones for your wallet. And you can frame one of the big ones."

"Yeah, I'll keep one with me," he said shyly.

Jeremiah cautiously touched Alonso's small foot, then his hand. Alonso grabbed on to Jeremiah's finger. His little face burst into a big smile. Jeremiah's eyes widened, huge with wonder.

"He's got a grip!" He stared at Alonso, transfixed.

Camila didn't say a word.

"I'm so tired," he sighed after a moment.

She ignored him.

"Alvarez! Cole!" the court officer yelled, even though they were the only people in the waiting room.

The same dreadlocked magistrate welcomed them back to the small office that functioned as a courtroom. "Do you have the finding of fact?" she asked Camila.

"No, I don't," Camila said, holding Alonso in her arms. Her voice was clipped and formal. "And I thought we'd resolved during our last court date that the case was being transferred to New York County." She spoke with the quick fluency of a put-upon courtroom attorney.

Jeremiah watched Camila's face, trying to follow along.

"New York County rejected the transfer, because of the order of filiation here in August." The magistrate spoke to Camila like she was confessing irritation to a sympathetic colleague. "And now because we don't have the finding of fact we can't proceed."

"Even though the divorce papers say there is no child," Camila said.

"Yep. We'll have to reconvene on the date we'd set earlier. Are you still receiving public assistance?"

"I am."

"Most likely it's going to be retroactive support from August, when the order of filiation was filed." The magistrate turned to Jeremiah. "Do you have any questions?"

He looked down and said nothing.

Brusquely, Camila translated the situation for him. "I have been on public assistance since the baby was born. You filed for paternity in August. That means you need to pay public assistance back what they've given me. Which is four hundred dollars a month."

He silently examined his lap.

"I lived in a shelter for six months with no support," Camila added.

Jeremiah continued studying his lap.

"Well, happy holidays!" the magistrate said brightly after a moment. "You have six weeks to do the DNA test." She called the next case.

Outside the office, Camila waited for Jeremiah to say something, but he just stood there, looking at his shoes.

She held up Alonso. "Want to hold him?" she asked dryly.

Jeremiah took the baby in one arm. He struggled to pull on his coat with the other.

Watching him engage in such unwitting slapstick, Camila's stony face finally cracked. She laughed at his contortions.

"Help me get my coat on?" he asked.

"Nope." She smirked.

He gave up and held the coat in his hand as he walked toward the escalator.

Alonso gripped his neck. "He's strangling me!"

Camila's grin broadened.

In only his thin thermal, Jeremiah carried Alonso through the icy air to the subway. Camila guffawed performatively, watching him try to get out his MetroCard with Alonso in one arm and his bulky coat in the other.

"I have new respect for women," Jeremiah said.

On the subway platform, he noticed a piece of lint on Alonso's eyelid. He informed Camila.

"And?"

"So I got to get it off?" he asked nervously.

She raised her eyebrows and nodded at him very slowly.

Jeremiah stared dumbly at the lint.

"Hold him with one hand and use your other hand to get it off!"

"I can't!"

"Yeah, you can. Like this." Camila mimed holding a baby and began whipping her hand around over her head like a lasso. "I cook like this, I clean like this." She paused for effect. "I go to the bathroom like this."

Jeremiah anxiously reached a trembling finger toward Alonso's eyelid.

As soon as they sat down inside the subway car, Jeremiah tried to hand Camila the baby. She ignored him.

Jeremiah noticed the breast pump poking up out of the diaper bag. "You breastfeed?"

"I do."

"Does it feel good?"

Camila just looked straight ahead.

"How does it taste?"

She didn't answer.

He was having fun now. "What if you need to eat cereal, would you eat it with our own milk?"

She pressed her teeth together.

"If you're homeless do you eat your own milk?"

Now she was offended.

Without a word, she unzipped her coat and took Alonso from Jeremiah's arms. She pulled down the neck of her sweater and freed her nipple from her bandeau. Alonso latched on hungrily.

"You can do that here?" Jeremiah asked, watching her like a kid trying not to bust up in class. The train slowed into his stop. "I'm out," he said, as he gave Alonso a final glance and vanished through the doors.

19

THANKSGIVING DINNER

Christmas lights glowed in the frigid air under the Brighton Beach elevated train tracks. Russian women cocooned in furs crowded against students on the B1 bus to campus as Camila gazed through the window at the yellow moon that hung huge and low over the ocean. Under her parka, she wore her Met outfit: her blue slacks, white rayon blouse, and gold-tipped flats. She'd dressed for Thanksgiving dinner. It was the only one she'd have this year, at Kingsborough, on the Tuesday before the holiday.

Lining a wall in a conference room in the Marine Center were fold-up tables laden with turkey slices, yams, beans, and rice in aluminum trays. Camila arrived and scanned the room for anyone she might recognize. There were about fifteen students. She'd never met any of them. Camila didn't really have friends at school, no one she could hang out with, not that her life was structured to accommodate any relationship.

She was messing around with Amare still, but that was just a booty-call thing. She didn't go out with the theater friends he was always clowning around with, who had a performance scheduled for that night. She cared little about Amare's involvement in it—something backstage—but she didn't want to miss the play. During

her freshman year at Buffalo, she'd acted in *Metamorphoses* and cho-
reographed the whole production. Camila looked at the clock hanging over the trays of food and realized that either she had to skip the
performance or she had to skip the dinner laid out before her. Despite the gnawing in her stomach, it was an easy choice.

"I just wanted to stop by and say hello," she said cheerfully to a
knot of middle-aged faculty members. "I have to pick up the baby,"
she explained, not wanting to offend anyone.

An adviser in a mud-cloth tunic insisted that she take some food
home. Camila politely refused and then relented, knowing she
could manage her hunger temporarily but not when she got home
to the Bronx much later that night. She examined the table for to-go
containers and couldn't find anything. With stealth, she scooped
some rice and beans and turkey into the disposable lid of a salad
bowl and wrapped a plastic shopping bag around it.

A reedy student blocked Camila's passage out the conference
room door. He stared her down. "You shouldn't be taking food to
go," he said.

She stared back at him. Did she need to explain that she had permission? That she was hungry? That she was living on food stamps?
Without a word, she pushed past him and fled to the box office
downstairs, humiliated.

Amare, in a pressed gingham button-down, was taking tickets at
the door. He leered at her flirtatiously, handed her a program, and
possessively looped his arm around her waist. She had told him the
week before that she had a boyfriend. It was a lie, of course. Camila
stiffened to express that she wasn't there for what he thought, she was
just there for the play. She'd arranged for late daycare—which she'd
have to pay for out of pocket—and after she put Alonso to bed she
had to write a paper on *Brown v. Board of Education*, but she loved theater and had promised herself this evening as an early holiday gift.

As the house lights dimmed in the theater, she found a seat in the
back row. Only then did she glance at the program. *Blood Wedding,*
by Federico García Lorca. Camila folded her hands in her lap and sat
erect, her head high. For the next hour and a half she barely
breathed, spellbound by its tale of tragically impossible love.

Through the long subway ride to fetch Alonso, Camila puzzled over the plot twists and replayed moments of connection and catharsis. She wrote herself into the narrative, imagined herself as the bride, and parsed the blood-soaked ambiguous ending as the B train hurtled under the cold streets above. When she arrived at the daycare center twenty minutes late, she was charged an extra thirty-five-dollar late fee, but it was worth it, she said. Her thoughts raced all the way to the Bronx, with her shopping-bag-wrapped Thanksgiving dinner on the seat beside her, the only Thanksgiving dinner she'd have that year, holding Alonso tightly against her heartbeat.

WINTER

1

CAMILA AND ME

At the shelter in New Jersey, Camila had painted a small canvas, a blue background with white brushstrokes that spelled out *A Mother's Best Friend Is Her Son*. The shelter had organized an art class so the residents could make paintings to hang on whatever walls they eventually found. But Camila didn't hang her canvas in her room on Sherman Avenue. The idea that Alonso would be her protection from loneliness wasn't something she mentioned anymore. With one exception, she felt, her life had become solitary.

Sure, there was the family in the apartment, but they didn't open their lives to her. No one in her own family came to visit. She wasn't tight with any of her old friends anymore—some slight or another had burned down many of those relationships long ago, or time and geography created distance. Moving constantly made it tough to maintain intimacies, and never feeling in control of one's own time, always having some sort of crisis or a waiting room unexpectedly claiming your day, didn't help. It wasn't like anyone was going to come up to the Bronx and hang out in her room with Alonso, anyway. Camila had begun to miss her family desperately. She talked about her father more and more and her sisters—her little sister

Tiana, whom she hadn't been talking to for a while, and Teresa, who sometimes said she'd come up to visit but never did.

But I did, always. I was there in her room. I was there on the subway commute. I was there in the waiting rooms. I was there to hear her yearnings and complaints, to talk to her about Amare, Jeremiah, Kevin, her reading on women in the prison system, her housing applications, her love of Rihanna and dismissal of Beyoncé, her family in the Dominican Republic, where she'd never been, where her father had a house he took Celia's daughter to but not her. I'd become her primary relationship.

Welfare was no longer paying Camila's rent, not since she'd left the shelter. She still had her public-assistance money and some income through work-study, but her savings account was shrinking by the day. She knew she wouldn't be able to keep writing checks to Jovanka for much longer. Meanwhile, I was writing the proposal for this book. Which meant that if all went as planned, sometime after New Year's I'd sell it and get an advance check. That would mean money I'd be earning to witness her poverty, which was steadily worsening. Money that would go toward the mortgage on the home I own, to pay for my daughter's music lessons, to bring wine to a dinner party.

When I met Camila, things were a bit middle-class tight for us. I'd gotten a six-thousand-dollar grant to fund my initial reporting, which was mainly gone by the time she went into labor. I was teaching and writing freelance articles when I wasn't with Camila. It didn't add up to much. We were feeling it, in payments for afterschool programs, in how quickly our daughter outgrew her clothes—not that my mother wasn't eager to know exactly what her granddaughter needed every time she drove by the Gap outlet, another privilege Camila would never know. These were middle-class problems; upper-middle-class problems, at that.

People feel their own scarcity based on the rungs above, not below. Above me were friends shopping in Brooklyn boutiques, taking vacations, grocery shopping at Whole Foods, attending fundraisers for their public schools in neighborhoods we couldn't afford. Subtle measures, socially encoded. Below, for everyone, wasn't a rung but a hole the ladder balanced over. It was the guy with the cardboard sign in Penn Station, a coffee cup with a bit of change in the bottom. Camila, me, the people purchasing condo floor plans, all of us weighed our privilege against that guy, the mythic foil to our financial anxieties, the icon of a martyr hanging in our urban cathedrals.

It was one thing to gripe on a subway ride about the $2,000 my daughter's braces would cost us out of pocket when things were tight. Camila seemed to feel solidarity in those moments, vexation on my behalf. I could worry about that $2,000 and mean it, and she could know I meant it. She expressed common cause with me. She was always good at finding that with anyone. Our solidarity, as she seemed to feel it, was what she appeared to lean into, not the economic chasm between us. But I hadn't begun to make a living off writing about her struggles yet. If all went as my literary agent anticipated, that was soon to change.

Meanwhile, Camila had found some temporary stability, but her housing was precarious at best, and everything else depended on it. Since she'd left the shelter, her natural optimism had atrophied. She knew she couldn't afford the permanent stability she needed, certainly not in this housing market. And I wouldn't be able to give her a cent of what I might be paid for reporting on her struggle. Compensating a subject or source is, of course, the third rail in journalism. Introducing money would not just discredit my reporting, but it would also present an even bigger problem than the usual journalistic issues of ethics and reliability. Her story was one about structural inequality, the housing crisis, the welfare system, single motherhood, and more. That was why she didn't have money or a home. If she had some money, I would no longer be able to witness how she succeeded or failed in making a life without it. We discussed this. She said she understood.

Yet my observation was hardly pure. My existence in her life had transformed it. I was observing a young woman, alone; only she wasn't alone, I was there, shining worth and interest upon her, taking notes, paying attention. And, by nature of my presence, providing companionship.

I felt the increasing dissonance between my days with Camila and the phone calls I would make to my literary agent. Camila was finding it harder each day to summon the stamina to achieve the goals she'd set for herself. I'd been amazed by her perseverance each day, her unflagging energy and focus, and it was frightening to see it falter. The exhaustion of her days and nights had begun to lull her to sleep on the crowded subway each morning on the way to school. Her success during the fall semester was born of those crucial hours studying on the train. Now her pale lids would lower over her eyes almost as soon as the car began its even, rhythmic ride; the metal walls could support her sleeping head—and shield her from any threat that might creep up behind her. Every time she rested her vigilance on the subway, she feared it would result in a knife in her back.

2

BRONX BABY

The holiday season meant donations. Camila hauled home all the toys she could from various charity organizations, encased in hard plastic, which she showcased in a neat line in the Pack 'N Play beside the bed. Her main source was the order of Sisters of Life, which maintained a convent in a brownstone on the Upper East Side. Camila had first gone there after she'd skipped her Planned Parenthood appointment. The entrance to the brownstone was flanked by shelves of pamphlets that graphically decried the evils of terminating a pregnancy. On a coffee table in a parlor was a massive book of full-color photographs of fetuses. After Alonso's baptism, one of the sisters had texted Camila to say they had something special for her. She'd mentally cataloged a list of things she needed for the baby, hoping, anticipating what awaited her. It was a homemade lemon-frosted cake. The sister texted again to invite Camila back for something special for the holidays. This time her expectations were tempered. A bag tagged with her name was filled with FitFlops, a plastic Mickey Mouse toy, and an enormous polyester blouse and matching skirt, which a nun informed her was a "careers outfit." At least in the bottom of the bag was a package of Pampers. Camila asked if she could trade them out for Alonso's size.

Back in the Bronx, she carefully laid the Mickey Mouse toy in Alonso's Pack 'N Play. The newness of donations seemed worth more to Camila than the things themselves. Infant socks, ridiculously packaged in tiny plastic foot forms far smaller than Alonso's nearly seven-month-old feet, had remained arranged on the shelf of her closet since she moved in, never to be unwrapped. The book she'd been given during pregnancy, *Where the Wild Things Are,* was kept hidden away, pristine in her trunk of keepsakes, its thin paper binding unbroken. The only book Alonso heard read aloud at home was *The Cat in the Hat*—which I gave him—because its hardback binding could withstand multiple opening and closings without obvious wear.

Camila was mainly too tired to read to him anyway, or too busy with schoolwork, when they were in the apartment. There was a television in her room, and she relied on it to occupy Alonso while she studied or showered. It had been months since she'd considered shopping for organic food, like she did in her early days in Park Slope. The only solid foods he had known were rice and beans in a takeout tin or the Gerber fruit purees that were covered by WIC, the Women, Infants, and Children nutrition program. They weren't even the good Gerbers, she'd grumble in the supermarket, examining the stickers on the ones she could purchase with her WIC check, adding up the prices in her head, making sure she didn't go over. Such calculations didn't make her a rarity: Alonso was among the 63 percent of all infants in the country—2.5 million in total—whose food was paid for by the program that year.

Her interest in natural healing, from the Brooklyn days of her pregnancy, had been replaced with a reliance on hot Coca-Cola to cure a cold, like her grandmother used to give her. To soothe Alonso she'd dig in her bag for Orajel or dissolvable teething pills found only in neighborhoods with low test scores and high crime rates. Park Slope's volunteer doulas felt like citizens in a distant country, the afternoons devoted to breastfeeding groups and walks in Prospect Park another time, another motherhood. Every day, that realm seemed farther away, she said.

Camila knew she couldn't take the time in the morning to drop Alonso off at the daycare center in Brooklyn anymore. She was always late to class; every evening was a panic to pick him up on time. Across Sherman Avenue, a sign for a daycare in one of the apartments peeked from above the security gate of a first-story window. She'd heard that Maria, the woman who ran the daycare, was Dominican. At least he'd learn about his own culture, she told me. Camila signed him up. That night, she put Alonso to bed telling him about all the new friends he'd make at his new school. She didn't bother informing the daycare in Brooklyn that he wouldn't be coming back. They never cared about him anyway, she said.

The next morning, Camila packed up the diaper bag and carried Alonso across Sherman. Practiced in the art of communicating refusal wherever men lingered, her jaw set, her eyes coldly fixed ahead, she brushed past the cluster of guys slouching outside on the curb. Above her, a dozen-odd pairs of sneakers had been tied together and slung high over the arm of a streetlamp. Pigeons roosted in them, burrowing into the high-tops, clucking and cooing. On the pavement leading to the front door of Maria's building, tires had been slashed open and painted white to make garden planters, dirty bouquets of polyester flowers thrust in each one.

Maria's door, metal and dented, was painted a dull brown. Inside, the shades were pulled down tight against the neighborhood. While a small girl in pigtails waged war between four off-brand Barbies, a baby sat in a high chair, staring blankly at a television loudly chirping Nickelodeon cartoons. A massive Dora sticker had been adhered to one wall. As a kid, Camila always hated Dora, she told me; always some fox waiting to jump out of the bushes. Most of the apartment's square footage belonged to the daycare—really just a living room, painted in chalky purple, yellow, and green. Maria and her husband lived with their ten-year-old son in the bedroom. In several weeks, a new baby would live in that small room with them, too. Maria, in a crocheted skullcap, her pregnant belly hanging over sweatpants, led Camila into the kitchen, where a telenovela blared to compete with the television in the living room. A round middle-aged woman was slicing apples while a cauliflower soup bubbled on the stove. Neither woman spoke any English. They'd have a real Bronx life now, Camila said.

3

SELF-CARE

Camila didn't have class on Fridays. That's when she'd schedule the weekly rounds of far-flung appointments—at the pediatrician's in Brooklyn, the welfare office in Lower Manhattan, the WIC center in the Bronx, and so on. On the rare Friday that wasn't scheduled, she'd drop Alonso off at Maria's anyway. She felt entitled to wash the heaps of laundry without having to quiet Alonso's cries at the same time, or she'd just take the day as a break from motherhood.

She had to take care of herself, she'd often say, in order to take care of him. Her own pleasures could coexist with his growth. Those pleasures were few, like filling the bored, lonely hours alone in the apartment after Alonso slept, attempting to mimic some sort of nightlife by queuing up an R&B playlist, squeezing into a minidress, and taking selfies. Or occasionally she'd put him to sleep in the stroller and turn it away from the bed, where she'd welcome another body to make her feel feminine, to make her shudder and twist her pillowcase, to transport her to a vibrancy outside the unrelenting grayness of her life. At least Alonso wasn't drugged asleep nightly, like she'd been during her childhood, she said: Eight o'clock was what Geraldine had called Nyquil Time, so she could be certain she and that night's boyfriend wouldn't be interrupted. Camila told me she'd had a pair of radio headphones with a little antenna that would allow her to fall asleep to music when she was a kid, drowning out the sound of her mother's moans. Alonso was young enough not to know better. And by the time he knew what was happening under those covers, he'd have his own bedroom. She wasn't going to deny herself constantly to protect her son. She said she'd seen what that did to women, how it had calcified her grandmother into wizened, unsmiling silence. That was no way to live, no way to make a life.

Some Fridays, when Alonso was at daycare, Camila would treat herself to a manicure. Self-care, she called it, using the language of her era. It never occurred to her that her poverty would bar her from a way of living that was considered a prerogative for women who had more money, a way of living that filled her Instagram feeds. *I need some me time,* she'd text when she wanted to get her nails done.

I knew how tight her money was. Part of me, which I kept silent, felt like a bit of a scold, thinking that she would blow thirty bucks on something so unnecessary and fleeting. But this was one of the small, achievable things that made her feel feminine, cared for, like anyone else. Most of the women at the shelter got their nails done whenever they could. Chipped polish was an embarrassment, like an overdue weave was often a mark of shame. Their lives might be a nightmare they couldn't afford to wake from, but their bodies were another story. Such grooming required an outlay of cash that wouldn't make a dent in their real problems. It was central to feeling self-possession rather than constant humiliation. I had never been as conscious of my ungroomed toes as I was on Fourth Avenue the previous summer, when I would try to remember to hide them under sneakers. I didn't mind how my feet looked in Manhattan, but at the shelter they felt like a dirty smock at a cotillion.

There was only one salon where Camila would go, a tiny shoebox of a place in Corona, where Mauricio had first taken her when she was sixteen. It wasn't just a place for a pedicure; it was a link to her past, to the only community where she ever felt she belonged, and possibly, if she timed it right, she might catch a glimpse of her father. Fridays were his day off.

Her increasing isolation had stoked a longing for her childhood, her Corona days. That week, on the way to the salon, she wanted to walk by the stout brick apartment building facing the Long Island Railroad tracks where they'd all lived with her grandparents and two aunts until she was nine. She and her sisters would stand on the other side of their chain-link fence, watching the boys with spray cans cover the cement wall below the tracks with graffiti, until they were scolded through the window to go back inside. She looked up to the second floor, to that familiar window. A FOR RENT sign hung in one underneath it. Camila took down the phone number. She knew it was unlikely that she could afford a room there, but she wanted to be back in that building, where they would put Judy Torres on the record player and dance.

We walked around the corner, past the bodega where her grandparents would send her out to buy sandwiches, across 111th Street from Flushing Meadows. Just over fifty years earlier, the World's Fair had assembled there on the theme of "Peace Through Understanding." The Italian American stronghold of Corona had already given way to an influx of Dominicans by the time the fair's twelve-story-high steel Unisphere was installed. When Camila was young, she'd play in the fountain that still spouted under its decaying hulk. Those were the good times, she said, when her dad would hold court at Christmas parties in the restaurant that hovered high above the park on concrete pillars, when everyone knew she was his daughter.

As the door squeaked open and we entered the salon, the three women hunched over feet at pedicure chairs, all in polyester blouses and liquid eyeliner, turned to look.

"Camila!"

It was a homecoming every time. She walked to the back of the tiny shop to lean down and kiss them all on both cheeks. Then she selected a Tiffany-blue polish from the wall rack and settled in at a manicure table with the bagel she'd brought in a paper bag. While Camila ate, she joined the conversation about a guy who had grown up in the neighborhood and was having a baby with a woman who wasn't his wife. Everyone in the salon had something to say about it; gossip and acetone filled the air.

Flaca, Mauricio's favorite, was finally ready for her. Camila pulled off her boots, rolled up her jeans, and hoisted herself over the bubbling pool of water into the pedicure chair. Sweeping her glossy bangs from her face, Flaca examined Camila's toes.

"I forgot you've got the same feet as your father," she said.

"Alonso has them, too," Camila told Flaca proudly. She turned to the customer sitting in the chair beside her. "Flaca gives the best foot massages—my dad won't let anyone else touch his feet," she declared. She turned back to Flaca. "Have you seen him?"

"Not in a while," Flaca said, sweeping polish remover across Camila's toenails. "Maybe today?"

We lingered at the salon for two hours. Camila wanted to make sure the polish was dry, she insisted, with an eye trained on the door.

4

CHRISTMASTIME

Christmas was inescapable in New York, every shop window trading in unrealistic expectations. Walking out of the Sisters of Life convent on the Upper East Side, where she was picking up a gift bag of holiday donations, Camila paused at the window of Pottery Barn Kids and admired the display. "Baby's First Christmas" stockings hung from a fake fireplace mantel; elaborate bassinets were garishly stuffed with holiday-themed bedding. Alonso wouldn't know what he didn't have this year, she said, but she deserved a present for herself, something one of a kind, to celebrate this year in which she had become a mother. It would cost a lot more than a manicure, but it would last forever.

One evening when Camila was eighteen, she had walked into a tattoo parlor in Little Italy, sat down in the chair, and asked for a *C* in blue on the inside of her arm. She was alone at the time and completely sober. It was her first tattoo. Her second was a heart with Pedro's nickname scrawled inside it, the one she'd once told me was her grandfather's name. Her father's upper arms were covered with half sleeves. She wanted a half sleeve, too. On her phone, she'd saved a picture of a tattoo she loved, a skeleton locked in an embrace with a woman staring intensely into his eye sockets. Even though he can't feel or show emotion, even though it seems like he's dead, she still loves him and he's still there with her, she told me, explaining why it resonated with her, why she'd chosen it months ago. But now she had something saved on her phone that suited a mother better, she said: a picture of Alonso, which I'd taken the day of the trip to the Metropolitan Museum. There was a guy in Washington Heights who went by the name of Rotten Apple. She'd seen his tattooing on Instagram. He might be expensive, she said, but he was good.

The tattoo parlor was down a tiny spiral staircase in the back of a barbershop, in a room carved from the bedrock of Manhattan, literally blasted from the stone hill under its ground floor, like a medieval cave. The walls were painted a glossy red and hung with *Scarface* posters and a flat-screen television. Camila arrived as Rotten Apple was switching out his *Reservoir Dogs* DVD for *Inglourious Basterds*. Spanish hip-hop thumped from an iPod speaker. She took a seat in his single chair. Showing him the picture of Alonso on her phone, she explained she wanted her son's face encircled in elaborate scrollwork that incorporated his name at the bottom, from just below her shoulder down to near her elbow. As Rotten Apple got to work, Camila felt nervous and distracted herself by scrolling through pictures of Kevin on Facebook with her free hand. She clicked on a video of him dancing at the gym. Her arm was bleeding from the needle, but she didn't wince at the pain. She just scowled at Kevin's pixilated face and wondered aloud what he was doing for Christmas.

Rotten Apple made conversation, asking Camila about her holiday plans. She'd met a woman about her mom's age at the supermarket, who'd clucked over Alonso and showed off pictures of her grandchildren. The woman had asked what Camila was doing for Christmas Eve. When Camila admitted she didn't have anywhere to go, the woman invited her for dinner with her family. She didn't tell Rotten Apple any of this; she just said she'd be with family. An hour or two passed. Then Rotten Apple said he was done. With mock gallantry, he offered her a hand to guide her out of the chair and over to the full-length mirror leaning against a wall. Camila rotated her arm slowly in one direction, then the other. It looked exactly like Alonso. His wide eyes seemed to glint on her skin.

"It's perfect," she said.

He told her it would be a total of $650.

That was more than she'd expected. Much more. She didn't care, she told me. Even though she had nothing, she said, she'd given herself something she could keep until she died.

At the shelter on Fourth Avenue, we were having a holiday party, and Camila wanted to come. It had only been five weeks since she moved out, but she said it felt like much longer. She hadn't seen Irina, and she wanted to celebrate; she'd just made it through exams and deserved to kick off winter break with a party, she said. I warned her it wasn't going to be much of a party, just donated gifts and takeout. Rose and the rest of the staff didn't even pretend they might stick around after regular office hours. When Rose learned that Camila would be attending, she sent me an email with a very clear message: Camila would be welcome, but she would not receive any of the donations.

The residents sat silent and passive, holding tight to their babies, who were all spending their first Christmases in a homeless shelter. Each resident accepted a paper plate of tacos and balanced it on a knee, trying to manage a plate and a baby, barely touching the food. Only Irina was vocal, trying to lift the mood in the room, despite a bad cold, while she awaited Camila's late arrival. Camila finally appeared and took a seat next to Irina on the couch. She lowered Alonso onto the floor next to Dima, who giggled and batted at his familiar face. Coolly, Camila surveyed the room, her eyes darting to the large gift bags stuffed with baby clothes at each woman's feet. She had her own apartment now, she told the room, with a Christmas tree. Until she enrolled at John Jay next year, she was in school full-time at the Justice Academy at Kingsborough. Alonso was in a great daycare, right across the street. She was looking forward to spending the holidays with family.

"You're such an inspiration," Irina said brightly.

None of the other women said a word, until one of them declared it was eight o'clock, the time the meeting ended. The residents began gathering up their gift bags and untouched food to bring upstairs. Camila said she had to leave. She didn't belong here anymore, she whispered to me, not that she ever did, she said. She didn't know these people. She thought it would be something to return to, but it wasn't. Before she left, she asked who had her old room. It was still vacant.

Camila and Alonso woke up on Christmas morning in the housing projects just south of Houston Street on the Lower East Side, a short walk up Eldridge Street from Geraldine's place. The woman Camila had met at the supermarket lived there—Grandma Harriet, Camila now called her. The night before, they'd eaten chicken and rice and watched Martin Lawrence in *Blue Streak*. Grandma Harriet had insisted Camila and Alonso stay over. Jovanka and Aaron were away visiting family in Pennsylvania, and she knew it would be lonely there, so she spent the night. That morning, she quietly sang "Feliz Navidad" to Alonso when he woke, careful not to disturb Grandma Harriet's family. Once they'd all risen for the day, Camila said her thank-yous and goodbyes and headed back to the Bronx to meet me.

Walking up Sherman Avenue, Camila tried to shut out the chaos of the block. A minivan blasted salsa at top volume through open doors. A crew of guys leaned against the hood, sucking liquor through straws out of foam cups. They silently watched Camila push the stroller past them, eyes tracking her ass like snipers. Upstairs, outside the apartment door, the hallway reeked of pungent weed. It smelled like Dreadhead's stock, Camila said. He was the dealer in the huddle of guys who hung outside, day and night. The door that opened to the rooftop was ajar. She looked anxious until she locked the apartment door behind her.

The unlit tree stood in the corner, Jovanka's laundry on the line next to it the only holiday garland. As always, the kitchen was a mess. Uncooked rice spilled over the floor like a colony of maggots.

Dishes crusted with beans, blackened tin saucepans, plastic souvenir cups from Medieval Times, filled the sink. Camila's spine drooped as she shuffled to her room. But then Mauricio texted to say she could come over for Christmas that evening. His invitation appeared to change her very body chemistry. Her muscles loosened; a glow replaced her pallor.

We opened presents. I'd bought her a bottle of perfume and Alonso a snowsuit. I knew she'd asked her dad for one, but I couldn't stand watching Alonso shiver in his stroller, and I didn't anticipate Mauricio would come through. Camila kissed my cheek in thanks and said that maybe he'd have two snowsuits now. Alonso slept for hours while Camila entertained herself by putting on makeup and a lace dress. Once he woke up, she dressed him for the holiday. All new clothes, nothing that smelled like the skin and sweat of strangers. Camila took selfies of the two of them reflected in the mirror.

She told me she couldn't wait to put her head on her dad's shoulder and veg out in front of the TV, just like they used to. He wasn't going to believe how much Alonso looked like him, she said, a little Mauricio. She told me about the time he took her shopping for a gold bracelet for Christmas. None of her siblings had a father who would ever do that, she added.

Much later that night, she texted me to say that the thought that she had been so excited to see her father now mortified her. There had been no coat for Alonso. No sense of reconnection with her dad. It had felt, from the moment she got there, like he was waiting for her to leave. When she finally got ready to go at midnight, she had to ask him to help carry the stroller downstairs. He wouldn't even walk her to the subway, much less drive her home. It took her more than two hours to get back to the Bronx. When would she learn? she wondered.

She hadn't mentioned Geraldine once all day. I asked her when she'd last spoken to her mother on Christmas. Camila said she had to think about it for a moment. Then she said the last time was ten years ago, when she was twelve years old.

At least Jeremiah had reached out on Facebook: *Merry Xmas to you and Alonso,* he wrote. He said he wanted to see the baby. Camila suggested Tuesday, now that she was on winter break. She didn't know what she'd do with all that time and no one to see. She'd already gotten her nails done and organized her room. On Monday, she texted to ask what plan they should make for Tuesday. He didn't write back.

For a week, she and Alonso mainly slept and stared at the laptop screen, streaming every episode of *Friends*. They barely left the room for her whole winter break.

Soon after the new year, I sold the book proposal.

I couldn't tell if Camila was excited or not. She wasn't expressing much of anything anymore.

5

THE LOTTERY

The subway to Kingsborough ran under a vast new apartment development rising in Downtown Brooklyn at the mouth of Flatbush Avenue. The building had just listed its affordable units. For a so-called "affordable" studio, an applicant would have to prove a minimum take-home of $57,000 a year. Camila was applying for two-bedrooms; she wasn't going to raise her son in the same room with her, she said. For a so-called affordable apartment that size, she'd need to make $142,000 after taxes—almost three times the national-average household income. This wasn't just the case on the rezoned blocks just across the bridge, but in all the new buildings that had turned the entire city into a giant development site. Even way out in Flatbush, near the Church Avenue stop, which Camila considered "the hood," a building that no one would consider to be luxury was renting $2,200 "affordable" one-bedrooms to families making $125,000 a year.

What the city deemed accessible was prohibitive to those who needed it most. While Camila searched for housing that year, the city saw construction of 6,844 new units that were categorized "affordable." Though there was a city bureau that oversaw affordable housing, each building with approved apartments had its own lottery.

Millions of New Yorkers were competing for those subsidized units, more than seven hundred households filing applications for each one.

The units were the tax for the new Gilded Age of luxury construction, a few pennies for a kingdom. In exchange for keeping 20 to 30 percent of a building below market rate, taxes were frozen at a rate based on the lot's value before a luxury residence was built. An empty lot, a foreclosed construction site, a teardown block of tenements—all would be taxed as though the rust and weeds remained, instead of the marble lobbies and floor-to-ceiling skyline views to come. As long as 20 to 30 percent of the units stayed below market, those tax breaks would remain in place for thirty-five years. As a result, the city lost $1.4 billion in property taxes that year alone, and it was estimated that these tax abatements would cost the city $10 billion more over the next ten years. All for apartments that Camila, and most everyone she'd ever known, couldn't afford to rent. That was often the case even if they doubled up on their applications, forging makeshift households.

A year before, when she was dating Jeremiah, Camila had submitted dozens of applications to affordable-housing lotteries. During the weeks they were together, she'd filled out the forms with Jeremiah's income as well as her own. He had the job at the dentist's office. She had a job at a pharmacy. She hadn't gone up to visit Kevin yet or soured completely on Jeremiah, and she had no idea she was about to get pregnant; she just knew she'd have a better chance at an affordable unit with two incomes instead of one. Who knew what might happen between them, she'd thought. Maybe they'd be together. If not, she figured, she could just drop him from the application. Maybe there'd be a better man to list on her forms by then. Maybe it would even be Kevin. Though it was unlikely she'd have the income to qualify for an affordable unit, she'd continued to apply for the lotteries—so many in the past few months alone, she'd forgotten she ever listed Jeremiah on an application.

January trudged into February. Subway miles logged, slush puddles skirted, classes attended, bottles fed, applications filed. The Bronx to Brooklyn, Brooklyn to the Bronx, with regular stops to check her mail on Thirty-fourth Street.

And then, one frigid afternoon, in the sterile glare of the post office, she found an envelope in her box. They'd been chosen.

A two-bedroom in Harlem, for $850. A rent she could afford if she split it with someone with steady money. The only problem was that she refused to live with the other person she'd listed on the application, Jeremiah. That, and her income was less now than it was when she'd applied, even with work-study included.

Camila thought that her brother Michael's salary from his doorman job could make up for it. Together, they could make it work. And if it didn't, she schemed, then Irina could take his room. Irina's time was running out at the shelter, and she'd been texting Camila that she was scared about not having a place to go. When I'd seen Irina the week before, she told me that her only plan was to go into the city shelter system and hope that someone there would help her find housing. She couldn't seem to gather the energy or initiative to put another plan in place. Having seen Camila and Sherice struggle to find affordable housing, she figured she'd skip those steps and jump right to the end point she'd predicted for herself anyway: exhausted, hopeless, and relying on the rusted and overburdened machinery of the city system. Camila scorned Irina's lack of motivation. But if she needed a roommate, she at least knew Irina would be a benevolent one, and she did miss her company across the hall.

Camila carried in her head the birth dates and Social Security numbers of every member of her disconnected family. She submitted Michael's requisite information and typed up a formal letter to the city bureau, asking permission to change her co-applicant. *I am a single mother living in the shelter system for over a year and I really need this housing. I beg you as a mother.* At school, she printed and faxed it, then made a copy and sent it in the mail. She'd have a home with the other person who had inherited her father's charm and smarts, and Alonso would have a man around, she said. They'd have family. Finally, she told me, everything was going to be okay.

Michael was currently sharing a room with his young siblings and an infestation of cockroaches at his mother's place in the Far Rockaway projects. Camila had not met her brother until she was eight. One afternoon, her father picked her up in whatever sports car he was driving that year. A boy her age was sitting in the back seat. She slid into the passenger seat and Mauricio started driving.

"That's your brother," her father said after a while, staring through the windshield.

No one spoke. They went to the movies.

Later, Camila heard the story about how her mother had learned that Mauricio got another girl pregnant. When Dorcas gave birth to Michael soon after Geraldine gave birth to Camila, Mauricio didn't say a word about it to anyone. Then, several months later, Geraldine heard a knock on the door. There stood a girl she recognized from the neighborhood, looking unusually gaunt and depressed, with dark circles under her eyes. She was holding a baby.

"Mauricio is my man," the girl said. "This is his son."

Geraldine studied the baby's eyes. They looked like her new daughter's eyes. She nodded.

Twenty-two years later, Michael still had his father's eyes. Of all her siblings, Camila was especially partial to him. Michael had dropped out of high school, but he got it together to get his GED. He hadn't gotten anyone pregnant yet. When he went to get his first tattoo, he chose a Keith Haring barking dog on a forearm. He was smart, like she was, she said. And Michael knew the pain of being rejected by their father, perhaps even more than Camila did. For years he'd reached out to Mauricio, yearning for contact, asking to have a relationship. Every time, Mauricio simply blew him off. Camila told me Michael used to say to Dorcas, "Dad wanted you to get an abortion. Why did you have me? Why am I even alive?" Camila had never asked Geraldine that question.

Camila told me she had to start packing and give notice to Jovanka. It was early February. She could tell her next week, and that would give her time to find a new tenant for March. Camila wondered how she should tell them she was moving out. She called the rental office to confirm that they had received her letter.

She was giddy when she picked up Alonso at daycare, scooping him up, covering his cheeks and neck in loud kisses, coaxing his giggles. "Valentine's Day is coming, Alonso! Would you be my Valentine?" she said.

In their room, on the floor, they ate cold leftover mangú. Fried salami, cheese, and plantains coagulated over stiff pellets of white rice. She put him down to sleep on her bed, lay beside him, and didn't mind, for once, the sound of Jovanka yelling at Aaron on the other side of the wall. She needed to get out of there. Now she thought she could. Such definitiveness may have seemed self-delusional, considering her abusive relationship with bureaucracy, plus the punishing bait and switch of the entire subsidized system. But her willful positivity had been armor and weapon alike as she'd successfully fought her way into courtrooms and classrooms. Maybe she wasn't kidding herself after all.

6

DARIO

At daycare pickup most days, Camila had taken to lingering in the kitchen, trading complaints and consolations, talking about how fed up she was living with Jovanka and Aaron. When Maria heard that a room was available in an apartment upstairs from the daycare, she suggested Camila have a look in case the Harlem place took a little while to come through. Camila had been calling three times a day to see if the housing officer had accepted her application change; finally someone had told her to check for a letter in the mail. It was Presidents' Day break anyway, so she had time to look at an apartment. All she was planning to do that week was go down to the post office on Thirty-fourth Street every day and study for a customs and border-patrol exam that was coming up, but she wasn't that worried about it; she was used to acing tests.

Camila got Alonso situated for the day, exchanged a little gossip in the kitchen, went up to the apartment number Maria had given her, and knocked on the door. A sleepy-looking guy opened it. He was her age and her complexion, tall and slim with a thin mustache drawing a straight line over his upper lip. He smiled and asked her how her baby was doing. Camila realized they'd seen each other before, from time to time on the block or walking into the building, though they'd never spoken. She told him she'd heard about a room. He said he'd be happy to introduce Camila to his landlord, not that he could recommend him. His own room was only slightly larger than a twin bed, just big enough to fit a small chair and a mousetrap. The heat didn't work. The roaches seemed immortal, uncontainable. The landlord entered his room without permission all the time, was constantly threatening to throw everyone out. He was looking for a new place, too, he said, but he'd seen worse.

Dario was his name. He was half Dominican, half Puerto Rican, one of six siblings born to a severely bipolar mother. Like Camila, he hadn't talked to his mother in a while; she was a drug addict, he said. Like Camila, he'd been in foster care, but for much longer. The first home was really bad. Savage beatings, constant fear; he'd been the one the foster mother took everything out on. His father died soon after Dario was placed in that home, and he never got to say goodbye. A family had adopted his sisters, and it seemed he'd lost them forever. But he still had his second foster mom. They were close; she'd helped him get this place—she knew the landlord. Camila learned all this very quickly. Dario was a talker. But there was a calm to him she responded to, she told me, a seriousness.

Before Dario even asked for Camila's number, he said to her, "There's something about you. I can see myself with you."

He took Camila to meet the landlord. It was a short meeting.

"I might have a room," the landlord told Camila. "Seven hundred a month plus a broker's fee and first and last month's rent. You've got to make thirty thousand a year to rent from me. Who is it for?"

"It's for me and my son."

"You got a kid? I don't want to rent to someone with a kid." He sized her up. "Or anyone on welfare."

That night she couldn't stand listening to Jovanka and Aaron fight anymore. Camila stayed in Woodhaven with her cousins. She brought them her extra food stamps in exchange for the night. Maybe tomorrow night she'd stay with Dario, she texted me.

Across the street from the post office was the pizza place she used to go to with her friends in high school. Camila bought two slices and a Coke for five bucks. Sitting at the counter, she informed me she had a boyfriend.

The night before, she and Alonso had spent the night with Dario in his twin bed. They kept each other warm while she did her best to ignore the cockroaches scuttling up the wall. In the morning, the landlord had banged on the door, yelling, "This isn't a hotel." They ignored him.

Dario told her he wanted to be with her the moment he saw her, but he didn't want to scare her away. She said he was so polite he didn't even want to kiss her when they woke up because he hadn't brushed his teeth. She told him to kiss her anyway. He said he had a wifey now. And he wanted them to live together.

Girlish and squealing, she pulled out her phone to show me selfies she'd taken of the three of them lying in the little bed. They were going to do laundry together tonight with Alonso, and Dario would come see her room, she said. Maybe he'd like it there. Maybe they'd stay at Jovanka's if the Harlem place took time to resolve. If he paid half the rent on the room, she could afford to stay there awhile longer.

Camila crossed the street to see if the letter from the management company had arrived. Nothing in her mailbox. Camila called the management company and spoke to an assistant, who clearly knew her voice by now. She called at least once a day.

"Check tomorrow," the assistant said.

It didn't frustrate her like it usually did.

Camila texted me that she wanted to go to a museum, maybe the Guggenheim, where she'd never been. I had a card the city gave families of public school kindergartners—covered in Halloween stickers to obscure the long-past expiration date—which let us into most museums for free.

On the Upper East Side, Camila waited for the walk light at Park Avenue beside a nanny escorting twins in matching navy wool princess coats. She turned down Eighty-eighth Street, skirting a stack of *Hamptons* magazines wrapped in twine. The majestic concrete curve of the museum peeked from Fifth Avenue. Inside, she gazed up at the swirling nautilus above her. She found the elevator and rode it to the top of the rotunda.

Down the gallery ramp, a video screen lit up a wall: *The Way Things Go* showed a kinetic chain of everyday objects exploding, tipping, spilling, and setting the next thing off, in a constant and precise causal flow. "It's hilarious," she whispered, giggling audibly at a firecracker hissing, a balloon floating. Everyone else was silent in their somber clothing, their serious faces. The video reminded her of her life, she said. One thing led to the next; everything had to line up for it to work, even if half were on fire.

The next morning, a frosting of new snow shimmered outside her window. As soon as she stepped outside she realized that her ski cap and University of Buffalo sweatshirt wouldn't keep her warm enough, but there was no time to go upstairs. Camila's broken headphones—acid-green Beats she'd gotten on Black Friday a few years back—had been working as earmuffs for the past month. They'd have to work harder today. She made it to the test center in Queens just in time to take her border-patrol exam. Four hours later, she was done. And proud. That night she'd celebrate with Dario. He said he'd take her to MoMA soon. Alonso had been calling him "Dada." People on the subway made space for them to sit together, assuming they were a family.

There was plenty to recommend Dario. He was clever. He played the cello. He said he loved her. He was willing to split her rent. Camila had relaxed in his presence like I hadn't seen her with a man before.

But he was also punishing, inventing reasons to berate her: yelling at her when he thought she was checking out men on the street, lambasting her for a pimple on her cheek, criticizing the way she walked. He admitted he was tough, he was bipolar, he was intimidated by her. She'd begun to strain against the effort of keeping her mouth shut.

Then, a few weeks after they'd started dating, Dario was late for their dinner date at a Dominican place near Sherman Avenue. She bided her time, entertaining Alonso at the table. When Dario finally showed, he was scowling, twitchy.

"I want to ask you a question," he said as soon as he sat down. "I know it's already been done, but why did you have a kid? Why would you do that to your life?"

He was picking a fight. Camila was no stranger to people's sudden surges of aggression—Lord knew she grew up expecting a lunge with a verbal knife at any moment. But this line of questioning caught her off guard. "Excuse me?" she asked, incredulous.

"And it's not like you even play with him. You should be paying attention to him." He was really going for it.

"Really? While I'm doing my homework? While I'm trying to shower? While I'm in school?" She began fully armoring herself. "What do you know about being a single parent?"

"I just don't know why you had him," he said.

Just last weekend, at Jovanka's birthday, Dario had been bragging that Alonso was his son, that he was a proud father who was going to raise him right. And that week, when Alonso was sick with the stomach flu, Dario woke with him, cleaned up his vomit, soothed him back to sleep, urging Camila to get her rest, that he was a parent now, too. He joined them at the pediatrician's office. But he couldn't keep it up, not even for a month.

"And another thing I don't like: the way you talk about your parents. You shouldn't say anything bad about them. It's disrespectful. You're lucky to have a dad. My dad is dead."

The waiter came to take their order. Camila felt too sickened to eat, despite the fact that she'd been hungry all day. She ordered anyway.

"And you don't even know about my goals," Dario said once the waiter turned away. "What do you think my goals are?"

"Trading?" She suddenly realized she was mocking him, that

she'd never believed in him. Furthermore, she'd lent him two hundred bucks to start a day-trading business. Now she knew what she'd suspected, that he'd blown it on menthols and weed, that the bottle he paid for at Jovanka's birthday came from her wallet, not his.

"No." He dismissed her with a wave. "That's just a hobby. Engineering," he said definitively, shaking his head, like she should know better.

This was too much.

He was just like any other guy, any other possibility. Men and housing applications—why did she even bother.

Camila was silent. They sat there for a minute, staring at each other.

"You know, Dario, this isn't working out." He reached over the table for her hand. She shook her head. "You can't take my hand anymore. You're not my man."

Camila sat while Dario ate and then asked to wrap up her food to go. They walked back to where their buildings faced each other on Sherman Avenue.

"Do you need help with the stroller?" Dario asked. Then he grinned at her. "Can I take you upstairs?"

"Nah, I got this," Camila said. "Take care."

She walked into the building without looking back, confident in how practiced she'd become in shutting the door on people she thought she could love, knowing she'd never speak to him again.

7

THE LETTER

That week, on Fourth Avenue, Irina's dark circles had deepened into navy blue, her skin yellowed gray. She'd had pneumonia for a month already. But that wasn't the worst of it. Once she hugged me hello, she lay Dima in a bouncer and went to fetch a sheaf of papers, which she handed to me in disgust. "They took away my welfare," she said.

The work-placement office had connected her with a job as a home-healthcare aide, making just over $15,000 a year. But the number of hours she'd worked in that pay period had earned her ten dollars more than welfare would permit. No matter that it was the system that had made the placement; it was the system that was also going to withhold her public assistance—half of her income. It took me a solid half hour of combing the documents, which were as dizzying and nonsensical as any I'd seen, to arrive at this realization. Irina's depression cleared the way for panic; she began to quietly hyperventilate. A new resident stared at her from across the room.

Irina tried to talk through her heaves. She said her doctor had told her she needed to stay home from work during those two weeks so she could start to recover, but she knew if she did, she'd lose her job. She was worried about infecting the woman she was caring for, but she felt she had no choice. Now she couldn't go back to work at all, since she'd lost her childcare voucher along with her welfare. It would be nearing spring before her lungs cleared.

She texted Camila, asking her what she should do. Camila said that she'd gotten an apartment in the housing lottery. They could be roommates. The boys could grow up together. Everything was going to be okay. She was just waiting on some paperwork.

Camila opened her post office box. Inside was a white envelope. She tore it open.

Bad news. The letter was from the Department of Housing Preservation and Development, which oversaw all affordable housing for the city. Camila pulled out her phone on the spot and called the number on the letter. After being passed from office to office, she was told the same thing that the letter said: Names on the lease must be the same as the names on the original application. The only exceptions are for death or divorce. And for either, there needs to be documentation. Jeremiah's name would remain on the application, and unless she signed the lease with him, she'd have to forfeit the apartment.

Most kids Camila knew didn't grow up with both parents in the same home, much less married. In fact, three-quarters of children who were raised poor didn't have married parents. This is how affordable housing was going to be regulated? she demanded, furious, after she'd hung up the phone. People couldn't break up unless they were married? You'd apply and wait for a year—or two, or more—for your application to be selected, and if any aspect of your family formation had shifted in that time, forget it? The only way your relationship could change, if you were poor, was to have the guy die on you? And they couldn't have told her this policy one of the fifty-odd times she'd called the office over the past month? During which she'd traveled to her post office box six days a week?

She was hungry. The day before, she had half an egg-and-bacon sandwich on the way to school and the other half for dinner after

Alonso fell asleep at nine-thirty. She hadn't eaten since then. There'd be Wi-Fi at Panera. She got a sandwich and opened her laptop to pull up affordable-housing sites, looking for new listings anywhere she'd be eligible. Slowly, she ate half the sandwich, saving the other half for the next day. When she was done eating, she closed her laptop. There was nowhere she could apply to live. Not with her income. Not even with the addition of Michael's. Camila nodded solemnly for a moment and then wiped her mouth daintily with a paper napkin.

I watched her retreat into her head, suspended in the dark awareness of how utterly alone she'd become. Securing a home was something bigger than I could solve by handing her a roll of cash. Securing a home was a question of social policy, of economic structure. Camila understood this. She knew it wasn't her fault, that it was a vast systemic issue, not a matter of individual failure. And that made it all the more hopeless.

8

CLOSED DOORS

What was she doing, trusting the system, she asked herself, focusing on a guy, wasting her time? She knew better. Instead of spending those weeks calling and calling like a fool, taking the subway to Thirty-fourth Street, and thinking she might have a man, a family, a home, she should have stayed in crisis mode. She should have been treating every week like an emergency. Anytime she didn't, it became one anyway.

Over the next weeks, she talked increasingly about missing Pedro. About how he would have treated her through this year, while she was pregnant, as a new mother. He'd have made sure there was a roof over her head. She would dreamily muse on the subway about what life would have been like if she'd stayed with him, if she'd kept her mouth shut. Respect had always been the most important thing to her, but taking a stand for it had become a luxury she couldn't afford, like so many others. At least not until she had a stable home for herself and Alonso. Respect had dropped below housing in her hierarchy of needs.

Camila had gone to The Door, an organization in SoHo, for counseling help after she moved back to New York with Pedro, when their brief marriage turned from bleak to menacing, when she was feeling desperate and afraid. She was feeling that way now, too, but she needed something more than counseling; she didn't have time for that, she said dismissively. Her entire focus needed to be trained on housing now. She thought the organization in SoHo had dorms for kids who had no families; she'd known people who'd been helped by them in the past—even Dario had been. Surely they'd help her, as well.

Her pilled gray sweatpants and oversized navy hoodie looked fine up in the Bronx, but downtown she became self-conscious, hiding her chipped manicure in her pockets as she turned onto Sullivan Street. People had queued up around the block for fifteen-dollar milkshakes that had become a recent food trend on Instagram. Overhead, construction was nearing completion on a new building, where a triplex was currently on the market for $45 million. Kanye West and Kim Kardashian would tour it with a realtor later that spring. Across Sixth Avenue and behind a door was a different demographic, a population of people who looked like Camila. A white guy in a newsboy cap pulled up her file in the system and printed out an ID with a picture from two years ago. She looked younger by a decade.

Camila disappeared into the office of a housing coordinator. Several minutes later she returned, her face gray, her eyes glazed. Because she had a kid, she was ineligible for any of their housing programs. Not unless she had mental illness, she said; then they would put her in a home for the emotionally disturbed.

"She just referred me to PATH." Her voice broke. "I don't know what I'm going to do."

Tears rolled in two paths down her cheeks. It was the first time I'd seen her cry and the first time I'd seen her lose her composure in public. Dazed, she pushed open the door to Sixth Avenue. I ducked to the side of a NO PARKING sign to make way for a woman in huge sunglasses, pushing her pug in a dog stroller.

"Don't split the pole! You split the pole!" Camila yelled. I had no idea what she was talking about. "You can't let the pole come between you and the person you're walking with in the sidewalk! It's supposed to give your family bad luck!" she frantically explained.

She seemed stunned at how rattled she felt, how hopeless. She tried to calm down. "I figure my family is just me and Alonso, and we can't have any more bad luck," she murmured.

Though it was unseasonably warm, she was shivering in the sunshine. I led us into a café and bought her a cup of coffee, sweet with cream and sugar. We sat in the window. After we finished, Camila noticed a slate-blue scarf abandoned on the street outside. She snatched it up, and looped it around her neck, European style. Her face began to regain its color, but she was silent on the subway back to the Bronx.

Another week, another attempt at getting into a private shelter, perhaps the last one. Camila had heard that the Henry Street Settlement on the Lower East Side had a private shelter that took in homeless mothers. A young nurse named Lillian Wald had established the settlement in a line of three Federal-style row houses to address the squalid conditions that defined Lower East Side living at the end of the nineteenth century; its services were still dearly required. Camila peered skeptically at its historic entryway, just blocks from her mother's place in the projects. This was no shelter.

Inside, her doubt was confirmed by dark antique furniture and the green-glazed tiles of a fireplace. The air had the dry, slightly musty smell of a country inn. She cautiously approached the reception desk. Despite her protestations, she was told to go to Helen's House, a place for battered women, down the street. She slunk back through the door. On the sidewalk outside stood a tall and broad black man in a black rabbit coat, leather pants, and alligator boots, his shaved head as shiny as his gold chains. He didn't notice the skinny girl with the ashen face looking down at a square of white paper. She muttered that she'd become invisible even to pimps. For a moment, she began to wonder aloud if she should think about a man who would give her a place to live in exchange— She didn't finish the thought. She couldn't, she said.

Helen's House was what Camila had been expecting. Instead of a preserved Georgian entrance, thick glass separated visitors from the industrial tiling and metal-rod railings inside the architecture of 1990s—not 1890s—social welfare. Camila's body relaxed a bit in the more familiar environment. She rang the buzzer. After a few minutes, a stout Latina in a white shirt and jeans came to the door.

"I'm a single mother looking for housing," Camila told her.

The woman opened the door about a foot and leaned her head and a shoulder out to hand Camila another square of white paper. The address she'd scrawled on it had been suggested to Camila many times before: the PATH intake center. Camila cowered as she read it. She folded the paper in half, slid it into her pocket, and shook her head. "That's not what I'm here for," she said meekly.

"You need to go to PATH in the Bronx. We don't take people off the street." The woman was about Camila's age but had the firmness of a warden.

"I've been to PATH," Camila said. "I was pregnant. I had to go to a shelter in New Jersey."

"Well, if you had stayed, they would have found you housing once you had the baby. They want them out of the shelters. Too many people and chemicals, not safe for babies. You missed your chance."

Camila just stared at the floor. She'd heard it all before but never when she felt this desperate. She thanked the woman and fled from the doorway, her head erect, striding at top speed past the pimp, past the historic row houses. She raced through the neighborhood she used to feel so comfortable in, where she'd rented her first room, where she'd gotten her own job at the supermarket around the corner. Suddenly these places felt as barred to her as her own mother's apartment, she said. Or a shelter for desperate women, she added. She was furious at the city. She needed to get out of here, she said.

As she sped past bodegas and boutiques, she indulged self-lacerating thoughts, doubts, remorse—all about Pedro. She just wanted him back, she told me. He would have found a way out of this situation for her. He would have never let her go back to a shelter. Not that there were any shelters she could even go to now, not without dropping out of school to sit in the PATH waiting room and end up God knew where. He'd told her that if she left him, she'd never find anyone like him again. He was right, she said. She used to never permit herself to think this way; she used to never look back. She said she didn't know herself anymore, this person whose thoughts were now constantly threaded with regret.

Camila stood before Pedro in a sterile-looking hallway. He was wearing a hospital gown. She stared deep into his dark eyes. Without looking away, she reached into her body and pulled out her intestines. She felt no pain, no emptiness. Solemnly and silently, she offered him the tangle of her organs. He grasped her shoulders and pulled her in for a deep kiss. She felt like she was soaring, golden and glowing.

Her alarm returned her suddenly to her bed and to the belief that she never should have left him, if only to have avoided this fate.

Two weeks into the new quarter and Camila was already exhausted. Two weeks of putting Alonso to bed in his bouncer at eight o'clock, taking a nap, waking to feed him two hours later, and putting him back to sleep in her bed, before she could sit down at her desk and do her homework. At school that morning, Camila had heard the dean's list for the second quarter was hanging on the wall outside the provost's closed office door. She walked by to check it out. There, listed right at the top, was her name. She was too tired to feel achievement.

9

MEN

The date for the next hearing at family court finally arrived. As she signed in, Camila scanned the waiting room for Jeremiah's braids. She noticed his head peeking out from a bench where he was slouched, his eyes closed.

"You tired?" she asked.

Startled, he straightened to attention, rubbing a sloe eye with a knuckle. They made small talk at first, about the subway, tourists, the neutral things New Yorkers riff about. Wary but warming up, they began to joke around, teasing each other about how young she was and about how old he was. That intimacy broached, they caught up about friends in common, friends who had known them as a couple. He was witty. She couldn't help but flirt a little, pushing back, giving him a hard time. He didn't look at her, though; he seemed scared to. They reminisced about the sweet sixteen she'd taken him to, an argument they'd had. Then they went quiet.

"Alonso's going to be nine months on Friday," she said, introducing a topic—a name—yet unsaid. "He's a grown man. He's talking a lot."

"A grown man," Jeremiah said soberly, studying the floor.

"He's starting to smell in his armpits." Camila grinned.

"For real?" Jeremiah asked.

"I'm joking! His feet do smell, though. He's sweaty."

"I sweat a lot. Especially under my arms. If he has that, I'm sorry." He smiled but still didn't look at her.

"Even in the cold, he'll be sweating."

"Yeah, I know. Like me."

"*Alvarez! Cole!*" The bailiff yelled their names.

A heavyset, ruddy-faced magistrate in a wide purple satin tie and lavender striped shirt sat on a raised platform in front of rows of courtroom benches. After gruffly confirming their names and addresses, he got down to business.

"Miss, who do you say is the father of the child?"

"Jeremiah Cole." I could tell she hated saying it, despite her slight defrosting in the waiting room. Chitchatting was one thing; parenting was another.

"Mr. Cole, do you work?" growled the magistrate, with plain disdain.

"Yes," he said.

"What do you do?" he growled louder. The contempt in his voice clearly stunned even Camila.

"I work at a restaurant."

"What do you do there?" He raised his voice again.

"Everything."

"Mr. Cole! I'm asking you a simple question!" Now he was yelling. "What do you do at the restaurant? Do you serve customers? Do you bus tables? Do you wash dishes?"

"Yes," Jeremiah said quietly.

"Where do you do this?" the magistrate bellowed.

"At a restaurant."

"Mr. Cole! *What restaurant do you work at?*"

"Fridays," Jeremiah whispered.

"Do you contest that you are the father?"

"I want a DNA test," Jeremiah said, afraid to look up at the magistrate.

The magistrate, his face flushed crimson, approved the DNA test. He scheduled another hearing for when the results would be due, over a month away. It seemed the process was endless, getting nowhere. All the days of school Camila had missed, not to mention Alonso's first year passing by without a cent of child support. The warmth she'd briefly felt toward Jeremiah vanished; her suspicions fully restored themselves. Once again, fury simmered under practiced aloofness. The longer this was drawn out, the longer she was responsible for caring for Alonso entirely on her own. Every bottle she prepared, every diaper she changed, every night alone in her room trying to get him to sleep, every early morning, every daycare drop-off and pickup. As though she had conceived his life entirely on her own. She may as well have.

Outside the courtroom, she began to cross-examine Jeremiah. "You only have one child, right? Just Alonso? There's no other child you need to support, right? Because if it's two children, it's a lower percentage per child. You know that, right?"

"No, I don't know that," he admitted, embarrassed.

"Alonso needs diapers. Alonso needs clothes. Alonso needs food. I pay for daycare, but that's not coming out of my pocket, that's the government paying for that. You've got to pay for it. You've got to be the father."

"I hope I'm the father."

"What are you saying?"

"I just want to be the father."

"You know you're the father." She was exasperated.

"I just get nervous," he said.

"Why? You've said to me Alonso is yours. They've cleared any doubt that he is my ex-husband's. We separated long before he was conceived. I already told you that."

"You sure there's no possibility on earth it's someone else's? I remember that other guy."

"Kevin? He is not the father." She reached into her bag for her folder. "I have the test results here."

Jeremiah grinned awkwardly and held up his hands in refusal.

"You need to see it so you can be sure." Camila pulled the printout from the folder. She held the DNA results in front of him and pointed to the conclusion of the page. "It says here the alleged father is excluded from paternity. That means he is not the father. It's a sworn statement. He moved on with his life. He doesn't want to be a part of Alonso's life. He's upset that I wasted his time. But he was there with me. He went to the doctor with me. He came to the hospital."

"How do I know that you're not with him right now?" Jeremiah asked.

"I told you I was pregnant. You decided to disappear. I told you I made an appointment to have my sonogram. I asked you to come. You didn't show up. You didn't respond. But that's the past. Alonso is here now. We just need to move forward."

"Especially seeing as he's not in the picture," Jeremiah said.

"At least he stepped up to the plate," she said. "You just disappeared. You didn't even ask me when the baby was going to be born. You could have contacted me before. You didn't. I have to tell Alonso that that's who his father was. That when he was born, I was living in a shelter and his father didn't do a damn thing. Even once he knew we were in a shelter, he didn't do a thing. He should know that if he's going to decide to trust you. Because I can't trust you."

Jeremiah was silent. He couldn't bring himself to look up at her.

"That's the relationship you chose," Camila said. She set her jaw and stared at him, her eyes cold. "You abandoned me. I'm never going to be your family."

"I'm just so scared of there being a surprise," Jeremiah whispered almost inaudibly. "I just want to be the father so badly."

Camila turned on her heel and walked away.

That night Camila dreamed that she had an appointment to have a C-section. She wasn't certain that she was pregnant, and her belly was flat, but the doctor insisted that she needed to have it anyway. She was lying on a table with her legs spread and her feet in stirrups. The doctor told her he needed to make sure the lining of her uterus was all right. She believed he was evil.

"You can't cut me to see if I have something in my uterus," she told him. "I'd rather have my future baby give me a uterus rupture than get one from a surgeon."

She pulled her knees together, lifted her heels out of the stirrups, and walked out of the room. Geraldine was sitting in the waiting area outside with a baby, trying to breastfeed and having difficulty. Beside her was Alonso's daycare provider from Brooklyn, the dark woman with the straight-ironed ponytail and the gold-rimmed teeth. A tall, lanky guy entered the waiting room. He approached her. She realized it was Kevin.

"Why is the doctor harassing you to get this unnecessary surgery without your consent?" he asked, concerned.

He leaned down for her to climb up onto his shoulders. Swiftly, not jostling her with his gait, he ran toward a back door. He pushed it open. They were free.

A snowy week eroded whatever fortitude she had left. First, she'd seen on Facebook that Kevin had been called up to participate in the NFL's Regional Combine Invitational. She texted to congratulate him.

Thank you, he replied.

I was thinking I'd come to Illinois. My sister there hasn't met the baby, she wrote, referring to one of Mauricio's daughters. It was a ruse, and she knew it.

So did he. *You take care,* he replied.

The following night she texted Kevin a picture of Midway Airport.

Is this the airport I fly into to come see you? she wrote.

I have a girlfriend, he wrote back. *With all respect, I think you should stay where you are.*

The mortification hurt more than the heartbreak, she told me.

Then, the next evening, Camila got a text from Pedro. It had been a year and a half since she'd heard from him. There he was, in words on her phone, like she'd conjured him.

I'm in the Bronx. Want to meet?

Yes, she replied immediately.

A few hours later he texted again. *I'm going to be straight with you. I don't want to chitchat. I just want to get my dick wet.*

Her humiliation was sickening. She put down the phone and walked into the kitchen to heat up some food, focusing on erasing the exchange from her mind. Aaron was standing at the sink with his back to her.

"Are you a home-wrecker?" He tossed the question ironically over his shoulder.

Camila didn't know what he meant.

Then she realized that the trickling sound she heard wasn't coming from the faucet.

He was pissing in the sink.

She turned away, shocked, and went to her room.

While Aaron and Jovanka argued late into the night, she looked up the word he'd called her. What an awful implication. Did everyone just think she was a whore?

"I'm the successful one with the master's degree, and I still have to cook and clean for you and take care of the kid," she heard Jovanka yell.

Alonso was woken by the argument. Scared. He started crying. Camila had to pee, but she was afraid to go into the bathroom while they were fighting. Her bladder ached most nights. The bathroom was crawling with roaches, anyway. No wonder Aaron preferred the sink. She shushed Alonso back to sleep and studied the exclusionary clause for her midterm before going to bed, only to be woken by a text from an unknown number.

You want 80 bucks for some head? it said.

Who is this? she replied.

Pretty girl like you, thought you'd be interested.

She tried to go back to sleep, but she kept picturing the pixels. There was only so much a person could shut out. She just needed something good to happen. She needed it so badly.

10

WINDFALL

During her first trimester, before she moved to the shelter in New Jersey, Camila had a job as a cashier at a small pharmacy south of Grand Central. The front of the drugstore was just a few aisles stocked with candles scented with amaranth and vetiver, "dry oil" that cost $54 for a tiny bottle, and European hair care. Camila would dress up for her shifts; she wanted to look professional. The other employees would remind her she was just a cashier. They'd sneer at her outfits, telling her not to go overboard.

In an office tower near the pharmacy was the Kate Spade corporate office, staffed with upwardly mobile women who would regularly drop in for beauty products. They loved Camila for the samples she'd press into their pale hands, for the vibrant, knowing chatter she'd sustain, remembering every detail about their boyfriends or work conflicts. One day, two of the women brought her a small baby-blue messenger purse, a Kate Spade sample, as a gift. The other pharmacy employees, women all, scowled at Camila. "You think you're better than us," they told her. It didn't help that the boss had a crush on her. She told me he'd come up with reasons to keep her late after closing, trying to lure her to a bar, or he'd bypass the formality of a drink, attempting to get with her in one of the aisles. Her rejections only aggravated his abrasive management style.

One morning, a FedEx delivery of nineteen heavy boxes of shampoo and body wash was left piled outside the pharmacy's tall glass door. The boss told Camila to move them inside. It wasn't her job—plus, she was pregnant, though no one at the pharmacy knew. When she refused, he threatened to fire her. Camila lifted a massive box and felt a pull deep inside her midsection. Then she felt pain in her shoulder that radiated down her arm. She told him she needed to go home.

"You can't," he said. "Take a Tylenol."

Camila moved the rest of the delivery inside, injuring her back. Once they were all stacked in the store, she pulled out her smartphone and took pictures of the boxes, just in case she needed evidence in a medical claim. She priced the items while serving customers through the remainder of her shift. Then she wrote up a complaint, which she told me the boss wouldn't file. The next day she was in too much pain to make it in to work. The following day she had to call in, as well. She was pregnant, looking for shelter—and now jobless.

Camila took her complaint to court. And then, over a year later, one gray early-March day, an envelope from a law firm appeared in her post office box, with a check inside. Eight thousand dollars. A onetime payment, in exchange for lost wages the previous year.

Camila hadn't believed it was ever going to appear. In fact, she never mentioned the possibility of it to me until it did. She said she'd use some to pay rent on Sherman Avenue, some for things Alonso needed. She'd hold on to some as emergency money, to make sure her account never dipped below $1,000, or for moving expenses the next time she needed to find another place to stay.

And with the rest, she was going to take herself to the Dominican Republic. The money she spent on a trip, she said, wouldn't change her situation one way or another. It wouldn't make her eligible for affordable housing. She was right about that. Still, I was worried about how much she might need that money in the future—for rent, or a new computer perhaps, or for Alonso's needs, not to mention an unexpected turn in her fortunes, an emergency. I told her so. But she was resolute. Camila had wanted to go to the D.R. since she was a kid, something that almost every one of her friends and relatives had done more than once before. She deserved to go as much as anyone else, she figured, to a country where everyone was her people. Her father had a huge house there; she'd seen pictures. Three floors. Cars. Two dogs he sent food to every month. Even her mom had gotten to go when she was younger and maybe still did, for all she knew.

Camila wrote her aunt who lived there to tell her we were coming to visit.

Her whole life, she'd told everyone it was where she was from; now she could finally see it. She'd visit the town where her father was admired for his fine house, where her grandfather had been revered on the police force, where she believed she belonged, and where there was family who might care enough to actually act like one—which, she told me, pressing a hand on her heart, was all she wanted. I was going to join her, to see what happened when her diaphanous fantasy of a homeland was rendered solid. Maybe she knew something I didn't, of kin and history and faith. Maybe she sensed a future for herself there beyond what I could imagine.

Spring was coming.

SPRING

1

STANDARDS

t was a brilliant day in late March. Camila's Minorities and the Criminal Justice System class had been canceled, so she had a free hour or two before picking up Alonso. She wanted to make a stop on the way back to the Bronx. Coming up from the subway in Downtown Brooklyn, she noticed construction had begun on the newest City Point Tower, where almost ninety thousand applications had been received for two hundred affordable apartments. Camila wasn't even eligible for a studio there, not by half. She'd given up on such hopes, anyway. She'd given up on short-term prospects, as well, not to mention private shelters. And she could only afford the room in the Bronx for a few weeks more, if she guarded the money she'd earmarked for her trip to the Dominican Republic. The flight to the D.R. was more than she'd anticipated. But she was committed to going, as much as I'd seen her committed to anything.

And she was feeling a new surge of optimism. She'd discovered a new city initiative dedicated to keeping the homeless in school. The announcement of the initiative specifically touted supporting heads of homeless families in college through the availability of stable housing. And yet, unless she dropped out of school, her income rendered her ineligible for any affordable apartment. How was the city helping heads of homeless families—like her—stay in school if she had to drop out to achieve any sort of housing security? Camila thought the initiative could give her some muscle to fight the denial of her affordable-housing application. She was going to the Legal Aid Society office in Downtown Brooklyn to talk to an attorney.

Camila found the massive office building she was seeking. Timidly, she stepped into the enormous dark lobby, her eyes adjusting to the relative murkiness inside, and rode the elevator up to the floor listed on the directory.

BE PREPARED TO WAIT 3–6 HOURS, said the sign at the front desk; luckily, the waiting room was empty. A receptionist in a pink cardigan over a *Star Wars* T-shirt, a huge gap between her front teeth, sat behind a glass partition. Camila gathered herself and approached the window.

"I'm here seeking legal representation," she said, her chin high, her face stern.

The receptionist looked at her skeptically and let out an annoyed breath. "You have a court case?"

"No, but I'm looking for a lawyer to represent me," Camila said. "My appeal was rejected from affordable housing and I want to push back." She explained her situation.

"The only way you can fight an application status is if it was clearly discrimination. That's tough. You just need to apply for another apartment," the receptionist said.

"Right, which I've been doing for the past two years," Camila said. "I was in a shelter for a year." She continued, her diction precise, "I believe there is a case for discrimination. Based on the Department of Homeless Services website, there is an education plan as of 2015 that says they want homeless people like myself to be in school. Therefore, they need to make affordable housing available for single mothers in school. My rejection for an apartment contradicts that plan. And that's what I'm here seeking to discuss with an attorney."

The receptionist allowed her to finish before snickering. "They're also trying to prevent homelessness in New York, and people walk in here every day evicted," she said. "There's nothing you can do, sweetie. You're not going to find anything here unless they clearly discriminated against you. And that means for your race or your disability."

"That I know." She was defensive. "I understand discrimination law."

"If it's because you're a student, that's not discrimination. We can't help. Because those apartments, it's a set rate. You make the amount of money they say, you can get the apartment."

Camila's gumption vanished. She looked down at her folded hands.

"Right," she said quietly.

The receptionist softened. "It sucks, I know. I see people clearly get discriminated against every day, and even that usually doesn't matter."

Camila listened, nodding.

"Once they get your application, they're looking for ways to disqualify you." The receptionist leaned forward. "I've been there. I applied, just me and my younger son. And I went into the interview and my older son was with me and they didn't want that. They were, like, that's it, you have another son, you're disqualified. My sister's been doing the same thing for two years, maybe three years, and she hasn't been called up once, so you got lucky."

Camila's eyes clouded. "For me and my son there are no other programs that would help us," she said.

"You're not in the shelter anymore?"

"No," Camila said. "And it was a private shelter."

"Oh, like a church shelter?" The receptionist shook her head. "Nah, no one will do anything for you from a private shelter. Where do you stay now?"

"I rent a room with another couple and their child."

"So there's three of you and the babies?" The receptionist perked up. She explained that Camila had an overcrowding issue she could claim, if she brought the city in to see her living conditions. That was the only way PATH was going to let her in.

It was beginning to register with Camila that she wasn't even eligible for emergency shelter through PATH. Her worst-case scenario was suddenly another out-of-reach hope.

The receptionist swiveled in her desk chair to call out to someone behind a cubicle wall. "Louis?"

Camila murmured that she hoped Louis was a lawyer. A wizened ebony-dark man loped around the reception desk, swallowed up by a patchy black leather jacket, his teeth far shy of a full set. The receptionist told Louis about the overcrowded apartment.

Louis replied in a high-pitched lisp, "She's got to say they don't want me there. And when I go back there, I'll call the police. And the police will say don't go back there. And then PATH's got to take her." Louis was getting excited. "And there was drinking and fighting and carrying on around your child. It's not safe for your child! And say you can't pay rent there," he added. "Once you're at PATH, your first ten days is your worst time. After that, you'll get used to it."

The receptionist nodded her head in solidarity. "So many people tell me they were thrown out from shelters and they won't let them back in, even with their babies in the cold. Everyone is just a number to the city. The only one who is going to help you is you."

Camila listened, stone-faced. They were saying her last and most feared option was only possible if she called the cops on Jovanka and Aaron and lied about the safety of their apartment, which would likely make their family homeless, as well. Legal Aid was telling her to subject them to the very same desperate situation she was facing, just to save herself. She maintained a polite mask until she was back on the elevator.

She'd never do that to them, she told me, no matter how annoyed she was with them every day. She had standards. So what did that leave, the street? Her eyes blackened and narrowed as she sped through the cavernous lobby into the sunshine outside. Elbows tense and sharp, she turned the corner and found herself staring up at the courthouse where she'd divorced Pedro. On Flatbush, she joined the crowd crossing the street as a middle-aged couple warily eased their gleaming Mercedes SLC into the mass of people in their way, their windows closed tight against the fresh spring air.

2

THOSE GOOD OLD DAYS

Bitter winter cold returned, sending people outside once more in dark, shapeless coats, but Camila wanted to look perfect. She dressed for the day in a pink cotton blazer over her pin-tucked blouse. It was Mauricio's birthday. She planned to take her father to lunch after Alonso's bimonthly WIC appointment. Weeks earlier, she had texted her dad a picture of her name on the dean's list. He still hadn't replied.

On the way to the appointment, Alonso's feet kicked outside the stroller cover. He'd outgrown all his shoes and wore only gray sweat socks, two sizes too small. While Camila pushed the stroller, she tried to hold the plastic sheeting in a position to cover his feet. It had been easy for her to get bags of donations for a small baby, but now that he was outgrowing those things, there was nothing to replace them. She fumbled her way across the Grand Concourse, trying to hold the stroller cover in place. The straps had all broken on it weeks ago, but it was the only way she could keep him warm. Alonso began to cry. Camila shook the stroller as she walked, shushing loudly against the wind's howl, trying to calm him down. His little hand grabbed at the plastic and tried to yank it off the stroller.

"I've got to keep you under here," she said pleadingly, her breath steaming in the frosty air. Camila had a bad case of conjunctivitis that wasn't healing. Her eyes teared in the blistering wind. "Sound good? Keep you warm?" Alonso smiled up through the plastic and kicked his feet.

The WIC office was a storefront overlooking a pawnshop. She signed in, was given a number, and waited. A little girl who looked around three, in lipstick and a weave, teetered over to peer into the stroller at Alonso. The girl pressed her face into the plastic cover and laughed.

Camila ignored her and pulled out her phone. She called Medicaid. On top of everything else, her account had been canceled. She didn't know why. No one answered.

It was chilly in the office. Camila tried to keep Alonso warm under the plastic cover. He stared up at the fluorescent lights from behind the wrinkled clear sheeting, kicking his foot until his sock fell off. Camila ignored the sock on the floor and called her dad. Voicemail. She tried again.

"Hi, Dad!"

"I've got to call you right back," he said.

Camila sighed. She looked mournfully at Alonso. He'd fallen asleep.

For the next hour while she waited, she made her way through all the forms she needed to fill out for her upcoming public-assistance recertification. She wanted to have everything perfectly prepared well in advance. The paperwork was complicated.

She wondered aloud how the other women at the shelter managed the convoluted language and intricate requirements of every document that stood between themselves and basic social services. Irina struggled with it, she knew, and Irina had a law degree.

Camila told me Irina just wasn't motivated to take care of herself, that she relied on the system to do it all for her. But to get any relief from the system you had to be vigilant and incisive; praying wasn't going to be enough to solve her problems. Camila said she thought Irina never had it in her.

Camila's number was called. The nutritionist, a heavyset young white woman with perfectly blown-out hair, sat at a desk under a poster of snowcapped mountains rising over a lake. GOALS, it said.

"Are you still breastfeeding?" the nutritionist asked.

"No."

"You just stopped? Any particular reason?"

"I didn't have time to pump. I'm taking eighteen credits."

The nutritionist scowled and made a note on a pad of paper. "Now that you are no longer breastfeeding, it will reduce your check to half the jars of baby food you're eligible for—just sixteen jars. And no more bananas for him."

"Even if his iron is low?" Camila asked.

"Yes." She handed Camila a check for the baby food. "You'll have to buy your own milk, eggs, and cheese. We don't pay for them if you don't breastfeed."

More money, gone. Camila thanked her and headed to the Fine Fare supermarket around the corner, which did a brisk business from the WIC office. She pushed the stroller over its stained and buckled tiles, looking for products approved for purchase with a WIC check. They weren't hard to find here; entire shelves were labeled with glaring orange WIC stickers. At the register, she signed over her last check for milk, eggs, and cheese alongside the new one for the jars of food for Alonso. Then she handed a dollar tip to the cashier and another to the bagger.

Back on Sherman, Camila steered the stroller around the glass of shattered car windows and liquor bottles. The twisted innards of a piano lay rusting on the street, right where it had been when she moved in. She decided to drop Alonso off at Maria's for a bit— she didn't want to share her father. Inside, Maria slowly opened the apartment door. She lifted Alonso out of the stroller while Camila followed the sound of Univision straight to the kitchen. Camila figured Maria's family needed the groceries more than she did. She unpacked the milk, eggs, and cheese onto the counter, while Maria set Alonso down in front of the television in the living room.

"I brought you some food," Camila called into the living room.

"Gracias, mi amor," Maria said, walking into the kitchen.

Camila went into the living room to say goodbye to Alonso.

Maria came back in, holding an envelope. She pulled out an official-looking letter.

It was a notice of child-care termination for Alonso. Her voucher would expire at the end of the month.

Camila had received neither warning nor notice that payment would be discontinued. Without childcare she couldn't attend school. Nor could she work.

She said she'd go home and figure it out right away. But instead she reached out to her father as soon as she unlocked the door to the apartment.

Hey, I want to come see you for your birthday, she texted.

No reply. She waited a bit. Then she called.

He answered.

"Hi, Dad, happy birthday!"

"Thanks," he said. "How you doing?"

"Good, how are you?"

"I'm working."

It didn't sound like he was working. She heard traffic, the car radio. "You're working now? You're at work?"

"I'm driving. Let me call you back."

He hung up.

Camila unfolded her laptop and opened up her photo-and-video file. She was searching for something in particular she wanted to show me: the video from her father's birthday last year. Celia carries in an elaborate cake made to look like a Romeo y Julieta box with a detailed fondant label, filled with cake cigars. They sing. He blows out the candles. Camila hit PLAY again and again, watching a loop of her father blowing out his birthday candles.

She clicked on another video. Christmas 2008. Her father's house. Camila is sitting in front of his huge television in the living room, wearing a Santa hat. Mauricio hands her a big gift-wrapped box. She's so excited she can hardly untie the ribbon. She rips off the paper.

"Let's look what my dad got me!" she says to the camera. "What? Are those condoms?"

"An appropriate family gift," her dad says.

Underneath the big package of condoms is a shoebox. "You got me the boots we saw at Macy's!" she cries, her beatific smile breaking wide open. "Oh my God, you got me the boots!"

Camila wiped away a tear, watching. She played it again and then scanned through a few more screens of family pictures. Confirmations. Mugging for the camera in short shorts during summer breaks. Then she let out a little yelp when she saw the still image of herself and her best friend from high school. She hovered the cursor over the white triangle in the center of the image, hesitated for a moment, and then clicked.

They're singing Mariah Carey. Camila knows all the words, every trill. She flattens her hands and slices the air high and low, according to the notes. Her friend's father shuffles in and out of the frame behind them, teasing the girls. But Camila doesn't break the flow. Her eyes filled with tears again, watching herself at sixteen with a best friend and a kitchen table to sit at.

"What happened to my life?" she asked aloud.

Pictures of her mother. Her eyes hard, her face thin. Unsmiling. Different hair colors over the years, different eyebrow shapes. She didn't want to think about her mother, she said. Instead, she clicked on a video she'd shot of herself in the hospital the day after Alonso was born. He's sleeping sweetly on her breast. She's smiling from her hospital bed, her arm outstretched to capture the moment on her cellphone. "Those were the good old days," she murmured.

Her phone buzzed on the desk. She pounced on it. It was a text from her dad.

No, he wrote in reply to her lunch invitation. *I'm very busy today.*

Her face flushed red. You don't want to spend time with your kid? You don't want to get to know your grandson as he gets older? You two could play baseball, go watch a game? You don't want to do that? She didn't write it, she just said it to me. She didn't reply to him at all.

Camila held her breath, trying to stanch the tears. She didn't mean to get her hopes up, she said, her eyes red. She should have known better. Camila became suddenly irate, not at her father, she said, but at herself. Angrily, she started pulling out clothes to pack for the Dominican Republic. The new maxidress she'd bought at Rite Aid for ten bucks. Alonso's donated red onesie—printed with *Oye chico . . . tu novia me está mirando*—that she'd been saving for the trip.

Camila said she'd wanted to tell her dad in person that she was going to the Dominican Republic, to Pinalito. She'd wanted to tell him she was going so she could finally see his house and meet their family. Her aunt hadn't written back. Camila said she figured it was because her father had told her aunt not to. He didn't want anyone to know the truth about who he was—how he abandoned her, how he let her become homeless, with a baby no less, she told me. Fine, she said, wiping the tears from her cheeks. She'd find her family herself.

3

EITHER THAT OR THE STREET

Camila dressed nicely for Good Friday, a turtleneck dress under a white jersey blazer, though she had no plans to see family and wasn't going to church. You didn't wear jeans on Good Friday, she said.

Daycare was closed and she needed a suitcase to bring to the Dominican Republic. That could be her Good Friday outing with Alonso, she told me. At T.J. Maxx in Manhattan, the cheapest rolling suitcase was marked down to fifty-six dollars. Nicole Miller, in a teal and blue chevron pattern. Fifty-six dollars wouldn't make a difference one way or another; she wanted everything to be really nice for the D.R.

On Sixth Avenue, pushing the stroller and pulling the suitcase, she passed a rheumy-eyed black man in a watch cap, a down jacket, and soiled pants, sitting on a cardboard box. Half a block down was another man on a cardboard box, rheumy-eyed, black, watch cap, down jacket, soiled pants. The picture of homelessness in duplicate. And then Camila, pulling her suitcase branded with the logo of an evening-gown designer, her own circumstances invisible.

———

Camila got a text from Irina. Her time was up at the shelter. She was going to PATH. It was either that or the street.

Irina was only allowed to bring two bags to the shelter office in the Bronx. She packed her pots and pans into boxes, her acrylic sweaters into suitcases, her baby gear into garbage bags, and moved it all from Fourth Avenue to Brighton Beach, where members of her church had offered to store her possessions. She told me she was going to get a new shelter placement in Brooklyn, near the church; she'd been praying on it. The worker at PATH sent her to a hotel on Tremont Avenue in the Bronx, where she and Dima could stay until a shelter had room. The hotel was infested with bedbugs, and she wasn't even allowed to bring a hot plate into her room to cook, but it was in God's hands now, she said.

Before she left, she'd told Rose that she had a friend from Russia who was here in New York and desperate: She didn't speak English, she had no one to help her, and she was just a few weeks from her due date. Rose was fed up with Irina and had only extended her move-out day a few weeks past the year mark. She'd thought Irina was someone who could improve her life, but it turned out, she said, that she had no initiative, not like her little friend Camila. Rose said she didn't want someone else in the shelter who was just going to wait for other people to take care of her. But when Irina's friend came to speak to her, Rose was impressed. There was certainly room for her.

No one had moved into Camila's room, still. Irina's was newly vacant. There was another room empty on the top floor. Only that week, Rose had finally offered Sherice's old room to a new resident. The day after the resident hauled her bags upstairs, she went into labor. A girl.

That week, Jovanka and Aaron had a fight that shook the walls. Camila turned up the volume on the television to drown out the sound so Alonso wouldn't get scared. She hid behind her door, waiting for them to leave the house. Her stomach growled furiously. She wanted to warm up some rice from her dorm fridge, but she thought the risk of setting Jovanka off was too great.

After the sun went down, she finally gave in to her hunger and went to the kitchen to use the stove. A drawer had been pulled out of its cabinet, its cutlery and takeout menus scattered on the floor. Cereal boxes were tipped over on the table and on top of the fridge. The only clean-looking thing in the room was the Dominican flag tacked to a wall. Then Jovanka appeared in the kitchen doorway. Camila told me later what had happened.

"I think this is not working out with you here," Jovanka said.

"I pay rent," Camila said. "I have to listen to you and Aaron arguing all the time. I feel like I'm in jail."

"We don't have a door on our room. Why don't we move into your room? You and Alonso can sleep in the living room."

"That's not the room you rented me. I just want to go home at the end of the day, go to school, raise my son, and be at peace." Camila had had enough. "I'm moving out," she announced. She went back to her room, where Alonso was crying for her attention, and shut the door.

She was going to the D.R. in a week, anyway. And she had a feeling, she said, that something magical would happen there. I didn't tell her what I was thinking, that her choices would be no better than Irina's. But I didn't know how much worse they could be.

4

THE LABYRINTH

Camila kept $1,200 in twenties in a binder clip. She'd gotten it as a tax refund on the tuition she'd paid for on her own. It was the biggest refund she'd ever received. She counted out ten twenties to change into Dominican pesos. She didn't put it in the bank account where she kept $1,000 for emergencies, since that would put her over the $2,000 limit she was allowed to have available while she was on welfare. Any more than that and she'd lose public assistance. The workers' comp check wouldn't count, she thought. It wasn't taxed like income was. It was money with different restrictions, she told me, since it came from a legal settlement.

Usually she carefully researched such policies. This time, it seemed, she'd deduced something that she needed to believe. It didn't sound right to me that the welfare office would have different rules about money like that. She'd just lost her childcare voucher. Medicaid had been canceled. She had no idea where she'd live next. And she was spending cash I feared she'd need, and soon, on her trip to the D.R. I worried that just as she'd tried to convince herself that Kevin was Alonso's father, because she needed him to be, she was willing this policy into existence, afraid to discover that it was written only in her mind. She was adamant, stubborn, when I asked her if she was sure. Each time she checked her mail at the post office, I worried there would be an envelope awaiting her with a crisis inside. But she didn't get a letter informing her she'd been kicked off welfare. She kept getting her checks. Maybe she was right.

Then, at her next appointment at the job center on Fourteenth Street, Camila was told that her welfare case had been closed. And nobody there could explain why or what she could do about it. Camila's neck and shoulders went rigid, as they always did when she was trying to brace herself against a wave of panic, her voice consciously quiet and steady. I knew her shock was genuine.

"Didn't you get a letter in the mail that you were getting cut off?" a monotone worker asked her.

"I did not."

"The application for recertification is incomplete."

"What does that mean? I submitted everything."

"Because the case has been closed, I cannot access it. Maybe it was transferred to DeKalb. You should go tomorrow."

Camila had missed a day of midterms to show up at this appointment. She couldn't miss another day of school to go out to the Brooklyn welfare office on DeKalb Avenue. She had another appointment scheduled later that week to recertify for her daycare voucher; she hoped they could help resolve the mistake. But at that next appointment, the worker verified that her file was incomplete.

"We can't see you, because your case has been closed."

"Can you explain why my case has been closed?"

"There's an incomplete."

"Can you tell me what is missing?"

"We can't do anything on our end."

"Can you please suggest who I might talk to who can clarify this?"

The worker just shook her head.

On Friday, Camila dropped off Alonso and took the train to the public-assistance office on DeKalb. She waited four hours to talk to someone.

"You have to reapply for welfare here. You have to start over."

Camila waited for another half an hour before they sent her to a different floor. Then she waited three hours to speak to a worker about reapplying.

The worker pulled up Camila's bank-account number on her screen. "We found out that you have eight thousand dollars in your bank. In order to qualify for welfare, you cannot have more than twenty-five hundred dollars."

"I no longer have that money. It was not income, it was workers' compensation," she said. "On housing applications it doesn't count as income."

"Here it does. You need to return with a bank statement that says you have no more than twenty-five hundred dollars."

"Can you pull up my bank-account information on your screen? I can show you right now that it is no longer in my account."

"No. You need to return with a statement. We will let you know within thirty days of submitting your bank statement, plus proof of address and how much rent you're paying now."

That meant a letter from Jovanka. Camila knew she'd never give her one now. She wouldn't risk asking. She asked the worker, "Does this mean that in the meantime I will not have cash assistance?"

"That is correct."

That meant no welfare check. No daycare voucher. Plus she still hadn't figured out why her Medicaid had been cut off. She only had $1,000 left. That had to cover the rest of her rent, her trip, and whatever it would cost to move and store her stuff when she left Jovanka's place.

Camila was sent back out to the waiting room without an explanation as to why she couldn't leave yet. There, for the first time, Camila began to talk about the advantages of dropping out of school. What choice was there? she said. It didn't have to be a mark of failure. She could follow another path to her goal, she told me. She worked through her rationale: Plenty of police departments didn't require bachelor's degrees. She could start with an entry-level police job, then move up to lieutenant, then captain, maybe chief of police. She could still be ambitious. So she wouldn't think about law school anymore; that never really mattered to her anyway, she said. She exhaled slowly, looked at the clock, and bounced an impatient foot. It would be thirty days before her case was resolved. If it was resolved. That decided it, she said. She would quit school and get a job.

School hadn't saved her, no more than anything else. There was no single solution to the prismatic impossibility of her circumstances. She'd elevated one hope above all else and worked to cultivate and maintain it, but the welfare system didn't care about the dean's list. Even once she graduated, her diploma wouldn't pay for Alonso's vaccinations or shoes or daycare. Her grades wouldn't cover her rent. She'd de-emphasized her studies and ambitions once she'd decided to go to the D.R. Somewhere inside that trip was her new salvation.

She couldn't cancel the trip now, she said; she wouldn't. She was leaving in less than a week. Before then, there was another paternity hearing with Jeremiah scheduled. And midterms. She just needed to get through the beginning of June. Graduation. Alonso's birthday. It would be okay, she said, as long as she got on that plane. As long as she got to Pinalito. She shook her head for a long time, and then fell silent for far longer.

We were quiet until the worker came out to tell her that she needed to go to Brooklyn, not Manhattan, for child-support enforcement. She'd have to start that process over, too, since cases didn't transfer from borough to borough; a change of address from Brooklyn to the Bronx, or from Manhattan to Queens, meant starting from scratch. A letter with an appointment time would arrive in the mail.

The worker said Camila needed to request new timekeeping paperwork from the Family Independence Administration to prove that her class hours and her work-study hours added up to sufficient hours of employment. The one they had was dated from March. It was no longer good, she said. The timekeeping document needed to be dated within the month, and it was now April, so it was invalid—that was the policy, the worker told her. Camila knew the document was still good, that there was no such requirement. She knew the policies cold. She showed up, always, with everything they could possibly need to see from her. But she didn't say anything to the worker except a clipped thank-you.

I sat beside her on the subway back to the Bronx, as she looked at her lap, murmuring the facts of her life, as though she was forcing herself to integrate them into her consciousness. No money coming in. No childcare. No place to live.

She began to mutter a litany to herself over and over: "I'm so alone, I'm so alone, I'm so alone." She rocked her torso along with each repetition. Her words were scarcely above a whisper and her rocking barely perceptible. It was the first time I'd seen other passengers look away from her with the self-protection reserved for panhandlers and street-sleepers.

Camila caught herself. Then she looked straight at me, her eyes wide and childlike. All she wanted, she said, was to sit down with her dad. She just wanted him to listen. She just wanted him to tell her it was going to be okay. She sent him a text.

He didn't respond.

5

TRUST

Alonso had outgrown his snowsuit, which rode up above his ankles and wrists in the spring chill. He was starting to stand, holding on to his mother's hands, keeping his legs locked until they'd wobble and collapse like a fawn's. Each month, his face seemed to look more like Jeremiah's—those sloe eyes, that broad nose—but perhaps I was searching for the resemblance.

I hadn't seen Alonso much for the past few weeks, meeting Camila at Kingsborough or in Manhattan while he was at daycare; Camila had been paying Maria out of pocket until her childcare case was straightened out. She hadn't mentioned him much, other than telling me how she'd been up with him at night. Her concerns were trained elsewhere: her welfare case, housing dead ends, homework. I knew that every day she'd dress him, feed him, put him to bed, since no one else did. But as his understanding of the world around him deepened, as did the development of his own stubborn and curious personality, it seemed like he had receded into the background. Another thing on her to-do list, another thing she needed a break from, another constant problem to solve.

Not that Camila wasn't trying to do right by him; she just had only so much right she could do. He was ravenous, for attention as well as food. In the hours I'd spend with him, I'd first find his fighting spirit thrilling—the will, the agency, like his mother—and then be exhausted by him within the hour, after he'd eaten half of my takeout rice and beans and tipped the other half furiously on the floor, or kicked and hit until he got the applesauce he wanted. It was easy to see how Camila could do little most days but yell at him to cooperate and then yell at him to go to sleep. Still, sometimes her exasperation would subside and she'd proudly text me a grainy video of him saying "ball" or "dog," taken late at night in the half dark of her room, or of herself singing softly as they kept each other company, curled together on Camila's narrow bed, his lips pursed just like hers.

Camila looked out the floor-to-ceiling windows of the waiting room at the Queens County Family Courthouse. The last time she was here, the park across the street was covered in snow. Now it was the pale green of April. She scanned the blond-wood benches for Jeremiah and found him sitting toward the back of the room, slumped over, elbows on his knees, braids hanging down. He wore a gray hoodie and sweatpants like last time, with no jacket to shield him against the spring chill outside.

She walked briskly toward him, the purpose and professionalism of her walk matching her sharp knit dress and tall leatherette boots; all she was missing was a briefcase. Camila took a seat on his bench and placed her backpack in between them, setting her face in a mask of indifference. He'd done nothing but blow her off since the last time they sat in this waiting room, she muttered. Not even a package of Pampers yet, she said, and Alonso was coming up on his first birthday.

"I hope we don't have that judge again," Jeremiah said in greeting. He pushed his sleeves up to reveal his skull tattoos and folded his arms around his small torso.

Camila ignored his comment, despite the fact that she shared his hope. She had other things she wanted to communicate to him.

Despite the desperation of those weeks, despite how alone she was, she'd decided to continue with school until graduation. And she wanted him to know it. She unzipped her backpack and pulled out a manila envelope, from which she removed a contact sheet of pictures. She pointed to one of her in a mortarboard and gown standing in front of a bookcase hung with a Kingsborough pennant.

"I picked this one for my yearbook," she said. "Now I have to pick the ones to give to my friends and my family." She handed him the contact sheet.

He looked at it, dazed. "I like this one," he said quietly, pointing to a different picture, where her face looked softer, a slight vulnerability revealed in her eyes and mouth.

"My nails were chipped, so I don't want to pick that one. You can see my nails."

Jeremiah was silent.

A heavyset woman nearby reached for her chiming phone and then broke the awkward stillness in the room.

"Yo, grow up!" she yelled, her voice cracking.

Every head jerked to register the reason for the howl. It was a similarly heavyset man, holding his phone on the other side of the waiting room. He looked at her pleadingly and then quickly studied his large hands in embarrassment. None of the couples in the room sat together except Camila and Jeremiah.

The court officer yelled that it was time to check in, over an hour behind schedule. Camila sprang up to get their names on the list first, then returned to the bench. That afternoon she had a midterm, and she feared it was going to be a long wait. She figured she might as well use the time with Jeremiah productively, get some information about her son's father.

"You're one out of how many kids?" she asked him.

"I'm one out of twenty? Seventeen? Something like that," he said.

"Are you Jamaican? Everybody keeps asking me where's Alonso from."

"Jamaican? Nah," he said. "My dad is Mexican and Cuban. My

mom is white and Haitian. When people ask me, I just say it's complicated. I just check off 'Other.' Alonso can figure out what he likes to check off."

She noticed him looking at the book a middle-aged white woman on their bench was holding. "Have you read that?" she asked.

"Yeah, I read that. *1984*. Also *Brave New World*. It's supposed to be like this utopia, but it's really a hell—everything is controlled. I read it in my literature class. We read that, we read a lot of Shakespeare. You know, *Romeo and Juliet*. It's good, but the other ones are more interesting." His face was growing animated. "Have you read *The Tempest*?" he asked.

"We read the sonnets. But that's all I've done in Shakespeare."

"The way he writes, you don't know if it's literal or not. If you just read it plain, you're not going to take it in. You've got to really work through it. It's radical work—for its day and also for now. In *The Tempest,* there's a witch, she was Algerian—that in itself was revolutionary. There were no black characters back then. Did you know Othello was black?"

"Really?" Camila was interested. "You should read it to Alonso, teach it to him."

"I'll read it to him. I'll teach him a lot," he said. He smiled hopefully, then immediately lowered his eyes to the floor.

This was not the impression Camila had given me of Jeremiah, that he had a literary mind, an appetite for critical thought. In fact, she'd made it seem like he lacked all possible sophistication. I wondered if she couldn't acknowledge his sophistication because she didn't share it herself. Or if she'd just decided, when she was done with him, that there was nothing there worth remembering. Either way, she was clearly beginning to recall how his keen mind had attracted her interest that summer.

"I know you're great in science," she said. "I prefer to learn about humans."

"Chemistry is about humans," he said. "It's about the basic building blocks of life."

"You learn about white blood cells and iron? Alonso's iron is low."

"I've always had low iron," he told her, looking back down at the floor.

"Yeah, but he eats," she said, smiling. "He loves to eat."

Jeremiah chuckled nervously. "That's how you eat. You don't play with eating. You left me one day because you were hungry. We were on the train. You went to the store, then you went to the house, and you just started eating—you didn't say a word to me."

Camila laughed. "You were walking slow! I was hungry!"

"It's like a main event for you when you eat," Jeremiah said, chuckling harder.

She darkened. "I only eat twice a day now," she said. "Or less."

Jeremiah dipped his head, quiet once more.

Camila crossed her legs, then uncrossed them. She shifted her weight from one hip to the other, trying to get comfortable on the hard bench. "I have this IUD," she said. "When I'm sitting, I feel a pinch."

Jeremiah smirked and shook his head.

"You must know what an IUD is," she said, incredulous.

"Yeah, I know what an IUD is. Certain things I would never do if I was a girl." He snickered. "I would not put anything in there. You just have to make sure you don't do it without protection."

"We used protection! That's why I got an IUD. I'm not trying to have another one. I'm on welfare."

He was quiet in response.

Camila tried to spark conversation again. "You're a Virgo, right?"

"Yup." He nodded slowly. "We're compassionate. Very emotional."

"Capricorns learn how to separate our emotions from business," Camila said, snapping her neck, ramping up. "You've got to make money. You've got to support your family. I show love as a role model, not by being broke and making nothing of myself. I need to advance myself, keep my brain active, make a career. That's how I show Alonso love."

Jeremiah didn't respond.

Camila was not about to slow down. "Yo, you should be grateful."

Jeremiah just studied the floor tiles.

She continued, "Alonso is my motivation. My parents didn't put their kids first, so I've got to give that to him. I don't have anybody. I get lonely all the time. I wish I had somebody to talk to every day, have a social life, go out. Someone to help me, to be there for me. But I don't."

Jeremiah said nothing.

Camila stared hard at the side of his face. After a minute she looked away.

"Alvarez! Cole!" the court officer shouted.

Camila hoisted her bag and strode toward the courtroom door. Jeremiah slowly rose and loped several paces behind her. The bailiff checked their names and ushered them in, handing each a piece of paper with a grid of numbers in decimal points and several lines of type.

The sheet of paper looked just like the one she'd pulled out of her folder to show Jeremiah the last time they were here, the one that said that Kevin's odds of fatherhood were impossibly low. As Camila walked to her seat facing the judge's bench, her eyes quickly found the same line of numbers at the bottom of the document. She lowered herself slowly into the chair, without taking her eyes off those numbers. Jeremiah lay his copy of the document on the table and took a seat, ignoring it.

The magistrate, the same one, in the same lavender dress shirt and purple tie, asked them to confirm their addresses. This time, at least, his voice was gentler, civil.

The magistrate looked straight at Jeremiah. "Mr. Cole, the likelihood of your paternity, according to the DNA test, is 226,801,687,408 to one."

Jeremiah knit his brows for a moment, bouncing his leg so rapidly that it looked to be vibrating. Then his face opened into an enormous smile. He looked over at Camila. Though she'd seen him and his smile, she refused to return his look. She clasped her sweating palms in her lap. She'd allow herself to react when it was over, and not until then.

"Mr. Cole, do you contest your paternity?" the magistrate asked.

"No, I do not," Jeremiah said, still smiling at Camila.

The magistrate introduced a surprising final order of business. "Ms. Alvarez, would you like to change the baby's last name to Cole?"

Jeremiah turned to Camila once more, his eyes huge and hopeful.

"No," she said, still refusing to look back at Jeremiah. "His name is Alvarez," she confirmed. "Alonso Alvarez."

The hearing adjourned.

Camila walked out of the courtroom toward the escalator, a few steps ahead of Jeremiah, who was scrambling to keep up.

"So can he come stay with me? Like, for the weekend?" he asked.

"No, he doesn't even know you," she said, eyes fixed straight ahead.

"What size is he?"

"What?" she asked over her shoulder.

"In clothes," he said.

"He's 2T."

"That's what it's called? So, like, if I go into a store, that's what I can tell someone, 2T?"

Camila finally breathed and turned around to look at him. Their faces were closer than they'd been since before her pregnancy test. She allowed her jaw to relax. "Yes," she said. "That's what it's called." Her cheeks slowly flushed pink under her ashen skin.

She told me later what she was thinking in that moment, what she permitted to wash over her: Maybe she really wasn't alone anymore. Maybe she had a partner. Maybe she didn't have to protect herself for once.

They walked outside into the bright sun of Archer Avenue. She impulsively kissed Jeremiah on the cheek. He raised his eyebrows in surprise.

"Let's go celebrate. Let's go to Corona," she said.

He paused, unprepared for this shift. "Nah, I don't have money to eat," he said, ashamed. "I only have enough to get a MetroCard to school. I don't want to just sit while you eat."

"I'll cover it. Don't worry. It'll just be eight bucks a plate. We should celebrate."

He searched her eyes. They didn't dim. She pulled him in for a buoyant hug. When she pulled back, he examined her face. It was bright and open. He grinned and nodded.

On the subway, they sat pressed together with their DNA records in hand, comparing test results like giddy teenagers all the way to Corona Plaza. Camila led him down from the train to her favorite place in the neighborhood. In Spanish, she ordered oxtail, yellow rice, and lemonade from the waitress behind the steam tables. He said he'd have the same. They found a table and sat side by side. Silence settled over them once more, but this time she was loose and aglow.

Her newfound vigor made him finally ready to talk. "It just hit me in there," he said. "'Cause before it's, like, I didn't know. I was—" He paused. "Unsure," he said very carefully. He suddenly opened his smiling mouth wide to mug his amazement. "I'm his dad," he said. He nodded firmly and said it a few times more. Under the table, Camila took his hand. "My dad was a ho, a man-ho," he said. "He loved women too much. The one person I had a parent relationship with passed away at a young age. My oldest brother. He treated me like I was his son. He got shot."

Jeremiah told her the story he'd never shared when they were together. One afternoon when he was just five, his eighteen-year-old brother took him to the corner store. On their way home, his brother's best friend jumped him with a gun. Every day for the rest of his childhood, Jeremiah had to walk past the same square of sidewalk where his brother bled to death. Camila didn't say anything, but she moved closer, her body easing against his. She decided she was ready to show him what he'd missed. She picked up her phone, located the photos from Alonso's birth, and placed the phone in front of him. He began swiping through.

"When I first met you, you didn't pay me attention," he said.

"It was summer," she said. "I was having fun. I wasn't focused on a relationship."

Jeremiah gazed at a picture of Alonso swaddled in his hospital blanket. "Now, there's you and me put together," he said. He reached up to stroke a lock of hair curling alongside her ear. "Academically, I hope he takes after me," he said. "You're on the dean's list, you said. That's very good. But I hope he takes after me, because everything always came so easy to me. I never had to try. They wanted to skip me, but my mom said I was going to grow up too fast."

The waitress arrived with their plates. Camila tucked right in, but Jeremiah just poked at his rice, moving meat around the plate.

"The name-change thing was interesting," he said. "You were like, 'Hell no.' And I was mad into it." He stared at his dish. "You could change your name, too."

Camila cocked her head and examined his profile closely. "That's like asking me to get married. That's a big proposal."

"It's not a big proposal."

"It is. I'm not married with you."

"You could be," he said, looking directly at her.

She nodded sarcastically. "That's your proposal," she said. "'You shouldn't have an IUD.' 'You should change your last name.'"

"No, in the future!" he cried. "We're not having another kid now. I know it's not the right time for either of us for that." He looked at her coyly.

She continued examining his face. His eyes fixed again on his plate. "Are you going to really propose right now?" she asked, amazed.

"No," he said soberly. "I can't do that right now. That's not how you propose."

"Yeah, but that was the moment!" she said, throwing her head back to laugh ostentatiously. "Are you at least asking me out?" she asked, lowering her chin and eyeing him flirtatiously. Her heart raced.

A bashful smile was his reply.

She wanted to give him a chance to prove he was worthy of her confidence, she told me when he disappeared into the bathroom. She wasn't going to let herself want it; she couldn't risk getting hurt. But now they could be a real family, she said. A mother and a father and a child.

"I'm so happy," she said, when he returned to the table.

He looked at her skeptically.

"For real," she said. "Feel my heart." She took his hand and pressed it against her chest.

Camila told him about her housing crisis, the Justice Academy, her dreams that seemed permanently deferred.

"What would it take for you to graduate from John Jay?" he asked.

"Finding a place to live," she said. "That's it."

"So let's look for an apartment."

"How are you going to pay for that? I get food stamps, but I can't contribute much more."

"Then I have to get two jobs."

"You'd do that?"

"I'd do that. I'll have to go part-time in school. I have a year left on my master's. It'll just take longer," he said.

"But I want you to graduate," she said. "We both have to graduate. That's the bottom line."

She began to narrate all her attempts to get housing. Eventually she got around to the building in Harlem with his name on the application, the one she waited on for nearly two years. He was horrified she never told him about it.

"You're just stubborn," he said. "I told you when you got pregnant, let me know your appointments so I can take you. Just like this, you didn't tell me about any of them."

This was news to me, even more than Jeremiah's interest in Shakespeare's plays or dystopian literature. Her story had always been that Jeremiah was nothing but a shirker, that he'd vanished and abdicated all responsibility, not that he was shut out by her. No wonder he didn't chase down information about Alonso's birth, when he thought it was another man's baby. No wonder he didn't give her money for Pampers. No wonder he'd been so nervous. Camila had treated him like he wasn't the father from the beginning, because she'd decided she wanted another man to be Alonso's dad. Or, perhaps, because she only knew men who let their women down. She'd never given Jeremiah a chance to show her otherwise.

"It's true, I did not tell you. But I didn't trust you," she explained. She stared him down again. "Men can tell me anything. Like my dad: 'I love you, I'm going to help you.' But he's not helping me. I'm tired of being lied to all the time."

He nodded, seeming to hear her. She watched him carefully. Then she told him about Jovanka's place in the Bronx, how they wanted her to have a guy there with her so they could raise the rent, how she couldn't afford it on her own anymore. He listened thoughtfully, pushing his rice around the plate. Camila didn't mention she'd told Jovanka she was moving out, that she was leaving for the D.R. in a couple of days, that her money was almost gone, that she'd lost childcare payments and Medicaid and public assistance. They could talk about that later. She suggested they try out living there together while they found a place for just the three of them.

Jeremiah smiled at her and nodded.

She put out her hand to shake on it. He took it to pull her close.

Camila leaned back to examine his face again. "I'm following my heart in this," she said, almost whispering. "I've been looking tough. I know. I haven't wanted to risk being let down."

"I'll come see it on Sunday," he said. He sized her up. "You got that IUD in?"

"You won't feel it at all." Her smile curled flirtatiously. "Why don't you come today?" Thank God Jovanka and Aaron were going out of town for the weekend.

He shook his head. "I have to work."

Then she said softly, "You said you wanted to make sure Alonso was your son. You had doubts. I understand."

They were both quiet.

"I haven't felt this happy since, my goodness, I don't know." She crossed her arms on her chest and squeezed herself tight, gazing up with her rarest and most beatific of smiles. "I think this is one of the best days of my life," she said shyly.

Camila pulled him in for a deep, long embrace. As Jeremiah nestled his face into her neck, she pressed her forehead against his shoulder, and, weeping, released herself.

Sunday was too long to wait. Jeremiah said he was coming over that night.

But by three A.M., Camila was crackling with exasperation, despite the euphoria of the afternoon. For two hours she'd been impatiently arranging her room, applying makeup and checking the time, her armor slowly sliding back into place. Why was it an hour between the text that said he was on his way back to Jamaica and the one that said he was on his way to the Bronx? Was he playing her?

I wasn't there for her impatience or what followed. This is how she told it to me.

Jeremiah texted that he'd arrived. As she let him in downstairs, brought him up the elevator, and led the way through the cluttered hallway to her bedroom, he noticed nothing, said nothing. He simply collapsed boneless on her bed, dulled mute with exhaustion. That afternoon he'd kissed her goodbye, taken the subway straight to the restaurant in Forest Hills, worked the closing shift, traveled home to get his book bag, and then made the two-hour subway trip all the way to Sherman Avenue. He said he just wanted to go to sleep. He had to be back at work before noon.

Camila curled her long body around him, reaching between his legs.

He turned over, annoyed. "That's what you want from me?"

She was stunned by the rejection.

"If that's all you want from me, if we're not going to really be together," he said, "I'm not going to have sex with you."

Camila continued her attempted seduction, trying to win him back with her slender fingers. He grabbed her hand and demanded she stop touching him.

"I can have anybody I want," she said. "I don't need to deal with this."

Ignoring her, he closed his eyes until slumber carried him away from her completely.

As he slept, Camila examined his tattoos and found the name of a girl he'd been with while she was pregnant. She lay beside him, sleepless, listening to the soft chorus of his breath and their son's. Her mind was busy, itemizing familiar evidence against him: his commitment issues, his financial ineptitude, his lack of respect for her, his absence over the past year.

After a few hours, the early sun dimly lit the room. Alonso cried out in hunger. Jeremiah woke and wanted to be the one to feed him.

Camila prepared a bottle. Alonso refused take it from his father, swatting the bottle away as Jeremiah tried to force the nipple into his mouth. Thwarted, Jeremiah stared as Camila fed his son.

"He's more like me than you," he muttered, and went back to sleep.

After Jeremiah woke again, he absently played with Alonso on the bedroom floor. Camila watched, trying to read him, but she couldn't. She tried to make conversation, but he was too withdrawn to engage. With the increasing awkwardness, her anxiety began to gather in her chest, primed to attack.

Jeremiah told Camila he wanted to take Alonso to Queens that night, to sleep at his sister's house, with him. She refused. He insisted.

"He doesn't even know you!"

"He's my son!"

"I don't know your intentions," she said. Accusing him of what, she wasn't sure, but she wasn't going to be made a fool by him.

"You want me to go to the train right now?" he yelled. "You don't trust me?" It was time to go back to work anyway. He gathered up his book bag and fled.

That night, alone again, after the long struggle of putting Alonso to bed, Camila typed *Jeremiah Cole* into Facebook to check if he'd announced his fatherhood yet. Two different pages for his name appeared, with two different profile pictures. One was a selfie Jeremiah had taken in a mirror, his hair unbraided into an enormous Afro. Another was the logo for Grand Theft Auto.

Why would he have two Facebook pages?

Clicking on the Grand Theft Auto image, she landed on a page with pictures of a somehow familiar-looking kid in glasses. She clicked on one with a big goofy smile like Jeremiah's, liked by Jeremiah's ex—the one he'd been married to long ago, when he lived in Buffalo. He'd never told her about the marriage, but she had looked into his court records.

He'd said he had no other kids.

She told herself, as she had so many times before, I refuse to get played.

Camila added the kid as a friend. She felt invincible as she typed out a message to Jeremiah's other son.

Jeremiah returned on Sunday afternoon, over an hour late, complaining about the two-hour subway ride, delivering a monologue about the Bronx, about how it was like an episode of *Law & Order*, all drugs and crime, how he liked Queens better. Camila sank inward. How could he leave her in a shelter for a year and then complain about where she was living? She noticed immediately that he didn't bring anything for Alonso.

Alonso needed formula and diapers, so they made their way to the Rite Aid on Grand Concourse, pushing the stroller down the wide promenade like generations of families before them. He told her he was hungry. And that he was broke. Camila breathed in to manage her disgust in him and scarcely breathed it out. Jeremiah began clutching his stomach in hunger, so she bought him a sandwich. She asked him where all his money went. He didn't reply.

At Rite Aid, a dollar bill was crumpled on the floor a few yards from two kids who were messing around in the aisle. Jeremiah kicked the dollar, attempting to hide it under a shelf. Camila scowled at him. She called out to the kids to see if they'd dropped it, then picked it up and handed it to one of them.

"Why'd you have to do that?" Jeremiah snapped.

She just shook her head and asked him how he paid for the enormous Batman tattoo across his back. He mumbled that his friend

did it for free. She didn't know whether to believe him. Either way
it was damning: He had no means, or he was blowing what he had
on bullshit while she was feeding and housing their son. All while
someone else was feeding and housing his other son. The familiar
sentence looped through her mind: I can't stand his character.

They walked to the supermarket. Blind to her clenched jaw and
narrowed eyes, he sparked up another monologue, this time on
how she was raising Alonso. "He's kind of difficult to handle," he
observed. "You've got to make him more manly or he's going to be
soft. He's got to know the streets. He's too attached to you."

Camila ignored him. She pushed the cart, stopping to compare
prices, while Jeremiah pushed the stroller.

Jeremiah scooped Alonso out of his stroller. He playfully whispered to him, "C'mon, let's leave Mommy." They disappeared.

Camila texted him. She called him. No reply. Pushing both the
cart and the stroller through the aisles, Camila roiled over Jeremiah's immaturity. He'd had a good dental assistant job, but he said it
was too much work for him. He had been getting paid fifteen dollars an hour, before he became a broke waiter. How the hell are
you broke and you had a good-ass job? She raged once more about
how he had never acknowledged that she'd been homeless or asked
a single question about the past year of her life. Nor had he said a
word about how she was about to be homeless again when she
couldn't pay Jovanka anymore. His son would be homeless, too,
again.

Back in the apartment, Jeremiah got down on the floor with
Alonso, who showed little interest in his father's attempts to engage
him.

Camila checked her Facebook messages. There was one waiting,
from Jeremiah, Jr.

Yeah, that's my dad, the message said. *I miss him.*

How old are you? she wrote back.

I'm twelve, the kid replied immediately.

When did you last speak to him?

Three years ago. What's his number? the son asked.

It hurt so damn much to reach out to her own parents. Jeremiah was something worse than broke, worse than a guy she couldn't trust. He was a father who remorselessly abandoned his children.

She was never, ever, going to subject Alonso to the kind of unmet longing she felt every day.

Camila looked up from her phone at Jeremiah, who sat on the floor, visibly frustrated with his son's lack of interest. Now that she had proof, she had no more patience.

"You have another kid," she said. "Is this true?"

Jeremiah glanced up at her like she'd expressed something ludicrous. "No, it's not true," he said. "What are you talking about?"

She stepped into full prosecution mode. "So you're telling me you were never married and divorced, either?"

"No."

"So if I show you a paper that shows that you were in fact married and divorced, you'll deny it."

He just looked at the floor.

"And you got a kid."

He pretended to focus on playing with Alonso. "Who told you that?" He laughed. "You're crazy."

She stared at him.

"You're making it up," he said. "I don't want to argue. You can believe whatever you want."

"I can prove that you're lying to me."

Camila opened up her laptop. A quick, familiar online search of the court-records database led her easily to a divorce citation. He watched as she began to pull up the document.

"You're right, you're right," he mumbled, staring at the floor.

"About the kid, too?"

"You're right."

"I am not going to allow myself to get hurt," she said sharply. "And I would never leave you alone with Alonso."

For the second and final time, he collected his book bag. He didn't say a word.

There was one thing Camila could not stand leaving unacknowledged. "I do a good job, right?" she asked Jeremiah, nodding toward Alonso.

He did not speak or look at her in response. All the satisfaction she got was a barely perceptible nod.

She was done with him.

Camila felt herself become impermeable, immovable, immune. She realized she had become so emotionless that she couldn't even cry.

6

SOY DOMINICANA

amila pushed the stroller into her constitutional-law midterm with an apologetic smile. The flight to Santo Domingo was scheduled for just a few hours later, which meant she had to bring Alonso with her to the exam, along with their luggage, or miss the plane. Camila hoped that a pacifier would keep Alonso quiet until she finished. She'd studied hard, she told her professor; it shouldn't take long. The professor gave Camila a chiding look and told her that if the baby cried, she'd have to take him out of the classroom.

As soon as Camila picked up her pencil, Alonso let out a scream that cascaded into a series of full-lung cries. She quickly ferried him out, pushing the stroller with one hand, wrangling two rolling suit-cases with the other, hoping the professor would let her take the exam during office hours. She'd told me she couldn't have left Alonso with his father—not that she'd become accustomed to that word in the two days since Jeremiah left her room in the Bronx. Yet he had called, checked up on Alonso, said he wanted to see him, wanted to know when they were flying, when they were returning, asked if she needed him to help them get to the airport.

Alonso was going to see where he really came from, Camila insisted, his real people, not the father who still had done nothing for him. She dreamily conjured what awaited them, describing palm trees and rum cocktails and beaches and salsa clubs and a whole country of people just like her—a world she only knew from postcards and Instagram. Her aunt still hadn't replied, but Camila said she had faith that it would all work out. Once she got to Santo Domingo, she'd figure out how to make her way to Pinalito to find her family, to find where she belonged.

She'd never been on an international flight, just one trip to Illinois and another to Buffalo. At JFK, Camila was flummoxed by the security line, the people carrying their shoes and laptops in shallow plastic bins like customers at a surrealist cafeteria. She looked for guidance through the bizarre choreography everyone else seemed so practiced at performing. But it all became familiar to her as we approached the metal detectors; as she told the TSA guard knowingly, it was just like court. Once we were through, the gleaming duty-free boutiques amazed her. "Michael Kors . . . Hugo Boss," she whispered as she passed each one. She marveled at how clean the terminal was, wondering aloud if Santo Domingo would be as spotless and shiny. Boarding had begun. Everyone crowded by the gate was Dominican, she noted with pride.

Once she'd settled into her window seat, Camila realized Alonso needed a diaper change. As the flight attendant moved past, she asked permission to use the lavatory.

"That'll be one dollar," the flight attendant said, straight-faced.

Camila reached into her bag to find her wallet.

"I'm just kidding, hon!"

Camila flushed, embarrassed. To make up for it, the flight attendant gave her extra peanuts during the flight. Camila carefully tucked them into the diaper bag next to the sandwich she'd been given for her meal.

The airplane began its descent to Santo Domingo Airport, drifting down through pink clouds, aglow in the setting sun. Camila gazed out the window, at the angled light transforming the sea's surface into giant metallic fish scales. Dense, rocky rows of green rippled up from the crag of the coast. Alonso slept in her lap as the plane circled in an elegant arc over clover-shaped clusters of base-ball diamonds beyond the hills, then over a vast forest of shipping containers, before landing in a country of ten million people she thought would be just like her.

One hundred years ago, the United States occupied the Dominican Republic. Even before the U.S. reign over the republic became official in 1916, the United States ran the customs office on the island, managing the country's finances at the pleasure of U.S. barons and banks invested in sugar cane. Then came the rise of Rafael Trujillo, the island's own homegrown dictator, tiny square mustache and all, who would rule the island with the vanity and brutality of a true gangster. Whatever wealth had not been channeled to the States flowed directly into Trujillo's personal coffers, or that of close party surrogates. Under his reign, disappearances became commonplace— shrouded in mystery—until more-open massacres became the way of law. While Trujillo's citizens starved, his own riches heaped as high as the mountain he renamed in his own honor, until 1961, when he was assassinated by one of the few opponents he hadn't murdered first. One of my favorite facts from the island's brutal past: Every year, the general who killed Trujillo commemorated the date by donning the same brown shoes and watch he was wearing when he fired that fatal bullet.

The Americans had looked the other way while Trujillo squashed the island nation under the heel of his Italian loafer. But a few years after his assassination, the Dominican Republic was once more deemed useful to U.S. power. In the hope of stanching communism that might ripple through the Caribbean from Cuban waters, the United States invaded again and once more took control of the Do-minican Republic. Immigration to the States was encouraged as part of the new occupation, to help cement American capitalism in a poor and furious country.

Meanwhile, the Dominican economy sharply declined. So did the availability of jobs, clean water, and electricity, inflating prices in response. As the Stars and Stripes flapped alongside the Dominican flag, most families could not afford basic groceries. In desperation, islanders began fleeing to America. At the time of Trujillo's assassination, about 12,000 Dominicans called the United States home. That number had risen to over one million by the time Camila bought her plane ticket back to her so-called homeland. Half of Dominican America lived in New York, in the largest Hispanic city in the country. New York had always been known for its Puerto Rican citizenry—its Marias and Bernardos—but Dominicans now outnumbered them. These days only 10 million Dominicans were left on the island, many of whom saw an American green card as their only hope for a future. Nueva York was the beacon to most Dominicans, and yet here in Santo Domingo, with its palm trees and patrimony, American Camila wanted to be nowhere else.

At passport control, Camila excitedly chatted up the policeman guarding the queue. She thought if she said her grandfather was a cop in Santiago, he might let her skip ahead.

"Dónde en Santiago?" he asked, bemused by her eagerness.

"Pinalito," she said.

He didn't let her jump the line.

As Camila inched ahead, she watched the tourists being fingerprinted. They smiled into a camera that automatically loaded their faces into a mainframe. She thought she might not be processed along with the other Americans, since, as she said, she was from here.

"Soy Dominicana," she told the immigration officer behind the desk.

"Your family is Dominican?" he replied in English.

"Sí," she said.

She handed him her American passport, and Alonso's.

"You're not Dominican, you're American," he said quietly.

He fingerprinted her and took her picture.

"Where is your receipt for the tourist tax?" he asked.

"I'm not a tourist here," she said defensively.

He looked her coldly in the eye and pointed his finger toward the payment window.

In the thick, inky darkness of the airport parking lot, Maria's brother waited for Camila and Alonso to emerge from the sliding doors that led outside from customs. Back in the Bronx, in the day-care kitchen, Camila had been giving Maria regular updates about her trip plans. When Camila's aunt still hadn't replied to her emails, and Mauricio never offered up his house, Maria insisted we all stay with her family in Santo Domingo. The house was small—her mother, brother, sister, nieces, and nephews lived there—but we could squeeze in, and she said it was in a nice middle-class neighborhood.

The brother, bulky and taciturn, barely spoke as he drove. Camila peered out the tinted windows, but it was too dark to see much of anything. When we reached the house, a stray dog, chewing at a hind leg, scuttled out of the way to allow the car to park. Across the street, a fluorescent lamp spilled a pool of white light over men playing dominoes at a card table. Maria's mother came to the top of the tiled stairway as Camila carried Alonso up to the front door, allowing Maria's brother to play porter with the luggage. Smiling warmly, she kissed Camila on both cheeks and reached for the baby as Maria's sister came out to greet us.

Maria had told Camila that her sister was a police officer, which had conjured something utterly different than the meek manner and rolls of belly fat that welcomed her into the house now. The sister graciously showed Camila the common spaces: the untouched formal couches hulking around a coffee table; the rusty kitchen where a teenage girl in a crocheted hairnet washed dishes in the cold-water sink. Two children, piled onto a single shredded armchair, refused to break their gaze from an American kids' show dubbed into Spanish. Camila whispered to me that she wasn't sure how many people slept in the three small, peeling bedrooms. The sister said not to worry: Camila and Alonso could have the bedroom with the luxury of air-conditioning and a double bed.

"What do you want to do while you're here?" the sister asked Camila.

"I want to party!" Camila said excitedly. "I want to go to Bahia, go to Boca Chica, go horseback riding, go zip-lining, go on motor-cycles. I want to do everything!"

The sister was silent for a moment. "We're near the zoo," she said quietly. "Do you want to take him to the zoo tomorrow?"

"What about the beach?" Camila asked.

The sister sat mutely.

"I heard Presidente tastes totally different here. So much better, right?" Camila asked.

The sister just stared at her dumbly. "Do you want to go to the Malecón?" she finally asked Camila.

Camila looked back at her, puzzled. She didn't know what that was, she told me, but she didn't want to ask.

She asked the sister how much money she made as a police offi-cer.

One hundred fifty U.S. dollars, the sister told her. A month.

Camila didn't tell her she was planning to do the same work or that her grandfather had been a cop in Pinalito. Somehow the mark-ers of identity that she broadcast at home, she was learning, seemed best unsaid here.

In a huff, she got settled in the bedroom, laying out Alonso's clothes on the nubby polyester sheets, white with small rosebuds. No one had asked about her family in the D.R., she said, beginning to explain her mood. There was no Internet, so she couldn't post on Facebook to show everyone where she was. And none of these peo-ple seemed capable of having a good time—they were all silent and serious, like her grandparents, she told me. But the sister had men-tioned that a friend of the family, a professional driver, could take her around. Camila hoped he wouldn't be like that silent brother. Maybe he'd be sexy, she said; maybe he could show her a good time. Maybe he'd take her to Pinalito to find her family.

The next day, the driver waited in a white car parked across the street from the house. Camila came outside, holding Alonso in one arm, shielding her eyes from the sun with the other to take inventory of her surroundings. In the bright light of day, she could see that the houses down the block were concrete, in varying chipped pastels. A mangy cat mewled in a pile of rubble near a woman filling up plastic buckets with a hose from a public tap. Camila crossed the pocked pavement to the car, memorizing the phone number painted on the passenger's side door. The driver got out to open the back door for her. Camila noted aloud how professional he looked in his white shirt and tie. He sized up her short shorts and lipstick and grinned. Alonso stared at his face and reached out a hand to touch his trim mustache.

The driver spoke no English. Camila asked him in Spanish to take her to the supermarket so she could change some money. At the market, the driver wasn't the only man grinning at her exposed legs—everyone else was wearing long pants. She exchanged two hundred dollars, slipped the cash into her bra, and laid a case of Presidente on the checkout counter.

Back in the car, she asked him if they could go somewhere to get frío frío. He didn't know what it was.

"How can you not know frío frío? It's Dominican!"

He just shrugged and shook his head.

Camila was quiet, sitting in the back seat with Alonso on her lap. He asked where she wanted to go next. She didn't know anywhere, so she told him to take them to the zoo, like the sister suggested. As he drove, she noted aloud how there were no seatbelts, no cup holders, just a dented ashtray.

The zoo parking lot was empty except for a few ramshackle yellow school buses marked with the names of the American suburban school districts where they'd been in service decades before: Bloomfield, Michigan; Sharon, Massachusetts. Another car pulled in nearby. A mother and daughter got out and stopped to admire Alonso, who was sitting in the stroller, alert and curious. They complimented Camila on her very cute baby. Camila thanked them.

"You talk different from us," the mother said.

"I am the same!"

The mother sized her up. "No. You're white."

They stared each other down for a moment.

"Thank you," the daughter said awkwardly in English. They hastened away.

"Leave your cellphone and money in the car," the driver told Camila, once they were out of earshot. "Don't let anybody come up to you. They're going to rob you in there." He waited in the car while we toured the zoo.

Back in the parking lot, Camila told the driver she wanted to spend the trip having a good time, going to the beach. He listed the beaches that tourists liked.

"I'm not a tourist here," she said.

He just laughed. It was the last time she'd make that claim.

"I want to do something else, too," she told him. "I want to go to Santiago, to Pinalito."

"I will show you the sights of Santiago."

"I want to go find my family there."

"I will show you the Monument to the Heroes of the Restoration."

Camila didn't know anywhere else to go, so she asked him to drop her off at the family's house. She put on a black swimsuit, leaving her bra on under it to hold her money. The mother mopped the tile floor. Alonso slept. The television droned, then, abruptly, it didn't; the electricity had gone off. When it came back on, her phone somehow picked up a bar of Wi-Fi.

Camila texted her dad. *I'm in the Dominican Republic. I want to know how to find our family.*

She nervously stared at the brief message long after it had been delivered to Mauricio's phone in New York. Then she wrote her aunt again to let her know she'd made it to Santo Domingo.

Finally the sister came home from work and the brother emerged from his room, where he seemed to have been sleeping all day. Camila said she wanted to go to the beach. The brother nodded and simply walked out to his car in response. Once the road straightened into highway along the ocean, we hit a traffic stop. A machine gun pressed against the back window, where Camila sat with Alonso crying on her lap. The sister said she was a cop, but the gun remained up against the glass, so no one said anything else. After twenty minutes, we were permitted to pass.

The beach was a thin strip of sand, strewn with plastic chairs and tables. Dogs prowled, looking for food.

"It's so beautiful! Look at the perfect sand!" she exclaimed to Alonso. She carried him into the water and took some selfies with her phone. "Look, the water is so clear!"

The brother and sister chose a table and ordered fish. Their silence was getting to her, Camila whispered to me. She pulled up some salsa music on her phone and set it on the table, moving her shoulders, standing Alonso on her lap to dance. There were no lights to illuminate the table as darkness descended. A massive whole red snapper arrived on a plastic plate in the quickly chilling damp air. Camila spiritedly chattered to Alonso as she fed small bites into his eager mouth while the brother and sister ate without a word.

The check followed: 6,200 pesos for a fish, $135 before tip. The brother and sister didn't make a move to contribute. Shocked, Camila remarked how expensive it was.

"That's because you're American," the sister said again.

I picked up the tab to thank the family for their hospitality.

Back at the family's house a couple of awkward hours later, Camila retreated into the bedroom. A small bar of Wi-Fi appeared. A text from her father. Three words.

Everyone is here.

Nothing more. It wasn't true that everyone was in the States. But what else could she say.

The phone rang. "It's an emergency," said the voice on the line.

Camila realized it was Geraldine's voice.

"Where are you?" Camila asked.

"It's Alonso. It's an emergency."

"Where are you, Mom?"

"I can't tell you."

Camila was back on Sherman Avenue. She ran down the stairs and out the door. Her sisters pulled up in a cab. They took her to a housing project. Not the building where her mother lived, but somewhere far more dank and foul, where rats skittered across the floor and men lurked in shadows. The elevator door was open. On the floor of the elevator was Alonso, swaddled, lying there alone. Camila realized he wasn't breathing. She rushed to him. As her face hovered close over his, he took a huge gasping breath. Camila turned around. Geraldine was standing by the doorway to the stairs, looking at her with blank eyes.

"You would have let him die," she accused her mother. "You were supposed to be responsible."

"The phone was ringing," Geraldine said. "I had to answer it. So I just put him down here. He's fine now." She turned away.

Camila woke up dizzy in the strange bed, covered in goose-bumps between the polyester rosebud sheets. Alonso was sleeping sweetly beside her, lulled by the churning air conditioner, until the electricity went out again and he woke with a cry.

She asked the mother to watch Alonso while she took a cold-water shower and dressed in a white T-shirt and a tribal-print mini-skirt in the colors of the Dominican flag. As she began to load up the diaper bag for the day, she heard chanting in the next room, over Alonso's screams. When she listened closely, she realized it was voices speaking in tongues, like her grandmother used to. She went out into the living room to see what was going on. The women of the household were all laying their hands on her son's wriggling body. They didn't see her. She felt too awkward to say anything, so she holed up in the bedroom until they stopped.

Camila tried to shut out the image of hands on her writhing son and ignore the glossolalia on the other side of the bedroom door. Another door to hide behind, another place she didn't fit in, she whispered to me, her voice tight with pain. She was never comfortable anywhere, she confessed, after all the months of performing how she could fit in everywhere. Camila listed the people who never made her feel like she belonged: Jovanka and Aaron; Pedro and his mother; everyone at the shelter; her dad. "I always feel I'm doing something wrong. I'm always overwhelmed," she told me, clenching her fists and then pressing them against her lips. But she said she had no idea it would be like this in the D.R. She'd believed this would be the one place where she belonged.

The lights came on. Electricity. Camila immediately plugged in her phone, which had gone dead overnight. It flickered to life with a message from Maria from the daycare in the Bronx.

Has my brother asked about the bargain?

Camila stared at the words, puzzled. *What's the bargain?* she wrote back.

The papers, Maria wrote a moment later.

Immigration papers. A green-card marriage. Camila was stunned by her realization. They wanted her to marry the brother. That's why she was staying there.

7

THE DRIVER

From the back seat, Camila announced to the driver she wanted to go dancing that night.

"Good," he said. "I will get a sitter for you. Just give her a couple of pesos and she'll take care of the baby. You like music?" He looked for her response in the rearview mirror.

She smiled gratefully at his reflection. Finally, someone who got her, who wanted to live a little, she told me. He turned on the radio so loud Camila felt submerged in the repetitive beat of a bachata song. Then he cranked up the music even louder and belted out lyrics in a full, clear voice.

"Tonight we're going to go to the club. But don't tell anyone in that house." He wagged a finger playfully in the mirror.

He sang along to the new salsa tune that came on the radio. Camila rolled down the window to let in a rush of air. She didn't ask where he was driving until he parked the car in the fifteenth-century Spanish Zona Colonial, on a street that came to a dead end in a pile of rubble.

"You're my tour guide," she said flirtatiously.

Passing gift shops along an empty pedestrian corridor, Camila recognized the same type of machete her grandfather had in the old

Corona apartment and racks of straw fedoras like his. She was amazed to see faceless dolls in flounced dresses and wide-brimmed hats like the ones her aunts had prized back in Queens. This was what she'd been waiting for, she told me with a sigh—a feeling of where she was from. The driver led us to a café by a park, where a trio played music for tourists.

"My grandfather played accordion like that," Camila said.

"I'm a grandfather," the driver said. "My daughter is twenty-three."

"That's how old I am," Camila told him, lifting Alonso out of his stroller, as the driver admired her slim curves.

Camila asked the waiter for frío frío. The waiter just stared at her, while the driver smiled patiently, amused.

"It's Dominican!" she said. "I know, I'm Dominican!"

"I don't know what that is," the waiter said.

Camila ordered mangú instead. Then she told the driver the story about being pulled over at the traffic stop, the machine gun at the window.

"He has tinted windows, so he looks like a gangster," he said about the brother. "They'll pull you over here and lock you up if you look like a criminal. They don't bother me, because I look professional."

How could Maria think she would marry a guy who the police assumed was a criminal? she said to me. She wanted a professional man.

"I want you to teach me English," the driver said, as the waiter placed the plate of mangú in front of her. Alonso opened his mouth for the rice and plantains like a hungry goldfish. As she fed him, the driver talked. "If I was in the United States, I could buy a house, and I could still send money home to my family. I know it's expensive in New York, but you can work hard. Here, there is no stability. Here, it is not sustainable."

He told her that his father and siblings had left for America thirty years ago. There was a problem, he said, and they couldn't bring him over. "They have good jobs in the States. It's only because of the money they send that we can survive here," he said. "In New

York I could have a better car," he said. He pointed to a Hyundai Sonata that was parked nearby. "Like that one; that's the car I want. What do you think of it?"

"It's very nice," she said politely.

Camila wasn't thinking about the car, she told me as soon as we were alone; she was thinking about the homes his family had in New York.

He smiled at her meaningfully. She understood what he was insinuating.

When the waiter brought the check, the driver got up to fetch his car. Camila sat with Alonso on her lap, calculating. It was $15,000 for papers—that's what people pay for a marriage, she said. She'd been asked enough times to know. She didn't want to be a welfare mom anymore, she said; she needed that money. She wiped away some food from the corner of Alonso's lips as she talked. He had family in New York. Maybe she could stay with them, maybe they could become like her family. He wouldn't try to get with her; it'd just be business. She hadn't planned on anything like this when she envisioned her trip, she said, but it made sense.

Alonso looked up at her. She kissed him on his tiny nose. Camila reached into the diaper bag for her wallet to pay the bill. She counted how much money she had left and wondered aloud if she could fall in love with the driver; he was her father's age, but he was fun. She shimmied excitedly in her chair and said her heart was racing. It was thrilling to think about: a real man, a successful family, money, a home, she said. She thought it could work.

The driver returned to the table and said he wanted to take Camila to the National Aquarium. While they were there, he insisted on carrying Alonso, who smiled in his arms as he pointed out species in the tanks, like a loving father. Camila wanted to take a selfie of the three of them. He put his arm low around her waist and pulled her in tight. She showed him the picture.

"It looks like a family," she said suggestively, raising her eyebrows.

He pulled off his navy-blue polyester tie and handed it to her, like a husband. She folded it up and laid it neatly on top of the diaper bag, like a wife. Then she ran a wand of burgundy gloss over her lips.

"I want a kiss," he said.

She leaned over and pressed her lips to his cheek, leaving a perfect mark. They laughed together.

Back in the car, he turned up the salsa loud and told her he was taking her to the beach.

"I want to see where I'm from," she yelled over the music. "I want to go to Pinalito tomorrow. In Santiago."

He nodded but didn't stop singing. "I want to see where my family lives," she said even louder. "It's important to me."

He turned to her, pressed a hand over his heart, and belted out the first line of an old song that came on the radio.

"Antony Santos! My favorite!" she cried. They sang it to each other, like lovebird duettists onstage, as the car raced along the sea.

By the side of a road, used clothing was piled in heaps on a folding table. The driver pulled over and motioned for Camila to stay in the car.

"People from New York send clothes to sell here," he explained.

The driver dug through the pile until he found a pair of red Speedo trunks and held them up toward the car and gestured for Camila's approval. "Thumbs-up? Thumbs-down?"

She gave him a thumbs-up.

He walked over to her window. She smiled up at him.

"Two hundred pesos," he told her.

Camila's face fell as she realized he was telling her to pay for his bathing suit. She reached for her wallet, counted out the money, and handed him the bills through the window. She didn't sing along during the rest of the drive.

Camila wanted to change clothes before she went out dancing. Back at the house, she fished through her suitcase for the maxidress, the most modest thing she'd packed. She didn't want the driver to think she was planning to go to bed with him. As Camila carried Alonso out of the house to take him to the sitter, her glossed lips and moussed hair glistening under the fluorescent streetlight outside, the mother clucked disparagingly.

The driver parked by a place that looked like an unassuming steakhouse in a sleek downtown area, near gleaming multistory malls filled with American stores. Outside the bar, a bouncer patted the driver down for weapons. Inside, lights flashed and bachata blasted. Hefty older men wore dark sunglasses, dress shirts unbuttoned, collars spread, their dates teetering on heels in skintight jeans and tighter Lycra tops. Camila said she was glad she'd chosen the long dress. A group of guys smoking a hookah at the next table stared at her tattooed arm. She ignored them.

A young, hunky waiter in a cowboy hat brought a tray of drinks. Camila pulled out her phone to take a picture of her mojito. "Wi-Fi!" she exclaimed; she could send pictures to Instagram right from the club. Still no word from her aunt, though. And nothing more from her dad. In the ladies' room, she took pictures of herself pouting and smiling in the mirror. Back at the table she uploaded a new profile photo, then she made a video of the dance floor and the bar and posted it. The driver was impatient for her attention; she'd been hunched over her phone or in the bathroom since they got there.

In a break from Dominican hits, a pop song from the States vibrated through the room, a new Rihanna hit Camila was crazy about. As soon as the patois over the vocal track rose over bass and keyboards, she dropped her phone on the table, lifted her hands into the air, and whooped, leaping off the chair and onto the dance floor. She kept her hands up while she got low, closing her eyes, moving her hips with precision and control. The driver came up behind her. They owned the floor until the song ended. Then, quick as she'd sprung up to dance, she was back on her phone. After a couple of songs, he persuaded her to dance with him again. She took a long pull of her mojito through a straw and followed him. They danced and drank some more. Between the rum, the rhythm of the music, and the freedom from Alonso, Camila unlocked herself. She felt the hunky waiter press into her as he made his way past to take orders, but she ignored it—she knew he knew she was sexy. When the driver rubbed his erection on her ass or against her long thigh, she tensed a little, but it was just dancing. On the dance floor, Camila finally surrendered all the awkwardness she'd been carrying, out of place and out of sorts and out of money.

Until the bill came. The driver went to get the car as soon as the waiter dropped the check. Twenty-one hundred pesos. It was more than she'd been expecting, but it was okay, she said; at least she'd had a good time. She left the cash on the table and made her way through the grinding bodies to the door. Then, as she stepped outside, she felt a hand grab her arm. It was the waiter.

"There was a problem with the computer," he said. "You owe a thousand pesos more."

Camila stared him down. Her composure fractured. She couldn't stand it anymore. Not after trying to keep her poverty in perspective here, only to be treated like an open wallet. Not after her hopes that in this country she'd finally find a family that would take care of her. All those months of not talking back, not permitting herself a flash of rage. Keeping her bed made, her son fed, her grades high, her documents up to date, her appointments met, her optimism impossibly in place after every crushing blow.

She rolled her neck. "You've got to be fucking kidding me," she said to the waiter in English.

"You owe a thousand pesos more," he repeated.

"Yo, nigga, I don't play that," she said, rolling her neck again before snapping it into position, like a cobra coiling itself before an attack. She stepped away, her eyebrows raised in haughty incredulity, but the waiter kept his hold of her arm. She jerked it from his grasp. "No fucking way!" she yelled in English. "I'm from Nueva York! I don't take this shit!"

The crowd outside the bar went silent. All eyes were on Camila as she raised her arms, her long fingers slicing the thick, humid air. Rolling her neck, she yelled louder, amplified by the thrill of exposing him in front of the crowd. "You've been pressing your dick up against me all night! You want more money for that? You think because I'm American you can lie and get my money? You think I'm stupid?"

The waiter shook his head and retreated inside the bar.

Camila wasn't going to stop there. "You don't fuck with me!" she screamed at his disappearing back. "Yo soy Trinitario!" The crowd gawked at her in silence. "You know what that means? *Yo soy Trinitario!*" She relished the surge of power she felt invoking not just her Americanness but Pedro's gang.

Then Camila dropped her arms and shook her head in disgust. She began to march toward the parking lot, away from the onlookers. "Fuck this shit," she said out loud, to no one in particular. "I'm going back to New York."

But first she was going to find her family.

8

FAMILY

The driver was steely and mute for the two-hour drive to Santiago the next morning. The air was thick with burning trash, and the streets were thick with people selling mangoes and selfie sticks between the crawling cars.

"Is it dangerous?" Camila asked him formally.

Without even glancing at her in the rearview mirror, the driver answered by reaching under his seat and pulling out a machete. He told her it would be another forty-five minutes at least to Pinalito, past Santiago, and would cost her more. The car began to climb up green hills, where tin roofs covered shacks made of branches, and occasional pastel-painted concrete houses dotted far hills. Mopeds and horses made up the sparse traffic on the road.

"You came all the way from New York to see this? It's nothing." His voice was scornful.

"It's where my family is," she explained.

Camila laid Alonso down on the back seat to change him. Her eyes were on the messy diaper, not on the gates of her family's town as the car passed through.

"Your mother's family?"

"No," she said. "Just my father's."

"Your mother is from here, too?" he asked.

"Yes, from Cibao."

"And you wanted to come up here instead of going there?"

Camila stared out the window with Alonso on her lap. She didn't reply.

She'd just assumed it was a city, she told me. Her family never showed her pictures from here or described the trees or the mountains. No one ever talked about why they left; they were just gone. They became Americans, that was all. Camila said she felt nervous. She didn't know what she was doing here, how she ended up here. It didn't feel like a place she was connected to, she said.

The road twisted past stepped fields gone fallow. An emaciated cow flicked its tail by the side of the road.

"Look, Alonso, a cow! And a plantain tree! Isn't it pretty here?" Camila lifted Alonso to stand on her lap; the little boy held himself up on the half-open window.

"There's nothing interesting about this." The driver sounded disgusted. "I'm hungry," he said.

He pulled up to the only place to eat that we'd seen for miles, across from a supermarket and an empty lot that had sprouted a few banana trees. A shellacked photograph of the Empire State Building hung on an exterior wall of the restaurant. Inside was a picture of the World's Fair globe down the block from where Camila lived with her grandparents in Corona. She asked the waitress if she knew anyone in the precinct and explained that her grandfather had been on the police force, but the waitress said she didn't live in this empty town. A young redheaded guy in an Aéropostale T-shirt stopped in for a Coke. The waitress introduced him to Camila. She asked if he knew anyone with the last name Alvarez.

"Mainly this town is Perez and Ferreira," he said, shrugging.

Camila's eyebrows shot up. "I have Perez in my family," she said. Perez was her grandmother's family name, the one she gave up when she married Camila's grandfather, the police officer.

"I work at the supermarket across the street. It's owned by a man named Juan Perez," the guy told her.

Juan Perez was Mauricio's uncle.

The waitress said she knew Juan Perez, too. "He's an old man. He's sick, no? He lives in Santiago now."

"That old man's got money," the redheaded guy said. "They have a nice house here."

"Here?" Camila asked.

"Yeah, just down the way. Do you want me to show it to you?"

Camila quickly paid the check. The redheaded guy led the way down the street and around the corner to a long lawn beside a wide stable. Beyond it was a sprawling wooden plantation house, pale pink with white shutters and Victorian trim, with a well-fed cat napping under a riot of bougainvillea. With Alonso on her hip, Camila walked tentatively up to the house, then along the driveway that led along the side. A tall window was wide open, framing a woman with an elegant gray bun secured at the nape of her neck.

Camila explained who she was, Juan Perez's grandniece, visiting from New York. The woman studied her face skeptically.

"Mauricio's daughter," Camila said.

The woman nodded. "I am your cousin," she said, a smile slowly transforming her face. "Come around to the back." She beckoned with a gracious hand.

Late one night when Alonso was an infant, back in the shelter on Fourth Avenue, Camila had taken a piece of lined paper from her spiral notebook and drawn something she carried in her head: her family tree on her father's side. She'd delineated the generations with markers, making green boxes around her grandparents' names, purple around her father's siblings, and red around his cousins. I recalled that one of the red boxes simply said "three children." This woman, slim and composed like Camila, was one of them.

On the broad and cool back porch, the woman took Alonso in her arms. "You came all the way from Nueva York! I'm so happy to meet you!" she cooed to him in English, tickling his nose. "Welcome! Somos familia!"

Camila relaxed on a wicker chair. The cousin wanted all the news from the family in the States. She filled in the holes in that family tree, talking about relatives who left, who was in Los Ranchos, who was in White Plains. I noted that she didn't say much about who had stayed.

Camila pulled up pictures of her father and his newest children on her phone. They fawned over each other, searching each other's eager faces for resemblances. The cousin went inside and lifted her daughter's framed wedding portraits from the wall to show off. Camila said she'd be graduating in a few weeks, with a special commendation. The cousin kissed her congratulations. An extravagantly plumed chicken strutted back and forth in the backyard like a sentinel. Camila breathed in the scent of the mango tree beside the porch and felt that she was where she was meant to be.

Camila's cousin told her a story. "There was a song about the police on the radio," she said. "And your grandfather—your great-grandfather," she whispered to Alonso, "would gather all the cops in the middle of town, in the middle of the night, and they'd stand there, singing the song, making fun of themselves, at the top of their lungs." She shook her head sentimentally at the reminiscence. "He was so funny, yelling that song in the street, waking everyone up. We used to have such a good time." The cousin nuzzled Alonso in her lap. "You look like him," she told him, running a finger along his cheek.

Camila bashfully covered her mouth with her hand. "I'm so happy. I can't believe I found my family," she said. "That's all I wanted."

This wasn't a place she could stay. But it was a place, for a moment at least, where she could belong.

"Somos familia," her cousin said again, reaching out to take her hand.

They sat like that, hand in hand, for a quiet moment, breathing the campo air. Then the driver emerged from under the mango tree, tapped at his watch, and the cousin let go.

9

TO ALL THE LADIES

Camila had just wanted to go home. She'd thought the D.R. would be home. It wasn't. Sherman Avenue wasn't. Fourth Avenue wasn't. Jeremiah wasn't. Pedro wasn't. Her dad wasn't. Her mom—she wouldn't even entertain the thought.

What was home? Was it family? Love? Shelter?

Returning to New York was more like blunt trauma than a homecoming. Camila's post office box was as bleak as the weather on Thirty-fourth Street: It contained a letter telling her that she was going to have to start her child-support case again, in a different borough. Seven months after she'd begun her proceedings, she'd have to open a new case in Brooklyn, since she had used the Fourth Avenue address on some paperwork.

It had been a month since Camila lost welfare and childcare benefits, not to mention Medicaid. Her money was just about gone. But she'd sent the public-assistance office the requisite documents, followed up with them on the phone to make sure all was shipshape, and even received the letter she'd requested confirming her case was recertified. At least those checks would be starting up again, since who knew when she'd ever get a cent from Jeremiah now that she had to start their case from scratch.

Outside the subway in Downtown Brooklyn, a relentless wind inverted pedestrians' black bodega umbrellas, their silver skeletons exposed powerless against the gale. Her nose was red, and the cover-up smeared under her eyes only highlighted the gray cast to her face. She had returned from her trip with another cold, made more miserable by the driving rain. It was already a bad morning and it wasn't even nine A.M. yet. Dropping off Alonso at Maria's had been awkward, with none of the previous ease they'd shared. Camila hadn't mentioned the papers, the brother, the family. She didn't tell her about the driver or what she'd imagined with him over those few days. There were bigger concerns now. She wasn't going to waste her time mulling over her momentary foolishness.

The child-support office was in the MetroTech complex, Bruce Ratner's—and Brooklyn's—first billion-dollar real estate development deal. In the vast marble-walled lobby, an enormous flower arrangement towered over a reception desk for J.P. Morgan, one of the building's main tenants. Camila barely noticed how out of place she looked in her sweatpants, her forehead broken out, her worn boots soaked through. The marble lined the softly lit elevator, too, but when its doors slid open on the sixth floor, fluorescent lights in a drop ceiling returned Camila to the more familiar reality of dark women with strollers waiting in line.

When it was her turn, Camila recited her case number.

Silence. Clicking. "Your case is closed. You need to go to DeKalb to open it again."

"So I won't be able to be seen today?"

"No," the worker said. "It's rejected for whatever reason."

"Does it give you the reason?" Camila asked.

"No. It doesn't matter the reason. It's rejected. You need to go to DeKalb."

DeKalb was the Brooklyn welfare office. Camila's case was still at the Manhattan welfare office; why would she have to go to the Brooklyn welfare office? Would she have to start her welfare case from scratch, too? Downstairs at Au Bon Pain, Camila counted out fifteen packets of sugar for her small coffee. As she ripped them open one by one, she shook her head, dumbfounded. She'd miss both class and work again.

She composed herself, looked up the DeKalb address on her smartphone, and braved the freezing rain to the subway. French tourists scrutinizing a guidebook blocked the exit of the G train in Bedford-Stuyvesant. Camila waited politely for them to let her pass and walked down Bedford to DeKalb. She was hungry. A sandwich board at the café next to the welfare office promoted a beef tongue confit on special. She decided she wouldn't be able to eat until she got back to the Bronx.

The DeKalb Job Center vestibule reeked of stale cigarettes and was tiled in 1970s gold and avocado. Wood-grained plastic paneled the elevator, the same untouched vintage as the entrance tiles. Inside, the air was redolent of weed, urine, and the body odor of the man rocking back and forth in the corner.

"They don't care. They don't care. They don't care," he repeated.

One floor up, an automated voice was competing with a news channel barking loudly from a waiting room television.

"Now calling CA52401. Please go to window ten. Now calling CB902306. Please go to window two."

Camila got in line behind a black-skinned woman in a greasy men's parka. The woman was leaning on a cane and lecturing the young Latina in front of her on the fallacy of body fat.

"These legs aren't fat. They're filled with feces. Feces. You understand? They look fat, but once I take a shit, I can walk better. They slim down. You understand?"

Camila's number came up to register. The worker at the window was an aging Caribbean woman in a wig and a polyester shirt. She did not look up from her computer screen when she spoke.

"What is your Social?" The worker barely opened her mouth to talk. Her words were almost indiscernible in the din of the room.

Camila recited the numbers.

"Your welfare case is closed," the worker said.

"Can you tell me why?"

Silence. The worker still had not looked up from her screen. "Do you want to reapply today?" she asked tonelessly.

Camila sighed in frustration and clenched her teeth for a moment to collect herself. "If I were to reapply today, I'd be submitting the same documents you already have," she said.

Silence. The worker continued to stare at the monitor. "Do you want to reapply again today?"

"A woman named Miss Selznick was working on my case," Camila said. "She sent me a letter that said she had all the documents. May I speak to her?"

"No, you may not. You may reapply and they will let you know the decision in forty-five days. So you want to reapply today?" she asked, finally looking up.

Camila clenched her teeth again and slowly nodded. The woman printed out a ticket and handed it to her.

This sort of exchange was commonplace. Camila knew that. Anyone who'd been in the system knew it. But the stakes were dire: Nearly one-quarter of the families that applied for emergency shelter in New York had lost their public-assistance cases in the previous year. Cases were often closed for "noncompliance"—that was the category Camila had just joined. Often the reason for noncompliance was mystifying. It could be something legitimate but unexplained. It could be a mistake on the part of an exhausted, underpaid worker, who was hardly motivated to ease clients' minds or help them through the system. Most welfare recipients reported hostility from workers, according to a recent study; one-third said they "always" experienced it at job centers like DeKalb or on Fourteenth Street.

But worse than that, the study—by the Urban Justice Center— had found that ten out of the city's nineteen job centers didn't even follow their own policies. Who knew why cases closed. Who knew how to find out why, without spending days in these waiting rooms; the study also said that over a third of welfare recipients reported that job centers "never" answered phone calls. A closed case was sheer catastrophe for the 356,350 New Yorkers on welfare that spring—up over 5 percent from the previous year. All this in a city with almost one million millionaires, more than any other city in the world.

Camila took a seat in the waiting room, where she became aware that there was piss puddled behind her seat. A tide of revulsion swept through her. Then she realized she herself had to pee. But the bathroom was on the first floor; if she went downstairs she might miss her next number being called by the automated voice. She'd have to hold it. Her hands started trembling, thinking about the series of efforts she'd made to avoid this exact catastrophe.

"Now calling PA50311. Please go to window number twenty-one." That was Camila's number.

Window 21 was a cubicle. An African American man in an argyle sweater asked her for her Social Security number. Mounds of dirt and dust were heaped under his desk; the linoleum under his chair had been ground down to a thin layer of grime.

"Your case is closed," he said. "Are you a citizen? Would you like to reapply today?"

"Yes," she said. "I also need to pay childcare."

"Then you've got to go upstairs." He handed her a ticket. "Go to the third floor and have a seat and wait. It might take a few hours."

The noise of the second floor was nothing compared to what assaulted Camila as the elevator doors opened on the third: wailing babies, television at top volume, strangers yelling at one another. The air carried the same ripe scent as the elevator.

She picked up a thick application booklet and found a place to sit among the rows and rows of occupied seats. As she slouched over the application, she began to list aloud all the dates she'd gone to the various offices. How many times she'd been to public assistance on Fourteenth Street. How many times she'd been to child support on the Lower East Side. How many times to family court in Queens. How many days of school lost. How many days of work lost. How many days of support unpaid.

Camila told me she felt like her chest was exploding. She closed her eyes, drew a breath, and stacked her spine into its usual queenly posture. Methodically, she continued to fill out the application. She completed it. Time stretched. She chewed the red polish of her fingernails and examined bits of tinsel still hanging from the stained ceiling. Next to her, a little girl in a stroller laughed happily and clapped her hands. In the chaos of the waiting room, Camila's eyes glazed over. She mumbled that she hoped Alonso didn't get sick. The weather made her nervous for his health, especially with no Medicaid . . . Her thoughts trailed off. She was quiet. Then she said there was nothing left to think about; thinking didn't make a difference.

The estimated three-hour mark passed.

Finally, she was called into a cubicle, where she was finally offered a reason for the loss of her welfare: She had failed to appear for an appointment with the Bureau of Eligibility Verification. The bureau was supposed to send Camila a letter informing her of the appointment. It appeared they didn't. Nor did anyone mention the appointment when she'd come in to reapply a month prior. The purpose of the appointment she'd missed was to show her birth certificate. That's how the bureau would verify that she was actually Camila Alvarez. Camila kept her birth certificate in her backpack, on hand at every appointment. It had been in her backpack when she'd come to recertify before. It was in her backpack now. She could verify herself to anyone at any time. And now she was not going to get her check because an obscure bureau hadn't sent her a letter for an appointment to do just that.

Plus, she was no longer eligible for childcare. The documents from Maria and Kingsborough that she'd gathered just last month were outdated now. She would need to make an appointment to apply for the voucher with new documents. Yes, the same documents, but they would need to be more-recent ones.

And she could expect that the earliest date to restart her child-support case would be in six weeks. In Brooklyn. If her public-assistance case was reopened by that time.

Mid-June. That's when she could expect her welfare checks to start up again. That was the best-case scenario—if they accepted her case, if she went to Midtown to check her post office box every day so she never missed a thing, if they didn't make another mistake. Two and a half months after her case had been closed without warning. Over a year into her motherhood.

Camila returned to the rows of chairs to wait for the printouts of each document she'd politely requested. There were just a couple of weeks to go until graduation. But she couldn't pay Maria out of pocket while she finished up classes and sat for her exams. And she didn't know how she was going to keep paying rent on Sherman Avenue. At least Jovanka hadn't asked when, exactly, Camila would be moving out. She knew she couldn't stay there much longer. But she had nowhere else to go.

I still hadn't gotten my advance check from my publisher, but I knew I'd likely receive it before Camila got her next welfare check. Regardless, I could have afforded to cover her rent and Alonso's hours at Maria's until her case started up again. I'd been through this year with her. We'd traveled hundreds of miles of subway track, flown to the D.R. and back, logged hours in waiting rooms and classrooms and bedrooms together. I'd calmed her baby, held her hand, been her confessor. She told me that she loved me every time we said goodbye to each other, always with a peck on the cheek. She didn't ask for my help.

The office was closing. It was the Friday before Mother's Day weekend. A woman her grandmother's age, with dark skin, a blond weave, and spidery fake eyelashes, called out to the whole waiting room on her way to the elevator.

"Happy Mother's Day to all the ladies!"

No one replied.

It was the first time someone had ever wished Camila a happy Mother's Day.

10

TERMINATED

Summer's heavy heat lowered over the city. Shave-ice scrapers appeared for their annual street-corner trade, scraping lemon and coconut into paper cones and contraband into tiny ziplock bags. Catcalls filled the mouths of most men under seventy. People hung out in parked cars with open doors, turning up the stereo, transforming vehicles into giant boom boxes for the block. Everything got louder in the summer.

Camila was tired. The night before, cops had gone knocking on every apartment door in the building while Telemundo news trucks parked on the street in front. A man in the building—a guy named Willie, whom everyone knew—had been stabbed to death in the sixth-floor hallway, right by the stairwell. He had a seven-year-old daughter. Camila heard he was murdered for his EBT card. She wondered aloud for a moment if they'd catch the guy who did it, what would happen to him. Then she shrugged, realizing she didn't really care.

Alonso's birthday party was planned for the coming weekend. Camila had bought party decorations at the dollar store and all the meat and chips and rice and beans her food stamps would cover. No way was Camila inviting Jeremiah to the party. He hadn't even reached out to her on Mother's Day. Camila had asked Alonso's godparents to come, but neither had replied. At least Irina said she'd bring Dima. At least her siblings told her they'd be there. And, though she remained outwardly skeptical about it, she hoped that her mother might show up.

On the Thursday before the party, Camila made the now-daily pilgrimage to her post office box in Manhattan to see if there was news about her case status. Today, two slim white envelopes awaited her. The first letter was from Medicaid. She needed to reapply with proof of residence, it said. But she couldn't use Jovanka's address, since it was an illegal rental in an overcrowded apartment, and she didn't even know if she would be there at the end of the month. Without an address she could claim, she and Alonso would continue to have no healthcare.

The second letter was from public assistance. It said the office was unable to verify her address before the recertification deadline. Her case had been denied.

11

COMMENCEMENT

All those class presentations and midnight cramming, all those after-class apologies for her lateness or absence, all those emails to professors pleading for makeup tests, explaining that she'd had to miss an exam for a court date, or an appointment, or because her son was sick. She was graduating. I'd given her a semiformal gown for the ceremony, something I'd bought on deep discount online, thinking it would work for one of us for the event. Camila was relieved it was backless, held up by thin spaghetti straps; the weather was forecast for eighty-eight degrees that evening. She pinned her hair up and said she hoped it wouldn't frizz too much. Alonso was dressed in what she called his Dominican look: a button-down short-sleeve shirt, madras shorts, a raffia fedora, and sandals he kept kicking off.

Though she'd invited everyone, no one in her family would be coming to celebrate her. I'd be there, with my husband and daughter. "You guys are my real family," she told me. I just squeezed her hand.

On campus, everyone stared at Camila. Her stroller didn't correspond with her gown; her gown didn't correspond with her huge tattoo of Alonso's face; her tattoo didn't correspond with the white lady by her side. She pretended not to notice as she hustled through the long corridors. The ceremony was being held in the hall where she'd lined up for financial aid that first impossible day on campus, when it felt like she wouldn't even be able to begin classes, much less graduate on the dean's list. As she approached the doors, she was handed a program of folded eight-and-a-half-by-eleven paper with a picture of a rose on the cover. She opened it to see her name in a florid font listed among the commendations inside.

Scanning the vast room, she noted aloud that she was the only student carrying a baby. Folding chairs were arranged around tables set with disposable tablecloths and bud vases of roses and baby's breath. A few tables were ringed with older women in bright hijabs, but most of the women wore wigs or weaves. Camila became self-conscious that every table but hers was filled with family members bearing bouquets and Mylar graduation-themed balloons. Her family should be seeing her graduate, they should be among the proud family members here, she told me, vexed. Why couldn't they just be proud of her? Advisers rushed up to her to offer congratulations and hugs. They fawned over Alonso, who was growing cranky. The attention was nice, but it wasn't family, she said; she didn't know these people.

The graduates were sent out of the room so they could return through the double metal doors to a tinny recording of "Pomp and Circumstance." Camila lined up with Alonso in her arms. He let out a wail. She felt his diaper—he needed to be changed. By the time Camila carried him back from the bathroom, still crying, she'd missed the procession.

As Camila tried to sneak back to the table, a dean in a suit at a podium intoned: "It's not what's before you or behind you but what's within you." Alonso screamed louder as Camila tried to focus on the dean's remarks. She bounced him in the back of the room, holding a pacifier tight against his wailing mouth as the succession of student award-winners thanked their proud moms. Finally, the top students were invited up to receive certificates for high achievement, one by one. Camila's name was called. She perched Alonso on her hip and strode toward the spotlighted stage, her gown sweeping the floor. Alonso suddenly quieted, his eyes focused on the lights.

"Congratulations, you've surpassed the standard of excellence," the dean said, shaking her free hand.

Camila nodded politely toward the dean and regally turned to face the audience. Her lips curved into a triumphant smile, as the entire room cheered for her. Then, for the first time in his young life, Alonso clapped, slapping his tiny hands together rhythmically, applauding his mother.

After the ceremony, a buffet dinner was set up for the celebrating families, but Alonso was crying again, and Camila figured there wasn't anyone to hang out with anyway. We gave her a lift to Downtown Brooklyn, to cut her subway ride to the Bronx in half. The car sped along Fourth Avenue, a delicious early-summer breeze teasing the curls from Camila's bun, until traffic slowed down near the shelter she'd left six months before.

She wanted to go in and show them all her diploma, she said. Rose should know what she'd accomplished. She looked up through the window to the third floor and saw that her old windows in 3B were dark. Nobody had moved in, still, in all those months. It was just an abandoned room, helping no one.

12

THE BIRTHDAY PARTY

Camila set her alarm for five-thirty to get up for Alonso's birthday party. She'd heard that the park got busy with families having parties on summer Saturdays, and she wanted to make sure she got there by six to stake out a spot. The night before, she'd organized the balloons, cups, and plates, made rice and beans, and seasoned the meats for the barbecue. She told me she needed to make sure it was an impressive spread, just in case her mother showed up. Aaron had said that he'd borrow a grill from his mom. No one had mentioned Camila moving out since Jovanka had cornered Camila in the kitchen weeks before. Camila had been wondering if she could afford to stay in the apartment for a little while more, even though she knew her bank account said otherwise.

Outside on Sherman Avenue, the air was thick and muggy, the sky heavy with low, dark clouds. On the door to the building a WANTED poster hung, offering a reward for information concerning the murder of the neighbor in the stairwell. Police klieg lights pointed at the building, blocking Maria's windows across the street.

In the park, Camila stood under a tree, trying to bounce Alonso to sleep, watching a team of women set up rented chairs with cotton covers with ribbons, two tents, and a table of gift bags. It looked like a wedding, but Minion characters on the helium balloons indicated otherwise. Children's birthdays were a big deal for all the families she knew, an opportunity to host an event, to put on a show. The month before, Jovanka and Aaron had a birthday party for their baby in a rented hall with a clown and an open bar. They'd saved up cans to recycle for cash to pay for some of it; Camila suspected that her rent had covered the rest. Camila felt ashamed that Alonso's party seemed so meager in comparison to theirs, to everyone's, she said. At least the food would be good, she assured herself.

I had picked up the cake she'd ordered from the Dominican bakery on the Lower East Side, our contribution to the party. It was large enough for forty people, three tall layers elaborately frosted in red, white, and blue and topped with a plastic Spiderman. There were Dominican bakeries nearby in the Bronx, but Camila had insisted it come from the place where her mother used to get their birthday cakes. I hadn't realized Geraldine had thrown parties for her kids and ordered cakes. "She's Dominican," Camila explained to me, like I'd missed something obvious.

Camila looked up at the sky. It looked like it was going to storm. Teresa texted to say she wasn't coming. She said she had to be at church. Aaron's blocky torso jostled down the asphalt path, carrying the cooler. Jovanka, dressed for the occasion in a red shirtdress and sandals, pushed the stroller a step behind him. "You should have worn Keds! You look better in Keds!" Aaron barked at her over his shoulder. Camila felt relief at their arrival. Irina came down the path next, holding Dima's chubby hand tight as he toddled next to her. She kissed Camila on both cheeks and announced that she had news.

After she had spent two months in a hotel room, PATH had found Irina a room in a shelter, a nice place, she said, with a kitchen, where she thought she might be able to stay as long as she wanted. Some people in the hotel had been waiting for years for such a placement, she said. But Irina had told her story to a social worker there, who'd called a local councilman every day for two months to advocate for her. Irina said the other homeless people in the hotel were furious that she'd jumped ahead of them. She'd tried to explain to them that she only had this good fortune because she prayed to God day and night. Now she'd have her own room, with two big windows and fresh white paint; she could stay as long as she wanted.

Camila's younger sister Tiana walked down the path next, her pale moon face lighting up at the sight of her little nephew. She and Camila sat wedged together on top of the cooler. She said quietly, "I think Mom is coming, even though she said she wasn't going to spend the money on a MetroCard." Camila just nodded and got out her compact to check her makeup. She ran a plum lipstick over her mouth and silently handed it over to her sister, who did the same. For a long time, they quietly stared at the path from the entrance to the park.

A woman with bleached-blond hair slowly sauntered down the path. Camila said she'd recognize that walk anywhere, even with the unfamiliar dye job. Geraldine carried a beach chair in one hand and a vanilla soft-serve cone in the other. Acid-washed-denim hips and long chain earrings swung as she neared. A lanky tween trailed behind her—Geraldine's youngest daughter.

Camila picked a sleeping Alonso up from his stroller and began fussing over him, ignoring her mother's arrival. Geraldine ignored Camila right back, setting up her chair and imperially settling in to finish her ice cream cone.

Aaron came over to Geraldine, gawking. "Wow, you must be Camila's mom," he said. "I didn't know you looked so much alike."

"You're like twins!" Jovanka said.

"Yeah, that's what everyone says," Geraldine said dryly.

Camila put Alonso back down, her movements reluctant, and joined the conversation. Matching her mother's dryness, she said, "They say I look more like Mauricio."

"No way," her mother said, pulling up Facebook on her phone. "Look." She swiped at the screen until she found a picture she'd posted of the two of them, side by side. "Look at the comments, Cam. 'Twins,' this one says. Look at this one: 'I didn't know you had a daughter.' They know just by looking at you."

Camila smiled tightly.

"Let me see the baby," Geraldine said.

Camila pushed the stroller over to her mother's chair. Geraldine looked skeptically at Alonso, who was restlessly trying to cling to sleep.

"Say hi to your grandma," Camila said.

Alonso opened his eyes, squinted at her, and turned away in the stroller.

"He doesn't like me," Geraldine said to Camila. Then she shrugged. "He doesn't know me." She scrutinized the food laid out on the nearby table. "Finally, food you cooked. About time."

Camila's only response was a quiet, deep breath to steady herself as she heaped a plate for her mother. She carried it over and explained everything she'd prepared: the rice and beans, the steak, the ribs, the chicken. Geraldine ate quietly, approvingly, and then asked for a second plate. "You use the little beans," she remarked.

"I know, you use the big ones," Camila said. "And I use more sauce."

"It's good," Geraldine said. She took another bite.

It was time for cake. Everyone gathered around to sing while Camila lit a candle in the shape of a number one, holding Alonso on her hip. Alonso looked puzzled but then grinned—his mouth wide and goofy, like Jeremiah's. Everyone applauded at his smile, which made him smile more. Camila began to relax.

Geraldine told Camila to hold up one of his fingers for a picture. "Then next year, two fingers," she said. "Then when you try to do three fingers, they won't do it." She snickered. "Already they won't do what you say. It'll come soon enough. You'll see."

"Mom, do you want to cut the cake, because you know how to cut it right?" Camila asked.

Geraldine asked Camila, "Do you have the perfect knife? Because if you don't have the perfect knife, it's too hard to cut it."

"We only have this knife," Camila said, holding up a disposable plastic one.

Geraldine shook her head. Tense again, Camila began to cut the cake, anxious about messing it up.

"He's supposed to hold the knife," Geraldine said. "The man cuts the cake."

"Mom, he's a baby," Camila said.

"You're right," Geraldine said.

"I had my graduation ceremony this week," Camila said as casually as she could, acting like she was focused on serving the cake. "I got my associate's."

"You did?"

Nodding slowly, Camila looked up, her eyes meeting her mother's identical ones.

"Good for you, honey. Good for you."

Camila smiled sheepishly.

As Camila held Alonso, Geraldine attempted to feed him forkfuls of cake. At first he arched away, but gradually, as he seemed to feel his mother relaxing, he did, too. He began to accept each bite, eventually eagerly leaning forward for what his grandmother offered him. Each time he opened his mouth for her fork, Geraldine's smile broadened.

She teased Camila familiarly. Camila teased her back. Their laughs came easily, in the same rhythm, Geraldine's a little huskier and more worn than her daughter's. They started catching up about the year they'd missed. Camila didn't mention that she had lost public assistance, childcare, and Medicaid. She didn't mention that she had lost child-support assistance, that she didn't have rent, and that she spent her money searching for something she couldn't find in the Dominican Republic. She didn't mention that she wouldn't be going to John Jay, that she wasn't even eligible for emergency shelter, and that she didn't know where she'd be living in a week.

"I want a photo of us," Camila announced.

She gathered her three younger siblings and her mother around her, and then she reached to pull me into the picture.

Geraldine said she had a night out planned with her man; she needed to go home and get ready. Camila just nodded and began to wrap up the rice and beans with her free hand, as she held Alonso on her hip. He grabbed for one of her fingers. She let him clutch it tight as she watched her mother disappear down the path and then pressed his small fist to her lips for a moment, her lipstick marking his hand.

EPILOGUE

Late that summer, I pulled up to an address in Queens. It was the home of a middle-aged man with a large belly and a mustache, an apartment on the first floor of a brick townhouse. There was a living room, a kitchen where Alonso was sitting impatiently in a high chair, a bedroom with a double bed strewn with Camila's clothes. Behind the house was a shed filled with the same cardboard boxes she'd first packed at the shelter. The man seemed equally intimate and annoyed with her. I didn't know who the man was, nor did I know how long she'd been staying there or what the arrangement was between them. I never found out.

Since her graduation and Alonso's birthday, I'd been increasingly out of town and out of touch. Not entirely, but compared to our prior intensity, it was noticeable and significant and, for me, necessary. While I dug through notes and began to sketch out this book, I had to keep her daily life, and voice, at a distance, so I could gain the necessary perspective on her life and the conditions surrounding it, perspective that would allow me to start writing. In my absence, she had cooled quickly. The curtain had to fall on her story at some point; we'd long discussed that I planned to limit the scope of the book to her first year of motherhood. I was still approaching our relationship as a journalist writing about a subject, albeit a subject I'd become tethered to, who perhaps had come to see our connection as simply personal, despite the presence of my notebook.

I was aware throughout my reporting that Camila increasingly cast me as her best friend, her caseworker, her therapist, her free lunch, her big sister, her mother—in the end, even her prom date. At her graduation ball in June, we'd lined up with all the other dates, mainly young men and women who had coordinated their gowns with cummerbund and bow tie sets, to have our picture taken together and laminated into a keepsake. When the DJ cued up "All the Single Ladies" and called out, "Ladies, grab your best friend!" Camila threw her arms around me, and we danced.

Considering the profound abandonment she'd already faced in her life, it was easy to see why any distance might feel like desertion, neglect. Still, the sudden and growing chill I felt from her, which hardened quickly into regular silences, felt both mystifying and concerning. I was used to being in touch with her almost every day, at least by text. Now she barely replied to me, and when she did, her words were cagey, provoking questions she'd just ignore. She wouldn't tell me where she was staying. I worried. I wondered if ours was the latest relationship she was closing the door on, if soon I'd hear the key click in the lock.

Of course, Camila proved entirely capable of working out her next step on her own. Her tenacity may have not been enough to rise up through the quicksand of the social-services system, but it found her housing nonetheless.

Buffalo State was in the State University of New York network that accepted her education grant. The college had a dorm that could accommodate students with children, and that was her newest shelter. The school also had a criminal-justice program and the added benefit of care for Alonso at the child-study center. As soon as the college gave her a move-in date, she wrote to see if I'd pack up my car with her boxes and haul them to the other side of the state. I knew how much she'd accumulated since her move from the shelter and borrowed a roof rack from friends, which filled up quickly. So did the way back and the back seat, which meant Camila and Alonso couldn't fit in the car with me. I set off for Buffalo, and they headed to Port Authority to buy an overnight bus ticket—the cheapest option—to their new home. Their trip would take more than eight hours, with frequent stops along the way.

I'd only known Camila to be effusive, greeting me with a hug, parting with a meaningful look and a peck on the cheek, even if I was going to see her the next day. This time, she'd barely glanced at me as I loaded up the car, and she walked away without looking back.

I crashed in a motel room in Buffalo late that night and found my way to her dorm the next morning. She didn't want to leave New York—her city—nor did she want to leave her family, no matter how absent they'd been. And yet, pulling up to that brick block of a building, climbing the concrete stairs, and opening a door that would be only hers, my heart began to lift with the feeling of real possibility for her for the first time since I'd met her, pregnant at the shelter the prior May. Behind that door was a furnished duplex. Upstairs was a bedroom for her and one for Alonso, plus a small study. Downstairs was an open-plan living room and kitchen. A home, for now at least, with space, air, room to think. To feel stable. To study and focus. For Alonso to learn to walk and talk and become a child. And with time, without the constant occupation of searching for a place to live, to devote to her schoolwork, to her motherhood, to build a life. She'd have this home for two years—graduation, his third birthday—or until another unforeseeable crisis.

We carried her boxes up the stairs and into the apartment. I wanted to talk to her about this next phase in her life and excitedly discover the facets of this new home. I wanted to help her settle in, to sit on her bed entertaining Alonso while she unpacked, talk like we used to only a couple of months before, get caught up on what I'd missed. I had so many questions. But she was distant, distracted, dismissive, avoidant. I knew she didn't want me there, despite how she'd clung to me since Alonso was born. Once the boxes were unloaded, she shooed me away. I left, wanting to respect her desire for space.

Once I left Buffalo, I began reaching out to her. First over text, our usual way to communicate when we were apart. She didn't reply. Then I wrote emails, in case there'd been an issue with her phone. Silence.

Camila wanted to go, so, reluctantly, I let her go.

To a point.

I wrote Camila at Thanksgiving and then again on Christmas. Still no reply. But then in January she emailed that she was coming down to the city in a few days. She was going with some friends to a Benihana steak house in Midtown that Saturday night and she wanted me to join them. I had another obligation that night but said I wanted to meet her on Sunday, if she had time, that I wanted to hear everything about Buffalo, that I'd missed her.

She replied that she didn't want me to waste her time.

It was a cryptic note, and an aggressive one. I didn't know what to make of it. I wrote her multiple times, offering to come up to Buffalo, offering to sit down and look at every page of the manuscript with her once it was written.

She didn't write back.

I did what all good reporters and any other person with an Internet connection would do: I looked her up online. She had blocked me on her social-media pages, as I'd seen her do when she decided to freeze out her friends and family in the past. Without seeing the lunch plates she was likely Instagramming or the motivational quotes she had a habit of posting on Facebook, there wasn't anything I could find, not for months. Then one afternoon I discovered her face, clear and smiling, on the page for the Buffalo State Criminal Justice Club. She was the club president, according to the website. There she was: at the shooting range, at self-defense training, with a police officer who'd come to speak to the club. She looked healthy, present, even preppy again.

It occurred to me then that she'd made a new life for herself in

Buffalo, with a new identity, one where she wasn't known as the pregnant woman I met in a shelter, a woman whose image wasn't identified by poverty. She looked like any other student in those pictures—maybe a little more statuesque and put together, but otherwise no different than the rest. Maybe, I thought, she no longer wanted the year I'd witnessed, or all that preceded it, to be her story. Maybe she'd made a new story for herself. Maybe she wanted this one to disappear.

I kept working on the book for a while. And then I stopped. I didn't declare to anyone, much less myself, that I wasn't writing it anymore. I just didn't touch the document. I was busy teaching and writing other things, I said. That was true. But what was truer was that I was paralyzed by her silence.

More than a year passed. And then I got an email from her old account, the one she used when I first met her. *Follow up,* said the subject line. What followed was rather opaque and brief. *I'm reaching out to let you know that I forgave you. Please don't take it personal. I'm sending this out to everyone.* Finally, the impetus for this email—and ostensibly the identical ones she was sending to that ambiguous "everyone"—was that she had found God and become a Christian.

I replied that I was happy to hear from her, I had been worried, I hoped we could reconnect. I didn't ask her what she'd forgiven.

She wrote back that she'd met a guy. They were engaged to be married. And she would be coming to the city in a few weeks.

We made a date. In her typical yen for nostalgia, she chose to meet at the last place we'd had lunch together, shortly after Alonso's birthday: a Chino–Latino place on the Upper West Side. Her new guy was going to join us, as was Alonso, of course. Once we'd made the plan, she texted me pictures of the three of them, asked if I was around to meet earlier in the week, and said she was excited to see me. She sounded like herself again. Still, I wasn't sure that she'd show.

But there she was. Her hug was as tight as ever, but she looked paler than I'd seen in the pictures, her skin broken out, her eyes more concave than I'd seen them. She seemed nervous, meek. Her boyfriend wore a tight pink polo shirt and a big silver watch. He used the word "entrepreneur" frequently and said he'd been saved by Christ. He explained how the covalent bonds that exist in cellular biology are proof of God's love. He cared for Alonso like he was his own son, cutting his food, making sure he ate, entertaining him in his high chair.

They'd met only a couple of months before, in the Rockaways. She'd come for a visit with her half brother Michael—whom she'd listed on that rejected affordable-housing application—and his mother, Dorcas. They sat alone together in Dorcas's kitchen, talking for hours. He was Dorcas's nephew, Michael's cousin. He felt like family. She'd told him her story, the same story I've told here. And he fell in love with her. Camila let him do the talking. He saw that she was a leader, he told me. They were looking for a place to move into together by the end of the month, in New Jersey. That's where he lived with his mother, who worked in the kitchen at a hotel in Times Square. The kitchen there was looking for a dishwasher and paying twenty bucks an hour. Camila planned to apply.

I was puzzled. Camila should have been just weeks shy of graduating from Buffalo State. I couldn't understand why she was even here in New York when most students were finishing up classes and preparing for finals. She was thinking about working as a dishwasher? Something had evidently gone wrong.

Over lunch she told me what happened. That family dorm was infested with mice, she said, and the school wouldn't do anything about it. She'd even taken her complaint to the local TV station. They ran a segment on the vermin problem, but it didn't make a difference. It was one thing when her kitchen was crawling with rodents, but when she found them in Alonso's room, she knew they had to pack up again. This was the worst move of all the ones she'd made over the years: a tenement on a bleak block downtown, where she didn't feel safe even running down the block. Her neighbors, she said, were all addicts. Opioids, I figured.

Meanwhile, Alonso had been coming home from daycare with bruises and bite marks. She had to move him into a private-nanny share and pay for an Uber to the nanny's house to drop him off and pick him up. There was no money to pay for the Uber, or the nanny, or the rent on their room, or anything else. Though she had finally gotten her public-assistance case recertified in New York City, she had to start a new case when she moved to Buffalo. She was caught in a system there that was even more dysfunctional and dehumanizing than what she'd experienced in New York. The welfare office wouldn't accept her school hours as work hours, so she'd lost any support she had as soon as she arrived—as soon as I'd dropped her off.

She fell into deep anxiety, depression, and despair. Her phone was cut off. There was no one she counted as a friend there, no one to talk to. And classes were boring. Mainly PowerPoint presentations, subjects she'd already studied, with no engagement to hold her interest. She failed a semester. Then she dropped out. She applied for temp work. But no one needed her skills. Unemployment was steadily increasing in Buffalo. Thirty percent of the city lived below the poverty line. Only half of high school students got their diploma. It was a tough city: the tenth most violent in the country. Before she'd moved back, Camila knew Buffalo made New York City look like easy living; her history visiting Pedro and her earlier student days had taught her that. But she'd never had to manage it as a mother before. Or without a partner, even one in a halfway house.

She was exhausted. She didn't have any options. "Nothing," she said quietly, shaking her head. "I had nothing and no one."

"I'm so sorry, Camila. I didn't know. I wish I had known," I said.

"You couldn't have known," she told me. "I see that now."

I knew what she showed me, yes. But didn't I also know better?

I had told myself that my brief encounter with her dorm in Buffalo was the setting for a vibrant college life, that the pictures I saw posted online were evidence of her health and progress. Surfaces, exteriors. In her silence, I had inadvertently retreated to the world of people who measured her need by her freshly made-up face, her future by her freshly laundered button-down. Yes, I'd worried about her. Yet I'd also felt relief in believing in those images I saw online, which, as ever, only obscured the truth of her struggle.

Without Camila, I was free from considering the ongoing gloom and trials, free to tend to the concerns of my own family without the constant contrast of her life. In retrospect, it was easier to assume she was fine than to let her silence spark a crisis when I couldn't sleep at night, or when I met with my editor, or when my friends asked how she was doing or if I'd heard from her. It became my own crisis, lived out in my stable home, or at an expense-account lunch in Midtown, or over wine at a dinner party. Respecting the distance she established meant I didn't have to drive to Buffalo, track her down, insert myself into her latest calamity. And why would I, when I'd seen all the evidence I needed to think that her life was finally under control?

You could say, perhaps, that we see what we want to see. We also see what people want to show us. Impeccable lip liner that says someone isn't homeless, even if she is. A pedicure that says life is under control. A social-media feed that depicts leisure and abundance, when neither really exists. The alternative, for over 43 million Americans who live under the line, is to reveal one's poverty, which our society tends to view as individual failure rather than a systemic one.

Poverty is a source of shame. Rather than prompting immediate compassion and sustained outrage, it provokes pity that dissolves into scorn. Reading about Camila's struggles, you may have heard your own internal voice articulating contradicting "shoulds": You should stay in school; you should drop out to work. You should be ambitious; you shouldn't be that ambitious. You should have had an abortion; you should have had your baby. You should apply for affordable housing; you shouldn't waste your time on it. You shouldn't tax the city system; you should just go to a municipal shelter. You should make choices to present yourself well and maintain your self-respect; you shouldn't get a pedicure. You should try to find any way out of New York or any family to help you; you shouldn't go to the Dominican Republic.

Some of these contradicting shoulds apply to almost any single mother. Some apply to almost any welfare recipient. Some apply to almost any student in poverty. Some apply to almost any homeless person. And some apply to Camila alone. The breadth of the system coexists with the uniqueness of our individual lives, prescribed and evaluated as it flatters the judge.

Camila and her boyfriend decided they were going to get married in August, as I was revising this book.

We'd all met up—their family of three, my family of three—for an afternoon at Coney Island earlier in the summer. I wasn't looking for information. I carried no notebook; my phone remained in my bag. I just wanted to see her, to hang out, to play with Alonso, to get to know her guy a bit better. I asked after her sisters and her mom. She answered carefully at first, studying my face. But as we slipped back into our old rhythms and shorthand, my deep and detailed knowledge about her family began to feel like a relief. We found our way back to each other, to a new form of the relationship we'd built together.

She texted me the next week that they'd set a date. He had cousins in Florida, and she wanted to get married on the beach, at sunset. I bought plane tickets for all three of us to go and booked a hotel room. Every few days she would write me looking for advice, about where to have the dinner afterward, about which florist to use, about which invitation I preferred, about whether they should rent chairs for the ceremony. They'd taken out a loan to cover the expenses. I found a florist and read my credit-card number over the phone. I didn't evade her queries anymore, asking her what she thought. I was there not to tell you the story anymore but to live it with her, to pin on her tiara, to be the person she nervously reached for before the ceremony, to hold her bouquet as she spoke the vows she'd written herself.

Her mother couldn't afford the flight for the wedding, nor could her sisters. But her dad could and did. I assembled a makeshift boutonniere from a spray of roses and affixed it to Mauricio's polo shirt before he walked Camila down the aisle. I was surprised that afterward, at the Italian restaurant in a mall where she'd booked the reception, she didn't ask him to make the toast. She asked me instead.

After I spoke, she stood up, luminous in her white Forever 21 sundress, and raised a glass to thank us all for coming. Then she toasted me, her friend, who was with her for her darkest days, she said. We both knew that part of what she said wasn't true, that I'd missed a tougher year than the one I'd witnessed. But the other part, for the time being, was unassailable.

They drove back to New Jersey—to her new mother-in-law's old apartment, where they were still staying—with glowing-sunset photos, an albatross of debt, and talk of saving to buy a house, to have another child, to start a business together. These were the most American of dreams, which, in a past America, for most children of immigrants this clever and dedicated, were not the gossamer of fantasy but the basic materials of living.

Camila had found love in her husband and someone to crash with, at least for the time being. I'd toasted her as the strongest person I'd ever known, and yet it seemed she'd been right that she couldn't manage her life alone. I was happy for her that she wasn't alone anymore, at least for now. But her not being alone was no storybook happy ending. Her marriage signified not just love but systemic failure.

The end of this story was contained in its beginning, to borrow from George Orwell. A shelter, a baby, a broken social-services system, a land of impossible dreams. And before then: Geraldine's abuse and privation, Mauricio's negligence and bravado. And before then: their parents, who moved here with nothing after their country was reduced to nothing, who despite their own impossible dreams remained with nothing. At least those prior generations had housing, though; they had a more functional safety net. Camila's wits, pluck, and beauty may have carried her to a different end in a different America. But without the tools of subsistence—housing foremost among them—as a human right and as a national commitment to human potential, there can be no happy end to this story for Camila, or for anyone barred from stability.

Our calamity of inequality, chosen and tolerated by other Americans with other American lives, is one almost no one can beat on their own, not even if they're as hell-bent and equipped as Camila.

I've discussed its ever-darkening bleakness in moments throughout this book: the emaciation of welfare, the cessation of housing vouchers, the rise of unchecked real estate development, and more. Looking ahead, it's only worse. Family planning defunded and its legality in question. Public assistance a shrinking and derided entitlement. The cost of childcare. Children as mothers' problems, mothers who must both educate themselves and work. And housing: an unchecked market, a safety net that touts inefficient short-term solutions instead of providing active homelessness prevention, and the very real impossibility of getting anywhere in life without stable shelter. Without a home.

What do we tell Camila? That she should have been born to different parents? Do we tell Alonso the same thing? If our own kids struggle, and theirs do, too, because of the catastrophic systemic failures we've permitted, is that the only answer for them, as well, that they should have inherited a different future from a different family? The circumstances of conception, we've determined, represent the full measure of what a life deserves: If your mother goes into labor in a homeless shelter, it's no one's fault but your own that you ended up there. As though you're born with a terminal illness and blamed for making yourself sick.

All four of my grandparents were born into poverty and prejudice, here or in the countries from which their families fled. It's never lost on me that their ascent into the American middle class was due to the drive and diligence that I found continuously echoed in Camila's clearest traits. But instead of a rise to the middle class, I saw walls materialize before Camila in an impassable labyrinth, one familiar to most anyone who lives below the poverty line in America: The maze of public assistance that dead-ended without welfare and childcare. The maze of affordable housing that dead-ended without the possibility of a stable home. The maze of emergency shelters that dead-ended without a temporary bed. And through it all, the psychic toll that left her dulled, her ambitions reset from a career in criminal justice to a job as a dishwasher. And a young son whose own behavior—screaming and clutching her leg during her wedding ceremony, as he did in most ordinary moments—indicated the toll exacted upon the next generation.

There's no doubt that inequity has become grievous and grotesque on our watch, as evidenced in the smattering of statistics I've included in this book. Like the dramatically shrinking welfare check; like the equally dramatic rise in rents. Like the overcrowding of shelters and apartments. You've followed a fairly steady descent through the narrative of Camila's year. It began in a crisis, going into labor in a shelter. How could it get worse? Now you know. Our national commitment to our brethren has traced a matching decline. Although I followed Camila's individual manifestation of this plight in New York, it's not just a New York story. Millions of people endure crises like hers in other big cities, small cities, poor suburbs, and rural areas alike. If you're not rich in America, chances are you're poor and similarly struggling today.

There's a reason Camila's mother, with five kids and no high school diploma, could maintain a certain level of stability in her children's lives a decade or two ago. Her reliance on the system may be exactly the kind of story that fed the notion of the undeserving poor, but that reliance allowed Camila and her sisters enough solidity so they could develop their own intellects and shape their own goals. The housing voucher she received from the city was the only reason her first three girls weren't homeless for much of their childhoods.

As any of the women on Fourth Avenue could tell you, their foundational need is a place to live. Once you have a stable home, it becomes possible to survive, but without that stability, you don't stand a chance. The rest of it matters: childcare, healthcare, accessible education, a living wage, a measure of public assistance that can permit a person to do more than barely tread water. These are problems that can be solved with better policy. Not easily, and not cheaply. But not necessarily at a greater expense than we believed our society's basic needs were worth in the past and as most other developed countries presume are basic rights in the present.

Stable shelter, though, is not just the baseline; it's perhaps the simplest fix. And one we have money to address simply by considering the fortunes of those who have egregiously commandeered and redefined our housing stock. The U.S. real estate market—most markedly in New York but also nationwide—has become a Swiss bank account to park cash from wealthy foreign nationals, with stunning tax abatements. Meanwhile, the wealthiest Americans are earning, and stashing, more money than ever before. Forget the 1 percent for the moment. Just focus on the top 1 percent of that 1 percent. Within that bracket, consider that the twenty wealthiest Americans own more wealth than half the U.S. population combined. Now imagine taxing that population, and their investments, and the investments of the global billionaires who sequester their money in homes where they'll never live. Imagine taxing developers who are turning our streets into theme parks for the rich. Would they feel the impact of those taxes on their daily lives? Of course not; it's a pittance. But it would transform daily life to channel that money into housing vouchers for those among us who don't have homes—as investments in their lives and futures, and in the lives and futures of their children. Imagine how little it would have required to invest in Camila's brilliant future in criminal justice and who Alonso could become as the son of a mother with the stability to achieve her ambitious potential.

We are defined by who we deem worthy of investment, as an economy as well as an ethical society. Today we are failing ourselves on both counts. That failure becomes increasingly villainous when you know simple solutions like housing vouchers exist to reverse the most dire foundational crisis for poor Americans. Vouchers that aid in rent payment are the most effective form of homelessness intervention. They're also the cheapest and the easiest to implement. And their effects are both multigenerational and multilateral. Families who receive vouchers are not only two-thirds less likely to experience housing instability. They're also two-thirds less likely to need foster care. And two-thirds less likely to experience domestic violence. The parallel numbers are hardly a coincidence. Nor are the reduced rates of single parenthood or the higher incomes and improved college attendance.

Of course, not everyone is college-bound or even has the skills to manage the brutal realities of independent living. It remains a mystery to me how Camila was raised in the abuse and instability of her family and emerged as skilled and shrewd as she did. Most women who appeal to Rose for a room on Fourth Avenue don't have the tools to get by without a measure of support. They come to her with severe mental-health issues, or addiction, or, as she once put it, they just can't handle paying their bills. This is why the rooms stay vacant, she explained to me. They need what is called supportive housing—an affordable place to live that also provides social services—and she can't offer that. It takes scaffolding to help them, having been failed by our system and by their own families, who likely were in turn failed by our system and their own families. They deserve a viable life, one with stability, as much as anyone, perhaps more than anyone. This is not a cycle that will break itself. I wonder what Camila's life would look like today if her mother had been able to raise her in such an environment. Yes, Geraldine had Section 8, but what if she had mental-health support and job training? What if her kids had the support she couldn't give them?

As I write this, Alonso is four and living at his sixth address— more than some of us move in our lifetimes. Camila has now packed up her trunk thirty-four times. Imagine her instead with stable housing, graduating and working. Imagine Alonso raised in a stable home, graduating and working. Imagine disrupting the pattern that dictates who Americans will become. Imagine not having to account for whether you deserve survival. Imagine not having to enter a lottery—a lottery, my God, where you're told, even after you win, that you don't have the income the developer requires—to have stable shelter for yourself and your baby. Imagine setting roots in a neighborhood, developing a community, eradicating the early-childhood trauma of continuous displacement, offering a different birthright. These rights, at least for free citizens, were once deemed essential in our flawed country. And though now, for so many, they're no more than impossible dreams, we cling to the delusion that they remain cardinal.

Instead, we are ruled by money. The private sector has all but replaced a public one. Our lawmakers and lobbyists genuflect to the unchecked capitalism that pays their way. Any ethic of fairness, or possibility, or hope mainly exists as founding mythology—the fairy tale that if Camila is smart and capable, she'll succeed. It's America, after all. But this America has gone upside down. The inheritance game is an exponential graph, with one line stretching up up up and another steeply descending—the apocalyptic physics of inequality. The graph is not theoretical mathematics; we can measure it, clearly, in numbers. Every year, with no end in sight, wealth consolidates and poverty expands. Those figures are shocking, but what's even more cataclysmic is how they are lived out. This story of our age isn't about following the money; it's about following the people.

Rose and I met for dinner a couple of months after Camila's wedding. She told me the shelter had a social-work intern now and newly renovated rooms. And a surplus: an income of $1 million this year. She was thinking about using some of those funds to hire a housing coordinator. It's what they want most, help finding a place to live, she explained. But, she added—and as I was thinking it—what good is a housing coordinator when there isn't any housing for them at all?

She told me nobody at the shelter ever received another housing voucher like the one Sherice ended up not being able to use anywhere. No matter how Rose fought city hall, quite literally, such privileges were reserved for the homeless in the city system. Which was where Sherice had ended up, Rose said. She'd moved in with her mom, but her mom died—an overdose, Rose assumed—and she and Tyrese had found themselves at PATH. She hadn't heard from Irina in a while, and neither had I, nor a word from Anselma or Tina. I knew Camila hadn't been in touch.

When I'd sat in Rose's office for the first time, the day she asked me to lead the Wednesday-night meetings, she had told me the story of a resident who found housing and work in Maryland, a woman who had left the shelter months before. Over dinner that night, she repeated it again. Then she told me a new story, about a woman who fled Nigeria for New York, who ended up at the shelter just before she gave birth to twins. She'd gone into the system after her time was up on Fourth Avenue. After some time in a hotel in Queens, she was given an apartment by the city. Rose proudly showed me pictures of her twins playing on the area rug in the living room, just as she'd shown me photos of the woman in Maryland four years earlier. Out of all those women, over all those years, she had just two stories to tell that rang with pride. The rest, blown to the corners of the system, human dust, forgotten.

Because I chose Camila to write about, and she chose me in turn, she may be less forgotten than others. Still, not even her mother seeks her out. Nor does her father. Nor Alonso's father. Curiosity takes courage—that's why people protect themselves from truths they fear will spark discomfort or guilt. Blindness is easier. That blindness is complicity. We must first look at each other in order to look after each other. Whether or not we choose to see the labyrinth of poverty, it's there, impassable. Whether or not we choose to see Camila, she exists.

ACKNOWLEDGMENTS

Any book, while it bears a single author's name, is the product of a wide community's support. That's especially the case when it comes to deeply reported nonfiction, which requires funding and access. My initial reporting on homelessness was funded by the Economic Hardship Reporting Project. The Reporting Award from NYU gave me the ability to invest time at the shelter. The MacDowell Colony and the Calderwood Foundation gave me space to write. At Yale, a Poynter fellowship encouraged me to bring the story's complications to light. The Maison Dora Maar offered me an extraordinary place to begin the end.

Jim Rutman saw this project through ups and downs, buoying me with his charm and grounding me with his guidance. The fabulous Julie Grau was the first editor to see the importance of Camila's story and, together with Cindy Spiegel and Annie Chagnot, offered incisive wisdom. Mark Warren took on the book when his desk was overcrowded and gently led my telling of Camila's struggles into the world. Natalie Lampert lent her research chops, Alissa Quart lent her subtitle sorcery, and Craig Hughes appeared by kismet to share his knowledge. Karen Mayer, Evan Camfield, Kathy

Lord, Robbin Schiff, Jess Bonet, Penny Simon, and the rest of the good people at Random House helped to deliver this book to a readership. I am grateful to you all.

Of course, Justin and Dahlia Lane have been there throughout. They've supported the absences that immersion reporting requires, and weathered living with a writer through a long book process, with patience and insight and love, each in their own way. It has been an extraordinary thing to watch my own daughter grow from a seven-year-old to a twelve-year-old against the background of this book, submerged in the ideas that simmer underneath it, already fighting to change the systemic injustice she sees. Dahlia's grandparents have shown up for what I've missed, expressing nothing but support for this work, as always. I am lucky.

My chosen family of friends read pages, offered analysis, and listened to me talk and talk: IFLYG. Of course, top on that list is John Williams, as dear as they come, and Eric Hynes, who covered these pages in ink and insight again and again. Thanks as well to my dear comrades at the OpEd Project and the Invisible Institute.

This book exists because the woman I call Rose opened the doors of the shelter to me. My thanks to her, and to the residents both inside and outside the covers of this book, especially women I call Irina, Sherice, Anselma, and Tina, who cracked open the door to their lives during trying and insecure times.

Of course, though, it all comes down to the extraordinary person I call Camila. I am still amazed that this private, self-protecting woman was willing to fully reveal her life to me, to expose her vulnerability and pain, to lead me through the emotional and logistical mechanics of her days, and to do so with humor and love and patience. The boy I call Alonso had no say in my witnessing his first year. He's now in school, mischievous in all the best ways, developing his own whip-smart responses to the world he lives in, leavened by his own beatific smile. I hope that his life evolves in a world where he has far more choice and agency than his mother has ever been afforded, and a safety net she never had, no matter what turns he takes.

THIS IS
ALL I GOT

LAUREN SANDLER

Random
House
Book Club

Because
Stories Are   TM
Better Shared

A BOOK CLUB GUIDE

QUESTIONS AND TOPICS FOR DISCUSSION

I lived with this book for five years before it was published during the first surge of the Covid-19 pandemic of 2020. During those years, the nation continued to shred our safety net, withdrawing support for those most in need and deepening inequality in the United States to levels not seen in a century. The public health crisis that greeted this book ruthlessly exposed our priorities as a society, further stranding Americans stuck in a system designed to fail them, adding still-untold numbers to their desperate ranks. Speaking personally, the experience of working on this book has filled me with questions about whether, in the absence of political will, we will ever truly make progress, and what difference we, as individuals, can make in the absence of leadership. Camila's personal decisions get debated as well, by people who know her by her pseudonym, and, Lord knows, by those of us who call her by her real name. I thought I would offer some questions that have arisen around *This Is All I Got,* as a spur to examine how you feel about Camila's experience, the country that has given rise to it, and your place in that story.   —LS

1. This book was written before the Covid-19 pandemic, and before the economic crisis the pandemic ushered in. How do you think Camila's experience would have been different if she'd encountered the year of her life recounted in the book—with a baby and no stable housing—in an even less stable era?

2. An overriding theme of the book is the issue of increasing income inequality in America. How does this theme play into Camila's life and plight?

3. Camilla becomes a student and scholar of "the system" and makes repeated efforts to secure benefits for herself and her son, but she encounters many bureaucratic hurdles. How did you react to these situations in the book? Have you ever had similar experiences? How do you think race or class affect her experiences, or yours?

4. The author feels that Camila understands the system better than many of the women who are in the shelter with her and has personal skills and attitudes that will stand her in good stead for getting what she needs. How does she do compared with these other women?

5. What are the pros and cons of the various forms of family that are presented in the book? What about the various forms of home?

6. What critical events or people might have helped Camila break the cycle of poverty?

7. What are Camila's attitudes and behaviors that you admire? Are there any that you feel negative about? Why?

8. What are the policy implications of this book? What policies could improve the lives of homeless families? Beyond achieving proper funding for social support services, in what other ways could access barriers be reduced?

9. Some people worry that bureaucracies will give assistance to people who do not really need it or who are gaming the system, and so processes are developed to ensure that this doesn't happen. We saw Camila spend hours navigating these systems. From what you read, are these systems fair and effective? Are they necessary?

10. What do you think readers moved by Camila's story can do as individuals to make a difference in the lives of people like her? Does making a difference feel more urgent or more impossible in times of economic upheaval and a public health crisis?

11. If you could change one of Camila's decisions, which one would you choose and how would you change it?

12. What do you think the author's purpose was in writing this book, and do you think she was successful?

13. Were you able to connect to Camila on a personal level, even if your circumstances are vastly different than hers?

14. Was there a particular moment in the book that had the greatest impact on you? If so, what was that moment?

Lauren Sandler is an award-winning journalist and bestselling author. For twenty years, her reporting and commentary has focused on inequality and gender. She lives in Brooklyn.

laurenosandler.com